Acknowledgments

I owe my first and largest debt to my wife – Divya, who supported my efforts way beyond what's fair to expect. Managing a kid of 2, and helping me in writing this book – both are equally herculean tasks. Thank you! Your name belongs on the cover of this book, every bit as mine does.

Next, a big thank you to my parents, my brother and his family for continuously believing in me and teaching me to think bigger and aspire higher.

A final thank you to Informatica® LLC and everyone at Informatica, for their help in every regard. A special thanks to Aashoo Saxena for his review and thoughts. I can't think of another organization that nurtures creativity and freedom of thought as much as Informatica does. Proud to be part of the Informatica family.

Foreword

This book is a modest attempt at sharing what I know of Informatica products, and to show why I love them as much as I do. If I did my job right, at the end of the book you will fall in love with them too. After reading this book, if you love Informatica Platform, it is primarily because of the simplicity and feature-rich functionality that the products offer. At the time of writing this book, Informatica's GA release is 10.2.0. Hence all labs and steps assume that you are using the same version of the Informatica Platform. Some screenshots may have been from other versions of the platform.

I'd love to stay in touch with you!

Supplemental material of this book is available at:

http://www.keshavvadrevu.com/books

Author can be reached at: vadrevu.keshav@gmail.com

Nope, that's not how it works!

Purchasing this book does not entitle you to free software
from Informatica!

A Note to my readers

Informatica Platform is a Graphical User Interface based software. Hence this book uses lots of screenshots. I've put in my best efforts to balance the size of the book and the volume, quality of the screenshots. However, I am limited by the physical space a page can offer. I made an attempt to group several screenshots together to contain the number of pages they consume. I have personally looked almost every single screenshot to ensure the necessary details are not lost. Despite these efforts, it is possible that some screenshots / instructions are not placed in an optimal fashion for the end reader. If you do notice such a placement, please do let me know and I will do my best to correct it in the next edition of this book.

Keshav

Table of Contents

Chapter 1 – Introduction and overview

This chapter gives an overview of the Informatica Platform's architecture. This chapter serves only as an introduction and certain topics will be covered in detail in relevant chapters. You begin with various components involved in the architecture, their role and purpose.

Informatica Platform

The Informatica Platform constitutes of the services and binaries that form foundation for various Informatica products such as PowerCenter, Informatica Data Quality and Big Data Management. Once the platform is setup, these products/functionality can be enabled by their corresponding licenses. Individual installations are not required. The platform also contains several connectors that are built-in, and that can be enabled by adding the corresponding license key. There may be some specialized products/connectors that require additional configuration/steps due to the nature of their connectivity, but most of the core connectors are available right out of the box.

Scope of this book

Since Informatica Platform is the foundation for many products, it is quite difficult to encompass all of them and yet keep the book readable and interesting. Hence this book focuses on Data Integration on platform. It is important to note that though Informatica PowerCenter services are also part of the Informatica Platform, Data Integration capabilities in

PowerCenter are beyond the scope of this book. In this book, you focus primarily on the Informatica Platform that form the foundation for Informatica Data Quality and Big Data Management i.e. Model Repository Service, Data Integration Service (DIS) and Developer tool. You will look at the Data Integration capabilities of this framework only and not the PowerCenter Repository Service and PowerCenter Integration Service. Reader should understand that PowerCenter and the Platform framework share many Data Integration capabilities and it is very easy to draw similarities/differences. However, these frameworks are very different and are built for very different use cases. You will not go through the comparison of these products in the book and will focus solely on the Platform framework.

Informatica Platform components

Informatica domain

Domain is the highest level component in Informatica environment. In simple terms, domain can be explained as an environment. If you want to setup development, QA and production environments, you will setup 3 different domains. Domains use the "share nothing" philosophy. So, any services and components within a domain have absolutely nothing in common or "shared" with those in other domains. A developer can connect to, and interact with more than one domain at the same time. A domain stores all of its information in a domain repository (database schema) that you define during the installation process. A domain stores information regarding various services that are part of it such as Model Repository

Service, DIS, group and user accounts, privileges and roles, object permissions and more.

Informatica nodes

An Informatica node is any node where Informatica services are installed. You can have any number of nodes in a domain. Some of these nodes can act as primary service nodes by hosting services such as Model Repository Service or can be used as compute/worker nodes for the DIS or both. Every participating node must have Informatica services installed on them. When installing Informatica Platform, you can choose whether you want to create a new domain on this node or join it to an existing domain. Once you do that you can configure what services run on the node in the Administrator console.

Model Repository Service

Model Repository is the collection of metadata created by the Developers and Analysts using Informatica Platform. This metadata is stored in a relational database. Model Repository Service (MRS) manages this metadata. The Model Repository can be configured either during the installation or post installation (in the Administrator console). The service translates the code stored in the repository in a meaningful way for the Developer tool to represent it in the UI. MRS allows you to centrally manage project level permissions, setup versioning, handle locks on various objects and much more. You can have as many MRS as needed, in a domain. Since each MRS is a code repository, they do not share objects. You can however migrate code from one MRS to another.

Data Integration Service

Data Integration Service (DIS) is a runtime service/engine that executes the mappings and workflows that you develop. DIS fetches mappings, workflow and other runnable objects from the runtime repository and executes them based on the logic within. DIS has several modules such as mapping service, workflow service, and profiling service built into it. Modules allow you to enable / disable certain functionality in the DIS. Disabling modules reduces the resources required by DIS to operate and also limits DIS' functionality at the same time. Depending on your license and usage, you may choose to keep some module disabled. For example, if you do not have any use-case for web services, you can disable the web service module.

Backup nodes

You can configure some of your services such as MRS and DIS to have backup nodes. When the primary node goes down, the service will automatically switch-over to the secondary/backup node. If licensed, you can configure High Availability so that the switch-over is seamless.

Informatica Grid

Grid is a set of objects grouped together to perform similar tasks. You can create a grid of nodes and run your DIS. When you run your DIS on a grid, jobs will be, by default, distributed across all nodes within the grid. This allows you to distribute the workload across various nodes.

Informatica Developer

Informatica Developer is an Eclipse based client tool where you can develop mappings, profiles and workflows. This is a single unified client for all developer needs including development, unit testing, code deployment, etc.

Informatica Analyst

Informatica Analyst is a web based thin client used by business users to build and manage data profiles, score cards and mapping specifications. Just like Developer tool, Analyst also relies on the DIS for execution of these objects. Unlike Informatica Developer tool which is used by IT personnel and developer community, Analyst tool is primarily used by business users and analysts. Both tools contain several collaboration features to facilitate the interaction between these different personas.

Informatica Administrator

Informatica Administrator (Admin Console) is a web based client to manage and administer the entire Informatica Platform. You can start, stop, restart services, manage users, groups, roles and privileges, and much more from this client tool. You can also manage database and other connections, monitor job execution from here.

Putting it all together

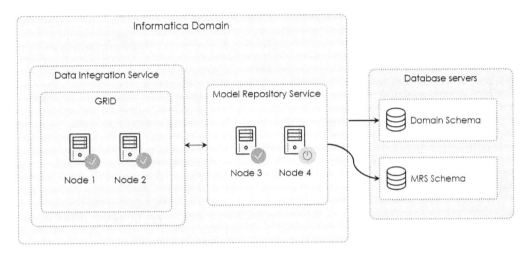

Let's take a look at it all together. You typically have an Informatica domain per environment such as Dev, QA and production. A domain may contain one or more Informatica nodes. The screenshot shown here represents an Informatica domain of 4 nodes. Two nodes are running DIS configured on a GRID. The other two nodes are running Model Repository Service on a primary node (node 3) and a standby node (node 4). MRS stores artifacts such as mappings, profiles, and workflows. You use Developer, a thick client, to design and develop design time artifacts. At runtime, you execute your jobs with DIS which can run on primary/secondary nodes or on a grid of nodes for load balancing. You can manage all these services using Administrator console (not shown in the picture) which is a web based thin client, where you can also create and manage users, groups, roles, privileges and various permissions.

The architecture diagram here shows a mix of physical nodes and services for easy understanding of the architecture.

Repository objects

The MRS can contain various types of objects. In this section you look at a few of them. We will cover them in detail later.

Projects

Project is a top level container within the MRS. It is a collection of all objects that can be stored in a MRS. You cannot create any objects outside of a project, within a MRS. Typically, you create a project for every application you are trying to build. For example: Enterpise_DataWarehouse. Projects are not recursive, but you cannot create a project within a project.

Folders

Folder is a container that allows you to group objects within the MRS. Within a given project, you may want to group objects based on their association or usage or functionality. For example, within an Enterprise_DataWarehouse project, you may have 3 folders such as: Source_to_Staging, Staging_to_ODS, and ODS_to_DWH. Similarly, if you want to group the objects by business unit instead of functionality, you may create folders such as HR, Finance, etc. You can create folders within folders.

Data Object

A data object as its name suggests represents an object in any data store. Relational data object represents a table in your RDBMS. A NoSQL data object represents a collection in your NoSQL database. A flat file data object represents any flat file you want to process. A social media data object represents the data you want to retrieve from Facebook, LinkedIn or Twitter and so on.

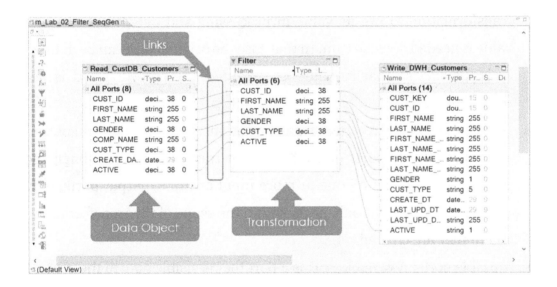

Transformation

A transformation is an object that can transform the input data it receives into a predefined/ user-defined output format. Sorter transformation orders the rows based on the user-defined keys. Expression transformation can be used to transform the data using Informatica's transformation language.

Ports

A port is a column within a transformation or data object. Typically, a port has a name, data type, and precision, scale. Ports can be of various types:

1. Pass through port (Input/Output): These are the ports that flow, unchanged, through a transformation. For example, in Sorter transformation, all ports are pass through.

2. Input only ports: Sometimes some ports are brought into a transformation to use its value in processing and only if transformed value is needed downstream. In that case the original port can be defined as input only so that its value is discarded after process, and is not carried forward.

3. Output only ports: In certain transformations, you create several output only ports. These ports originate in that transformation. Though the output ports depend on one or more input or input/output ports, they are referred as output only ports within the scope of the transformation where they are created.

4. Variable ports: A variable port is a port that is visible only in the context of a given transformation and its value is retained across rows until it is subsequently changed. Variable ports cannot be transferred to another transformation. If you want to pass on the value of a variable port to a subsequent transformation, create an output only port and assign the variable value to it.

5. Special ports: Certain transformations have special ports that are very specific to them. For example, a Sorter transformation has sort key ports. The ports marked as sort keys are used to sort the data. Similarly,

Aggregator has group by ports on which data must be grouped by to calculate aggregations. You will learn more about them when you learn about corresponding transformations.

Links

A link is an arrow that you draw to define the data movement between two or more objects. These objects can be data objects and/or transformations or both.

Mapping

A mapping is an Informatica repository object that allows you to define how to read the data from a data object, transform it as necessary by applying transformations, and then write it back to another data object. A mapping is the most basic processing unit in the platform. Mapping is the Informatica Platform's UI based approach to code your transformation logic.

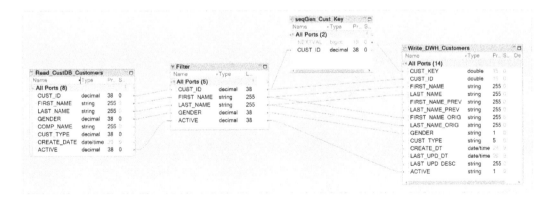

Workflow

A workflow is Informatica's orchestration entity. It is the place where you can define the order of execution of the mappings, set dependencies between them, and execute them together to form a process flow. A sample workflow screenshot is provided here for better understanding:

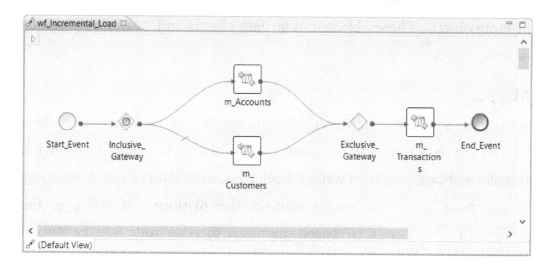

Chapter 2 – Installation of Informatica Platform

This section takes you, step by step, through the instructions for installing Informatica Platform. This book will use Oracle database for its Informatica installation. You can use any supported database.

Pre-requisites

Let's first take a look at the pre-requisites involved in setting up the Informatica Platform. It is important to understand, at the outset, that Informatica Platform is an enterprise software, and is hence setup for scale. Informatica has a consistent install procedure regardless of the number of users leveraging it. As the numbers of your users grow, you just have to ensure the underlying hardware has enough resources to scale up, and Informatica Platform will adapt to the hardware resources. For first time users though, the steps involved may sound somewhat complex. But once you understand the overall procedure, it starts becoming clearer as to what is needed and why. At a high level, this is what you need:

1. OS user to host Informatica services - recommended, not mandatory
2. Database accounts
3. Disk space

Just like any other data integration software, it is recommended that Informatica Platform be installed and configured in a dedicated application account. An application account is typically just another OS user with no login privileges. Individual user accounts are usually bound to certain policies within the enterprise that require them to change the password regularly. Using an individual account for hosting an application such as Informatica causes administration and maintenance overheads. When passwords expire, jobs start failing; necessitating manual intervention. Application accounts solve this problem. Having application accounts also helps in security. DI jobs at times require to access and process sensitive information. Having a dedicated application account helps in granting necessary elevated privileges to the application account that individuals do not have access to. This keeps the auditing and security simple and clean. In this book, you will create an application account called "infa". You will use this account to host Informatica Platform. Similarly, you can use any name of your choice. You can also add Informatica Platform version number as a suffix to the account name such as "infa1011", "infa102", etc., though this is discouraged. Having a version number requires you to create a different account every time you upgrade. This can cause a huge overhead in a multi-tenant environment as you will have to reapply all file level access, which will have a direct impact on production jobs. On UNIX platforms, you can host more than one Informatica Platform under the same user account and run various jobs from both versions of Informatica Platforms at the same time.

Disk space

In general, when accounting for disk space, you need to consider various factors:

1. Disk space required for Installer: The Informatica installer is about 25 GB in size and is a unified installer for all Informatica on-premise products. Once the installation is complete, you can delete these installers and reclaim the space. Alternatively, you can archive the installer to a different low cost storage for future use.

2. Disk space required for an Informatica instance: When you run the installer, you will point it to a location where you intend to install the binaries. This will be your INFA_HOME. This is the location where you will run the Informatica Services from. You will continue to consume this disk space as long as you intend to have an Informatica instance available. This space is typically around 25 GB.

3. Disk space for the repositories: The code you develop in Informatica is stored inside the repositories (more on this later). These repositories are created inside database schemas that you create and associate as part of the installer. If you are a large enterprise and have tens of developers actively building code, the repository schema will grow accordingly.

4. Logs: You will need to account for the logs that Informatica Platform will create. Depending on the Informatica products you are licensed for, and you plan to run, you will have various services running within the platform. Each of these services will maintain a comprehensive log of activities. You will need to provide them enough space to retain the logs for audit and future reference purposes. You can configure how long these logs should remain on the disk. Service logs typically grow gradually, and not exponentially

over a period of time. However, there is another set of logs that grows fast. When you execute Informatica jobs (mappings or workflows), each invocation of the job creates a log. Developers can customize the level of logging for the jobs. These logs are stored on the disk too. Just as with the service logs, you can control how many days these logs should remain on the disk before they are purged.

5. Backups: In Informatica Platform, the code you develop is stored inside a repository. Hence it is important to have regular backups of the code. Depending on how large your enterprise is, you should plan for enough backup disk storage.

6. Upgrades, patches: You may also want to account for additional disk space required for upgrades and patches. When upgrading or applying patches, you would want the upgrade/patch installers also available on the same server(s). So, you will temporarily need enough disk space to hold them along with your Informatica services.

7. Data files: Every data integration application has certain sources and targets. Some of them may be inside a relational database or stored as files. If the databases are on the same servers as Informatica or on the same file system as your Informatica server, you need to account for those as well. It is important to note that the growth of this part of the disk purely depends on the architecture (i.e. how often the mappings land their data), archival and auditing requirements of the application itself. The Informatica Platform or the services have no bearing on these.

8. Cache files: As part of your jobs, you may choose to use certain transformations that cache the source data for faster processing. If the data volumes are high, these caches may spill over to the disk. The number of caches that are created varies per job (depending on how the mapping is built) and the data processed.

NOTE: You do not need to allocate disk space for all of the above types to begin installation. As described above, some disk requirements are more or less static (such as INFA_HOME), whereas some are completely dynamic (such as cache files and job logs). Depending on whether you are setting up a sandbox or a production environment, you need to plan accordingly.

Database requirements

This section of the book only talks about the database requirements of Oracle. If you are using another database in your setup you can skip this section and continue to the next one. But remember that you should still meet all the prerequisites mentioned in Informatica Installation and Configuration Guide for the database you are using.

Open cursors

Informatica Platform needs Oracle's open cursors to be set at 4000 or higher. To check the current value for open cursors you can use the following command:

```
SELECT VALUE OPEN_CURSORS FROM V$PARAMETER
WHERE UPPER(NAME)=UPPER('OPEN_CURSORS')
```

You can change the open cursors using the following Oracle command:

```
ALTER SYSTEM SET open_cursors = 1000 SCOPE=BOTH;
```

For further details or other ways of configuring this property, please reach out to your DBA.

Database schemas

Informatica Platform relies on a couple of database schemas. These schemas are used to store the repository content. Depending on your usage of the platform, you may need one or more repositories. At the minimum, you need two repositories created: Domain Repository and Model Repository. For the functionality you cover in this book, you are going to create two additional schemas as well: Monitoring / Runtime and Workflow Service. We will cover more on the schemas in a later section.

You can use the following commands to create the users and grant them necessary privileges:

```
CREATE USER infa_domain identified by infa;
CREATE USER infa_mrs identified by infa;
CREATE USER infa_monitor identified by infa;
CREATE USER infa_workflow identified by infa;


GRANT CONNECT, RESOURCE, CREATE TABLE, CREATE VIEW, CREATE
SESSION, CREATE SYNONYM, CREATE SEQUENCE TO infa_domain,
infa_mrs, infa_monitor, infa_workflow;
```

Note that for simplicity sake, I have used a very simple password. It is highly recommended that you use a much more complex password with a combination of lower case letters, upper case letters and numbers for your database accounts.

In an enterprise environment, you may want to suffix the usernames with the Informatica version. For example, instead of infa_domain, you can use infa_domain_1011 or infa_dom_1011. By suffixing Informatica version number at the end, you can have repositories of multiple versions of Informatica Platform within the database without any conflicts. This is also very handy when you want to perform upgrades of Informatica without upgrading the databases it relies on.

Software and license

To install and configure Informatica Platform, you need to download the Software and license keys. You can get the download links by requesting Informatica Global Customer Support. You can create a shipping request in the Informatica support portal to get the download links and the license keys. You get a different license key for production and non-production environments. During the initial steps of the installation process, you will be prompted to provide the license key. So, you will need to keep it accessible on the servers. Once the install is complete, you can remove the license keys from the server(s). The platform will store your license internally and you will no longer be required to keep it on the disk.

Installation procedure

In this book, I have executed the installer on the Linux platform. So, I have downloaded the Linux installer as shown below:

```
[infa@mahathiDownloads]#ls -l *.tar

-rwxrwxrwx. 1 infainfa 8810127360 Nov 20 23:04

1011_Server_Installer_linux-x64.tar
```

First you must un-tar the installer to a location. In this case, I am un-archiving the installer into a directory called 1011_Installer. The un-archive process goes through every single file in the installer archive, which may take a while. During this process, you will notice that the un-archive process appears to have paused. Let the process run its due course. Some sample lines from the un-archive process are given below:

```
[infa@mahathi 1011_Installer]# tar -xvf
/mnt/hgfs/Downloads/1011_Server_Installer_linux-x64.tar
./
./properties/
./properties/UIDesign.properties
... ... ... ... ...
./properties/version.txt
./properties/copyFiles_OverWrite.properties
```

I have already copied the license key into the same location as the installer.

```
[infa@mahathi 1011_Installer]$ls -l *.key
-rwxr-xr-x. 1 infainfa 5568 Jan 20 21:07
License_201701.key
```

Let's look at the default code page on the server:

```
[infa@mahathi 1011_Installer] $ echo $LANG
en_US.UTF-8
```

Run the installer by invoking install.sh. Installer will take a few minutes to initialize. When prompted to continue, choose "Y".

```
[infa@mahathi 1011_Installer] $ ./install.sh
OS detected is Linux
unjar task is in progress...........
\***********
\* Welcome to the Informatica 10.2.0 Server Installer.  *
\************


Before you continue, read the following documents:
* Informatica 10.2.0 Installation Guide, Informatica
Release Guide and Informatica Release Notes.
* B2B Data Transformation 10.2.0 Installation,
Configuration Guide and Release Notes.


You can find the 10.2.0 documentation in the Product
Documentation section at https://network.informatica.com/.
```

```
Configure the LANG and LC_ALL variables to generate the
appropriate code pages and
create and connect to repositories and Repository
Services.
Do you want to continue? (Y/N) Y
```

You will be prompted to either install or upgrade the Informatica services. In this case, I choose to install it instead of upgrading an existing environment.

```
Select one of the following options to install or upgrade:

  1. Install Informatica.
. Choose this option if one of the following conditions is
true:
   * You want to install Informatica services on a machine
that does not have Informatica version 10.2.0.
   * You want to install Enterprise Information Catalog
10.2.0.


  2. Upgrade Informatica.
. Choose this option if one of the following conditions is
true:
   * You want to upgrade the Informatica services on a
machine that has Informatica version 10.1.1 or an earlier
version installed.
   * You want to upgrade Enterprise Information Catalog
version.
```

```
   3. Install or upgrade Data Transformation Engine Only.

     Choose this option to install or upgrade only Data

  Transformation Engine.


  Enter the choice(1 or 2 or 3):1
```

In the next step, you will be prompted to run the pre-installation checks. I have already gone through the installation and configuration guide and checked all the pre-requisites. So, I will choose option 3 to directly run the installation after skipping the pre-install checklist.

```
--------------------------------------------------------------
-

Checking for an Informatica 10.2.0 installation.

To verify whether the machine meets the system

requirements for the Informatica installation or upgrade,

run the Pre-Installation (i10PreInstallChecker) System

Check Tool before you start the installation or upgrade

process. Informatica recommends that you verify the

minimum system requirements.



Select one of the following options:

1. Run the Pre-Installation (i10PreInstallChecker) System

Check Tool

2. Run the Informatica Kerberos SPN Format Generator

3. Run the Informatica services installation
```

```
Select the option to proceed: (Default: 3)3
```

You will be prompted with terms and conditions. You will have to accept them to continue.

```
***************************************
Welcome - Step 1 of 9
***************************************
[ Type 'back' to go to the previous panel or 'help' to
check the help contents for this panel or 'quit' to cancel
the installation at any time.]
WHEN YOU SELECT 'AGREE' AND INSTALL THE INFORMATICA
PLATFORM, YOU AGREE TO BE BOUND BY THE PRODUCT USAGE
TOOLKIT END USER LICENSE AGREEMENT, WHICH IS AVAILABLE AT:
http://www.informatica.com/us/eula/en-support-eula.aspx.
AS FURTHER DESCRIBED IN THE EULA, YOUR USE OF THE
INFORMATICA PLATFORM WILL ENABLE THE PRODUCT USAGE TOOLKIT
TO COLLECT CERTAIN PRODUCT USAGE AND FAILURE INFORMATION.
YOU MAY DISABLE THIS FEATURE AT ANY TIME. FOR MORE
INFORMATION ON HOW TO DISABLE THIS FEATURE, SEE THE
INFORMATICA ADMINISTRATOR GUIDE.


I agree to the terms and conditions
    * 1->No
      2->Yes
(Default: 1):2
```

You will be prompted to install Informatica Service or Informatica's Enterprise Information Catalog. Enterprise Information Catalog is the framework that powers Informatica products such as Enterprise Information Catalog. You will choose the Informatica Platform.

```
*************************************
Component Selection - Step 1A of 9
*************************************
[ Type 'back' to go to the previous panel or 'help' to
check the help contents for this panel or 'quit' to cancel
the installation at any time.]


Select one of the following options to install Informatica
10.2.0 services or Informatica Enterprise Information
Catalog:
    * 1->Install Informatica Services.
Select this option to install Informatica 10.2.0 services.
      2->Install Informatica Enterprise Information
Catalog.
Select this option to install Informatica Enterprise
Information Catalog and services.
(Default: 1):1
```

You will then be prompted to choose whether or not you want to enable "Kerberos". I am disabling the Kerberos in my environment.

```
Enable Kerberos network authentication for the Informatica
domain.
    * 1->No
      2->Yes
(Default: 1):1
```

Prerequisites and pre-installation tasks are displayed. Press <ENTER> to continue with the installation.

```
*************************************
Installation Prerequisites - Step 2 of 9
*************************************
[ Type 'back' to go to the previous panel or 'help' to
check the help contents for this panel or 'quit' to cancel
the installation at any time.]


Verify the installation prerequisites and complete the
pre-installation tasks before you continue.


Disk Space: 13 GB


Memory(RAM): 6 GB


Database Requirements
- Verify the Oracle, IBM DB2, Microsoft SQL Server, or
Sybase ASE database version.
```

```
- Verify the database user account. The account must have
following permissions on the domain configuration
repository, reference data warehouse, and Sybase ASE
(applies only to the domain connection):


- Create tables and views.
- Drop tables and views.
- Insert, update and delete data.


Pre-installation Tasks
- Get the Informatica license key.
- Verify the minimum system requirements.
- Set the environment variables.
- Verify the port availability.
- Set up the keystore file.
- On UNIX, set the file descriptor limit.
- On UNIX, configure POSIX asynchronous I/O.
- Download and extract the Informatica installer files.
- Run the Informatica Pre-Installation
(i10PreInstallChecker) System Check Tool.
- If you are enabling Kerberos network authentication, run
the Informatica Kerberos SPN Format Generator.


Press <Enter> to continue ...
```

In Step 3, you will be prompted for the license key and the directory where you want to install Informatica services. You need to provide absolute paths for both of these. If you do not have a license key, just log on to the Informatica Global Customer Support portal at http://network.informatica.com to create a shipping request.

```
****************************************
License and Installation Directory - Step 3 of 9
****************************************
[ Type 'back' to go to the previous panel or 'help' to
check the help contents for this panel or 'quit' to cancel
the installation at any time.]


Enter the license key file (default :-
/home/infa/license.key)
:/home/infa/Installer/License_8696.key
Enter the installation directory (default :-
/home/infa/Informatica/10.2.0) :/opt/Informatica/10.2.0
```

Pre-installation summary is displayed. Press <ENTER> to continue.

```
****************************************
Pre-Installation Summary - Step 4 of 9
****************************************
[ Type 'back' to go to the previous panel or 'help' to
check the help contents for this panel or 'quit' to cancel
the installation at any time. ]


Product Name        :        Informatica 10.2.0
Installation Type       :        New Installation
Installation Directory     :        /opt/Informatica/10.2.0
```

```
Disk Space Requirements
Required Disk Space        :        10,165 MB
Available Disk Space       :        47,464 MB
Press <Enter> to continue ...
```

In Step 5, installation will begin. It will take several minutes for the file copy process to complete.

```
**************************************
Installing - Step 5 of 9
**************************************
Installing... 5%
Installing... 10%
Installing... 15%
Installing... 20%
Installing... 25%
Installing... 30%
Installing... 35%
Installing... 40%
Installing... 45%
Installing... 50%
Installing... 55%
Installing... 60%
Installing... 65%
Installing... 70%
Installing... 75%
Installing... 80%
Installing... 85%
```

```
Installing... 90%
Installing... 95%
Installing... 100%
```

Once all the files are copied, you will be prompted with Step 5A for domain creation. Here you have a choice of either creating or joining a domain. If you are installing Informatica on multiple nodes, on the first node you will create a domain, and on every other node you will join the domain you already created. Domain is an equivalent of an environment. If you want to setup say 3 environments for your enterprise: Dev, QA and Production – then you will install 3 domains. In this step, you can also choose to enable or disable security for the domain. If you enable secure communication, all nodes interact in a secure mode (SSL). You can also enable HTTPS for the Informatica Administrator console. You use the administrator console to administer and manage the services. SAML authentication can be enabled for the domain. In this demonstration, it is being disabled (option 2).

```
*************************************
Domain Selection - Step 5A of 9
*************************************
[ Type 'back' to go to the previous panel or 'help' to
check the help contents for this panel or 'quit' to cancel
the installation at any time. ]


    * 1->Create a domain
      2->Join a domain
(Default: 1):1
```

```
Enable secure communication for the domain
    * 1->No
      2->Yes
(Default: 1):1
    * 1->Enable HTTPS for Informatica Administrator
      2->Disable HTTPS
(Default: 1):2
Enable SAML authentication
    * 1->No
      2->Yes
(Default: 1): 1
```

If you choose to create the domain, you will be prompted for the database details. The domain requires a repository / database schema. This is where the Informatica services configuration, user, and group information is stored. In this book, I have used Oracle database. So, I have provided the Oracle login and schema details, and the JDBC URL associated with the database.

```
********************************************************
******
Domain Configuration Repository - Step 5B of 9
********************************************************
******
```

```
[ Type 'back' to go to the previous panel or 'help' to
check the help contents for this panel or 'quit' to cancel
the installation at any time.]
Configure the database for the domain configuration
repository:
Database type:
    * 1->Oracle
      2->SQLServer
      3->DB2
      4->Sybase
(Default: 1):1


Database user ID: (default :- infa_domain) :


User password: (default :- ) :


Configure the database connection
    * 1->JDBC URL
      2->Custom JDBC Connection String
(Default: 1):


Database address: (default :- mahathi:1521) :


Database service name: (default :- XE) :


Configure the JDBC parameters?
      1->Yes
```

```
     * 2->No
(Default: 2):
```

Then you reach Step 5c where you will be prompted to provide encryption keys. It is very important that you memorize the encryption key you provide here or store it in a safe place. There is no way to retrieve the encryption key post this step. The encrypted siteKey is stored by default inside the Informatica home directory. You can choose a non-default path.

```
*******************************************************
******
Domain Security - Encryption Key - Step 5C of 9
*******************************************************
******
[ Type 'back' to go to the previous panel or 'help' to
check the help contents for this panel or 'quit' to cancel
the installation at any time.]
Keyword: :
Encryption key directory: (default :-
/opt/Informatica/10.2.0/isp/config/keys) :
Information !!! The encryption key will be generated in
the /opt/Informatica/10.2.0/isp/config/keys
with the file name siteKey. Save the name of the domain,
the keyword for the encryption key,
and the encryption key file in a secure location. You need
to specify the domain name,
```

```
keyword, and encryption key when you change the encryption
key for the domain or move a repository to another domain.


Select a Choice
    * 1->OK
(Default: 1):
```

In Step 6, you need to provide the node and domain configuration. In this setup, I named my domain as Domain_Dev, where Dev stands for development. You are required to specify the hostname, and provide a node name to it. The node name is an Informatica reference to the hostname. You will also provide the port number on which Informatica services should run. You can also configure the default Administrator account at this time. This will be your master account to administer all Informatica services. I am choosing to configure the default ports. You can choose the advanced port configuration page to define individual port numbers for each Informatica service.

```
************************************************************
******
Domain and Node Configuration - Step 6 of 9
************************************************************
******
[ Type 'back' to go to the previous panel or 'help' to
check the help contents for this panel or 'quit' to cancel
the installation at any time.]
```

```
Enter the following information for the Informatica
domain.


Domain name: (default :- Domain) :Domain_Dev

Node host name: (default :- mahathi) :

Node name: (default :- node01) :node01

Node port number: (default :- 6005) :

Domain user name: (default :- Administrator) :


Domain password: (default :- ) :


Confirm password: (default :- ) :


Enable SAML-based Single Sign-on
    * 1->No
      2->Yes
(Default: 1):1


Display the Advanced Port Configuration page?
    * 1->No
      2->Yes
(Default: 1):1


Configure the Model Repository Service and DIS
    * 1->Yes
      2->No
(Default: 1):1
```

Installer will now create the domain, and Administrator console, and will ping it.

```
Executing the Command...
--

Defining the domain...
-

Registering the plugins...
-

Starting the service...
-

Pinging the domain...
-

Pinging the Administrator service...
-
```

Since I chose to create a MRS service in the previous step, you will provide the database schema details to store the Model Repository content.

```
************************************************************
******
Model Repository Service Database - Step 7A of 9
************************************************************
******
```

```
[ Type 'back' to go to the previous panel or 'help' to
check the help contents for this panel or 'quit' to cancel
the installation at any time.]


Configure the Model Repository Service database:


Database type:
    * 1->Oracle
      2->SQLServer
      3->DB2
(Default: 1):1


Database user ID: (default :- admin) :infa_mrs


User password: :


Secure database
      1->Yes
    * 2->No
(Default: 2):2


Configure the database connection
    * 1->JDBC URL
      2->Custom JDBC Connection String
(Default: 1):1
```

```
Database address: (default :- host_name:port_no)
:mahathi:1521


Database service name: (default :- ServiceName) :XE


Configure the JDBC parameters?
    * 1->Yes
      2->No
(Default: 1):2
```

In the next step, you provide the names for Model Repository and DIS.

```
***************************************************************
******
Service Parameters - Step 7B of 9
***************************************************************
******
[ Type 'back' to go to the previous panel or 'help' to
check the help contents for this panel or 'quit' to cancel
the installation at any time]



Model Repository Service name: (default :-
Model_Repository_Service) :MRS_Dev


DIS name: (default :- Data_Integration_Service) :DIS_Dev
```

```
HTTP protocol type:
    * 1->http
      2->https
      3->http&https
(Default: 1):


HTTP Port: (default :- 8095) :


Creating the Model Repository Service...

-

Enabling the Model Repository Service...

-

Updating the Model Repository Service...

-

Creating the Model Repository Contents...

-

Creating the DIS...

-

Updating the DIS...

-

Enabling the DIS...

-
```

Post-installation summary is now displayed. Once you go through this, press <ENTER> to continue. You will notice that the administrator console URL is displayed. You will use the administrator console to manage the services and Informatica domain from hereon.

```
**************************************************************
******
Post-Installation Summary - Step 9 of 9
**************************************************************
******
Installation Status SUCCESS


The Informatica 10.2.0 installation is complete.


The system services are disabled by default after the
installation is complete.
You must configure the services and then enable them in
the Informatica Administrator tool.


For more information, see the debug log file:
/opt/Informatica/10.2.0/Informatica_10.2.0_Services_2017_0
2_03_14_36_00.log


Installation Type :New Installation



Informatica Administrator Home Page::
http://mahathi:6008


Product Name:   Informatica 10.2.0


Press <Enter> to continue ...
```

Client Installation

This chapter talks you through the various steps involved in the Informatica client setup. Informatica client installation is a very simple and straightforward process. If you don't have the client installer, you can create a shipping request on the Informatica Global Customer Support portal at http://network.informatica.com. Once you download the client, extract the zip file contents. To install Informatica client, run the install.bat as an Administrator by choosing the "Run as administrator" in the windows explorer. This will give the installer elevated privileges so that it can add necessary values to the Windows registry as well. Once the installer launches, you will be prompted to choose either to do a new installation of the Informatica client or to upgrade your existing client. If you are installing the client for the first time, choose "Install Informatica client". If you already have a client that you want to upgrade, choose the "Upgrade Informatica Clients". Upgrading clients will replace your existing Informatica client with the version of installer you are executing. It is possible for you to have more than one client installed on the same machine. To do so, you will have to install each version of the client to a different location / directory.

 Note that each Informatica client can connect to the same version of the Informatica Server. If you still want to connect to your older

version of the Informatica server, you should perform a new installation instead of upgrading the Informatica client.

Installer will prompt you with the pre-requisites. Informatica client requires about 7 GB of disk space. Click "Next" to go past this screen. You will be prompted to choose the clients you want to install. There are two Informatica clients available: Informatica Developer and PowerCenter client. Informatica Developer client is used for the Informatica Platform (i.e. to connect to MRS and run the jobs via DIS). PowerCenter client is used to interact with PowerCenter services i.e. PowerCenter Repository Service and PowerCenter Integration Service. In this book, you will only discuss Informatica Developer. You are then prompted to choose the location where you want to install the client. Default location is `C:\Informatica\10.2.0`for this book; I am installing it to a non-default location `C:\Software\Informatica\10.2.0` Pre-installation summary is then displayed followed by the installation process. Installation will take about 15 minutes to complete. Once the installation is complete, a post-installation summary is displayed. You will notice that the Installation Status is set to SUCCESS. If you see any warnings, go through the log file mentioned on the screen and rerun the installer again.

Chapter 3 – Understanding the client UI

In this chapter of the book, you take a look at the client UI. This chapter introduces the user interface and various components in the Informatica Developer tool. Informatica Developer is an Eclipse based Graphical User Interface (GUI) that lets you design, develop, manage and deploy all Informatica Platform code objects. It is important to note that the Informatica Developer tool is not used for managing the Informatica environment. Environment management and administration is performed through the Informatica Administrator console and it is built for administrators. Administrators can also use Command Line Interface for automating the administrative tasks. Developer tool, as its name, suggests is used by developers to perform all aspects of code in a single, unified, user-friendly interface. You can launch the developer from the start menu. In Windows 8 or later, you can search for Informatica and you will notice that the "Launch Informatica Developer" menu item appears. When you launch the Developer for the first time, you will have to configure it, which you will see in the next section.

Understanding the UI components

When the developer is launched for the first time, you will see the screenshot as shown here. You will have to click on the "workspace" icon on the top right corner. This will launch the Developer workspace. Once developer workspace is launched, you will notice that several windows and panes will appear. Let us look at them one at a time. Please refer to the annotated screenshot for this.

a. This is where the menus and toolbar icons appear. Both of them are contextual – meaning that the menus / icons appearing here will change, based on the current activity you are performing or the current window open in the workspace.

b. Object Explorer: This is where the contents of the Model Repository will be displayed in a hierarchical order. This navigation is very similar to the navigation in the Windows Explorer. Here you will see objects such as Projects, Folders, Mappings, Mapplets, Profiles, Workflows, etc. You can open them, copy-paste them, delete them – right from this object explorer.

c. Outline: When you have an object such as a mapping open, outline pane displays all the objects within that object. This pane is very helpful for large objects. For example, if you have a mapping with 30 transformations and you are looking to quickly get to a specific transformation, instead of visually searching for it in the mapping, you can use the outline pane to quickly find it.

d. Workspace: When you open an object such as a mapping, this is where it appears. You will use the workspace to interact with the object, make any modifications and in some cases preview the data or run the object.

e. Properties pane: When you have an object open in the workspace, this is where all the properties associated with it appear. This pane is context sensitive. If you open a mapping in the workspace, this pane shows mapping properties. If you select a transformation in the workspace, this pane shows the transformation properties and so on.

f. Welcome pane: This pane is often used by beginners to understand
    their way around the UI. Once you are familiar with the UI itself, you
    can close this pane.

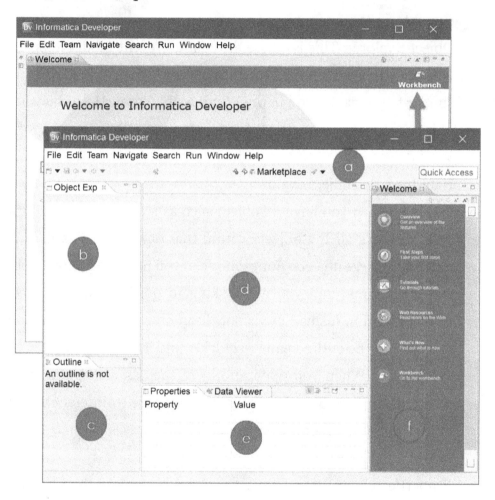

Connecting the Developer to Informatica Domain

What information do I need?

Since you have launched the developer for the first time, you need to configure the domain and Model Repository Service (MRS) that you want to connect to. You can connect to as many domains/MRS services as you want. You can also do cross-domain, cross-MRS operations such as copying a connection from one domain to another and copying a mapping from one MRS to another. Before you connect to a MRS, you should configure the domain that hosts the MRS service. To connect to a domain/MRS, you will need the following information:

    a. Name of the domain

    b. Hostname of any node in the domain

    c. Port number on which that node is hosting Informatica services

If you do not have access to this information, reach out to your Informatica administrator. This is how your Informatica administrator can provide you the details.

    a. Log into Informatica Administrator console. This is by default available at http://<host name>:6008/administrator.

    b. In the Domain tab, click **Services and Nodes**.

    c. In the domain Navigator, select master gateway node. Note that the names listed here are not the actual hostnames. These are the names that you have provided for the hosts during the installation of Informatica Services. They are typically named as node01, node02, etc. Click on the node name.

d. On the right hand side properties, you will notice the physical hostname and the port number.

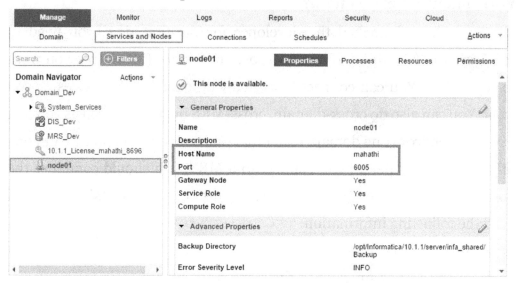

Configuring the client for first time use

Once you have all the information needed, follow the below steps in Informatica Developer to register the domain and MRS.

    a. In the **File** menu, click the **Connect to Repository**.

    b. This will open the **Connect to Repository** dialog box. Click on the **Configure domains** hyperlink.

    c. This will open the **Preferences** dialog box with available domains list. Since this is the first time you are accessing it, the list will be empty. Click on **Add**.

    d. **New Domain** dialog box will appear. Provide the domain details here. You will need name of the domain, hostname of the nodes in the domain, the port number on which the services are running. Click

Test Connection to test the values you provided followed by **Finish**.

e. You will now be back to **Connect to Repository** screen. Click **Browse...**

f. **Choose Service** dialog box appears. Double click on the domain or expand it by clicking the triangle icon appearing before the domain name. Then click on the MRS you want to connect to and click **OK**.

g. You will now be back to **Connect to Repository** screen and you will notice that the Domain name and MRS name are listed in the screen. Click **Next**.

h. You will be prompted for a username/password. Provide the login credentials provided by your administrator here and click **Next**.

i. **Open Project** dialog box appears. This is where you will typically see all available projects. Since you are connecting to an empty MRS, you will not see any projects here. If you are connecting to an existing MRS, you will see the projects list here and you can choose (select) the projects that you want to load to the developer. Any projects that you leave unchecked will still continue to be in the MRS, but will not be displayed in the developer UI. Click **Finish**.

j. You will notice that the MRS is now listed in the object explorer, but is empty (since you don't have any projects yet).

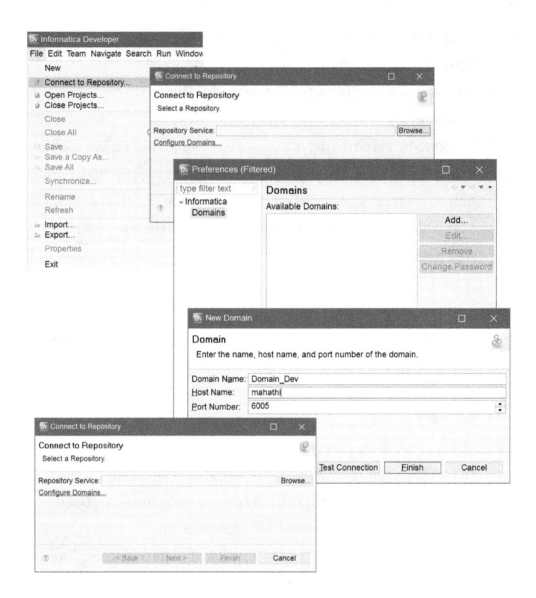

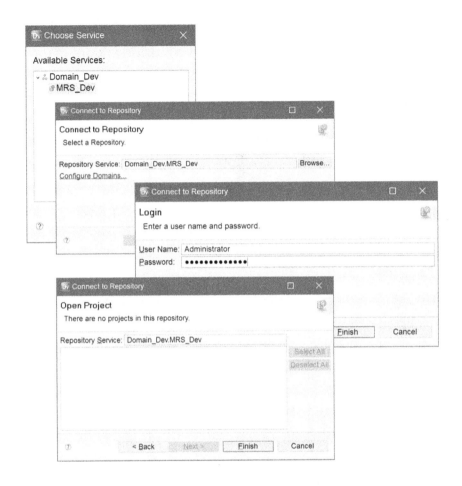

Organizing your code into projects & folders

Now that you have connected to an empty MRS, let's create some containers. There are two types of code containers that you can create in MRS: Projects, and Folders. Project is the top level container. You need at least one project inside a MRS. Objects such as mappings, profiles and workflows can be created only inside a project. These objects cannot be created outside a project. Inside a project, you can organize your code into various folders. You can have any number of folders inside a project. You can store your code objects directly in the project or inside folders within a project. For example, you can have all shared objects such as sources/targets inside the project itself and organize your mappings into various folders. Depending on the application that you are trying to build, you can organize your folders differently. For example, in a Data Warehouse project, you can have a Staging folder, an Operational Data Store folder and a Data Warehouse folder. Alternatively, you can have one folder for each business unit that interacts with the Data Warehouse such as HR, Finance, etc. For the examples listed in the book, you will use a project named INFA_Platform_Labs. To create the project and a folder within it, let's follow the steps listed below:

a. Right click the MRS in the object explorer. Click **New → Project**.

b. In the **New Project** dialog box, provide the name as **INFA_Platform_Labs** and click **Next**.

c. You can configure which users have access to this project. In this example, you are leaving everything to default. If you are creating the project in an enterprise MRS, you can click **Add** to add users/groups and assign them **Read / Write / Grant** permissions on the project. Click **Finish** to close the dialog box and create a project.

d. In the object explorer, right click the **INFA_Platform_Labs** project and click **New → Folder**.

e. Type the Folder name as **Part_1_Basics** and click **Finish**.

f. Similarly, create another folder called **Shared_Objects**.

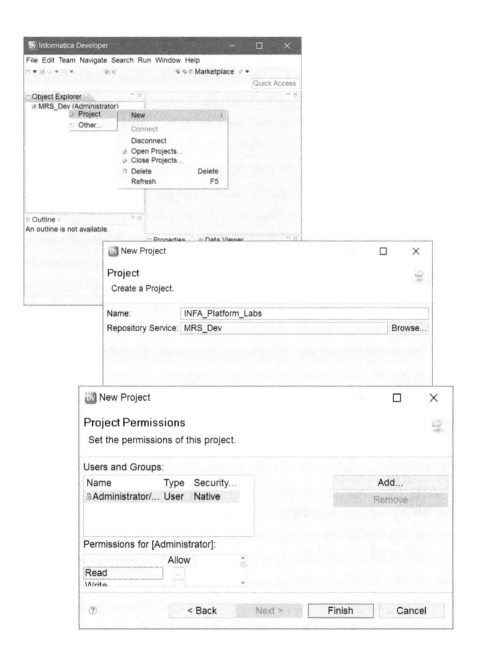

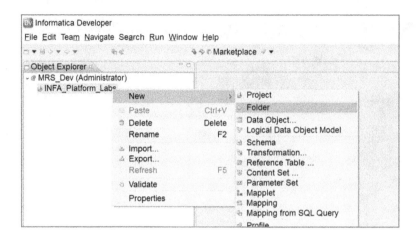

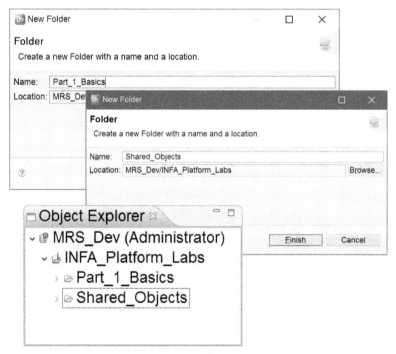

Monitoring console

Informatica Developer is primarily used to create, manage, organize and deploy code. Though it does have basic monitoring capabilities, it isn't the primary monitoring tool in the Informatica Platform. Monitoring console is automatically setup when you install and configure Informatica Services. This monitoring console is used to monitor all types of jobs including mappings, workflows and profiles. In this section of the book, you get a basic understanding of the monitoring console. You can access the monitoring console at the following URL: http://<Informatica hostname>:6008/monitoring, where 6008 is the default port number. Your administrator may have configured a different port number for the monitoring console. The monitoring console leverages same port number as the Administrator console.

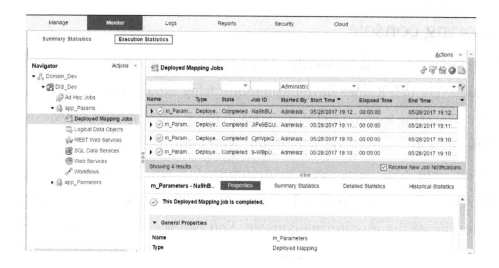

Chapter 4 – A simple case study

In this chapter, I will outline the use-case that you are trying to solve through the labs in this book. As part of the labs, you are trying to build a Data Warehouse using Informatica Platform. This use-case involves a fictional bank that is building a Data Warehouse. This bank offers various kinds of services to its customers: Savings account, checking account, credit cards and so on. Each customer may have one or more accounts with the bank and each account can have one or more customers (individual accounts, joint accounts and business accounts). The bank has several legacy systems that maintain the data and also deliver it to the other applications within the company. The primary purpose of the Data Warehouse being built is to improve operational efficiency and provide customers better services. As you build each lab in this book, you will move one step closer towards completing the Data Warehouse.

> If you are not planning to use the examples given in this book, you can skip this chapter and move on to the next. If you are planning to use examples in this book, please note that this book does not strictly abide by the Data Warehousing concepts that are in practice in the industry. It takes several liberties to teach the readers the Informatica technology and does not focus on the Data Warehousing in general. It is not the intent of this book to teach you Data Warehousing.

Understanding the source system(s)

There are several source systems that you use as part of this project. CustomerDB is a RDBMS system that hosts the customer master data, and this constitutes of the following tables:

Table name	Description
Customers	This table contains the master customer information
Accounts	This table contains both active and inactive accounts
Cust_Acct_XRef	This is a cross reference table that represents the active customer-account combinations
Cust_Acct_XRef_Arc	This is a cross reference table that holds all the historical/non-active customer-account combinations
Cust_Addr	This table stores the customer physical address information
Cust_EAddr	This table stores the customer e-address information such as phone number and email
Trxn	This is the transactions table

Data Warehouse structure

The Data Warehouse used in the labs of this book is completely denormalized. It has the following tables:

Table name	Description
Customers	This table contains denormalized information on all the customers. It also contains their physical addresses and contact information
Accounts	This table contains the account information
Cust_Acct_XRef	This is the Cross reference table between customers and accounts and is a Slowly Changing Dimension Type 2. It holds both historical and active records with flags to indicate the latest record
Geo_Dim	This table contains geographical information that are associated with customer addresses
Sum_YearMon_Trxn	This is a summarized version of the transaction table with data aggregated for year and month

Chapter 5 – Your first mapping (Lab 1)

Now let's get right into building an Informatica mapping and executing it. You will begin simple, and build complex mappings as you go further onto the subsequent chapters. In this chapter, you will focus on building a straightforward mapping that will perform a pass through operation of loading the data from a source system to the Data Warehouse. You will call this as Initial load mapping that will overwrite all the customer information you have in the Data Warehouse and load it completely from the source.

Prerequisites

To begin building a mapping, this is what you will need:

a. A source database/schema having the customers table with data already loaded.
b. A target database/schema with the empty customers table.
c. Username, password, connectivity details to both source and target.
d. A complete Informatica Setup
  a. Informatica Platform setup on 1 or more nodes
  b. MRS and DIS services
  c. Developer account in the Informatica Platform with privileges to create and execute mappings, create connections and access to at least 1 project
  d. Informatica client installed on a workstation

Summary of the steps

At a high level, here's what you will do in the 1st lab:

a. Setup connections

   a. Create a connection pointing to the source

   b. Create a connection pointing to the target

b. Setup the DIS

   a. Select the DIS on which you want to execute your mappings

c. Import data objects

   a. Import the source data object

   b. Import the target data object

d. Create a mapping

   a. Create a pass through mapping connecting the source data structure to the target structure

e. Execute the mapping

   a. First preview the data in the source

   b. Then, execute the mapping and load the data into the target

f. Monitor the mapping

   a. Study the Informatica Monitoring console to verify that the mapping executed successfully and look at the monitoring statistics

Setting up the connections

Now, let us begin by creating a connection to the source. Open the developer and login to the domain, if you haven't done so already. Then follow these instructions:

 In PowerCenter, connections are a repository level object. In the Informatica Platform, connections are domain level objects and hence can be reused across multiple Model Repositories.

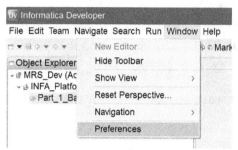

To create connections, go to the Informatica Developer tool → **Window** menu → **Preferences** menu. This will open the preferences dialog box. In this dialog box, choose **Informatica** → **Connections** on the left hand side navigator. On the right hand side, select **Database** → **Oracle** folder and click **Add**.

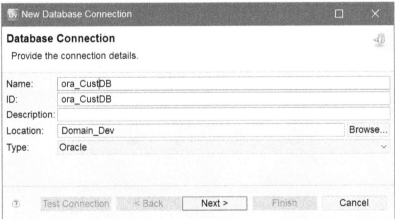

A New connection dialog box appears. Type the connection name as ora_CustDB, and click **Next**. In the second step of the wizard, there are many properties. These properties are typically grouped into 3 sections:

general properties, Metadata Access properties and Data Access properties. General properties are common properties for both metadata access and data access. Metadata access properties are used by the client (Informatica Developer) to access the database. These properties are used to import the table structures/metadata into the Developer tool. Data Access properties are NOT used by Developer tool. They are used by the DIS to access the data when the mapping is executing. You create two such connections: one for the source and one for the target.

Property	Description
General properties	
Username	Type in the username that has access to the tables you want to import
Password	Corresponding password
Metadata access	
Connection String	This is a JDBC URL to connect to the database. Informatica Developer always uses JDBC to import the metadata
Advanced JDBC security options	If the database you are trying to access has additional security enabled, such as encryption, Kerberos – use this property to define those
Data access	

Property	Description
Connection String	This is the connection string that DIS uses to connect to the database. DIS always relies on the native connectivity (unless you are creating a JDBC connection). This connect string must be accessible from the DIS node(s)
Environment SQL	You can use environment SQL to invoke any SET commands that are usually applicable only for that database session
SQL Identifier character	This is by default set to double quotes ("). Other options include a single quote (') and none. If set to none, Informatica will use the tables names exactly as specified in the data object properties – which is set during the import process. If quotes are set, it will always embed table names in quotes. This is helpful if your table names are case-sensitive

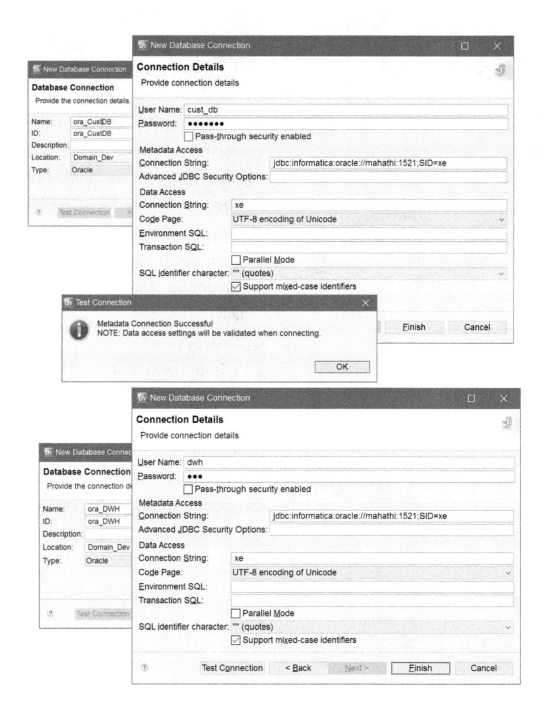

Import Physical Data Objects

Now that you have setup the connections, let us import the physical data objects (or data objects). A data object is a representation of a physical object that stores your data such as tables, files, etc. For example, you may have customers, accounts and trxn data objects each representing a table in your source system. Informatica Platform supports various types of physical data objects including flat file, relational, social media (such as Facebook, LinkedIn, Twitter), NoSQL and so on.

In this section, you will import two data objects: the customer table in the CustDB database and the customers dimension in the DWH. You will store all our data objects in a subfolder called "Shared_Objects".

 In PowerCenter, you import table definitions as sources/targets. In Informatica Platform, you import them as data objects. Once imported a data object can be used as a source, target or lookup. This keeps the metadata in the Informatica Platform well organized and avoids duplication of objects.

Import Customers table

Right click the **Shared_Objects** folder and click **New → Data Object**. In the **New** wizard choose **Physical Data Objects → Relational Data Object**. In the **New Relational Data Object** dialog box, click **Browse** next to the Connection. Choose the **ora_CustDB** connection and click **OK**. You will be back to **New Relational Data Object**. Ensure the "**Create data object from existing resource**" is selected. Now click **Browse** next to the **Resource**. Developer tool will connect to the database and load all the tables and views it can access through this connection. In the **Select a Resource** dialog box select **CUST_DB** (Schema) → **Tables** → **Customers** and click **OK**. You will be back in **New Relational Data Object** dialog box. Name the data object as **CustDB_Customers** and click **Finish**. Data Object is created and opened in the workspace.

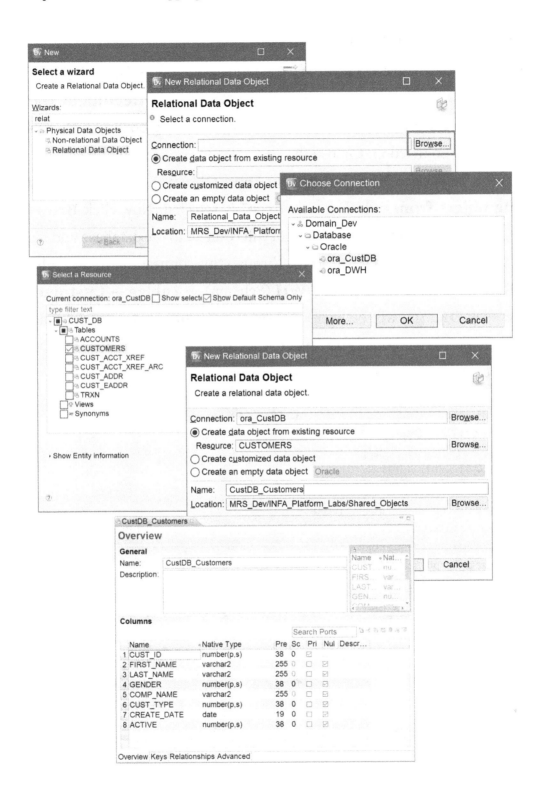

Import Customers dimension

Right click the **Shared_Objects** folder and click **New → Data Object**. In the **New** wizard choose **Physical Data Objects → Relational Data Object**. In the **New Relational Data Object** dialog box, click **Browse** next to the Connection. Choose the **ora_DWH** connection and click **OK**. You will be back to **New Relational Data Object**. Ensure the "**Create data object from existing resource**" is selected. Now click **Browse** next to the **Resource**. Developer tool will connect to the database and load all the tables and views it can access through this connection. In the **Select a Resource** dialog box select **DWH** (Schema) → **Tables** → **Customers** and click **OK**. You will be back in **New Relational Data Object** dialog box. Name the data object as **DWH_Customers** and click **Finish**. Data Object is created and opened in the workspace.

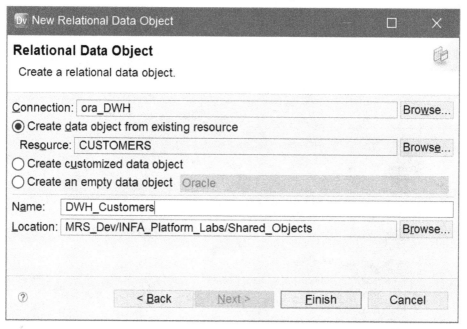

Setup the default DIS

Developer client allows youers to configure a default DIS. When an Informatica domain has multiple DIS, users can configure the default DIS on which they want to run their mappings. This way, the developer client doesn't have to prompt the user for a DIS every time they run a job. To set the default DIS, you go to the preferences dialog box by clicking **Window** menu → **Preferences**. On the left hand side, select **Informatica** → **DIS**. On the right hand side, your domain name appears. Expand it to see the DIS available in the domain. Select a DIS and click **Set as Default**. The string **(Default)** appears next to your DIS. You can select a default DIS per domain.

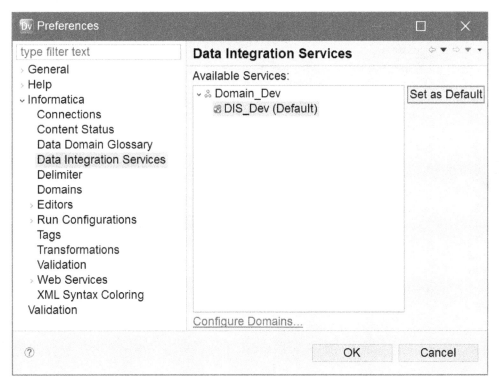

Data Preview

In the workspace you can switch to the data object CustDB_Customers. In the bottom half, switch to the Data Viewer tab and click **Run**. You will see a dialog box indicating the execution of 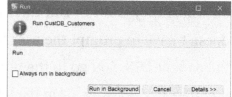 the data viewer and then you will see the data from the table. Note that since you have not executed any mappings, there will be no data in the DWH_Customers table. By default, data preview fetches only the first 1,000 records from the data source. This options is configurable in the preferences dialog box

	CUST_ID	FIRST_NAME	LAST_NAME	GENDER	COMP_NAME
1	1	Nannie	Ehigiator	0	<null>
2	2	Audrey	Briles	0	<null>
3	3	Madlyn	Doster	0	Raytheon Co.
4	4	Kellye	Hormuth	1	U.S. Bancorp
5	5	Shaquita	Monfore	2	Family Dollar Stor.
6	6	Sibyl	Schoolcraft	0	<null>
7	7	Theron	Gaspari	1	<null>
8	8	Shavonda	Germer	2	Federated Depart.
9	9	Darrel	Caliguire	1	Pfizer, Inc.
10	10	Antione	Laggan	2	<null>
11	11	Maegan	Bahe	0	Hughes Supply Inc
12	12	Susann	Paulseth	0	<null>
13	13	Sacha	Blide	0	<null>

Row 1 to 1,000

Properties　Data Viewer　Alerts
Configuration: (Default Settings)　... Run　Show: (All Outputs) Choose...
Output
Name: CustDB_Customers

Creating the mapping

Now that you have metadata of both our source and target data objects
imported into the repository,
let's go ahead and create a
mapping. To do so, right
click   the   folder
Part_1_Basics   in   the
object explorer and click
New → Mapping. Name it as

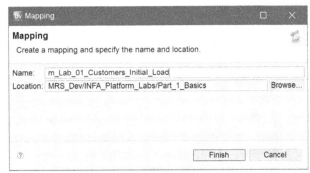

m_DWH_Customers_Initial_Load and click **OK**.

Drag the data object **CustDB_Customers** into the mapping workspace.
Add to mapping dialog box appears.
Choose **Read**. In the Read operation,
you will notice there are two sub options:
As related data objects (which will be
grayed out) and **As Independent data
object(s)** – which will be enabled by
default. Click **OK**. The   data   object

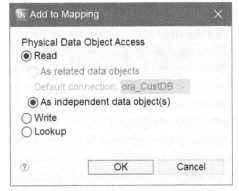

appears in the mapping canvas. The options listed in the Add to Mapping
dialog box are known as ***Operations***. An operation is an action you can
perform on the data object. Relational data objects have **Read**, **Write** and
Lookup operations.

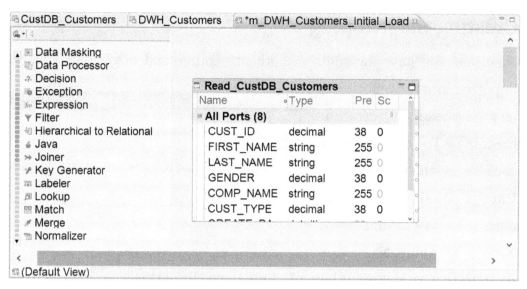

Now, drag the data object **DWH_Customers** from the object explorer into the mapping workspace. **Add to mapping** dialog box appears. Choose **Write** and click **OK**. Target data object is created.

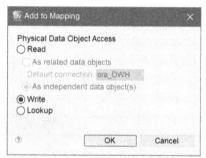

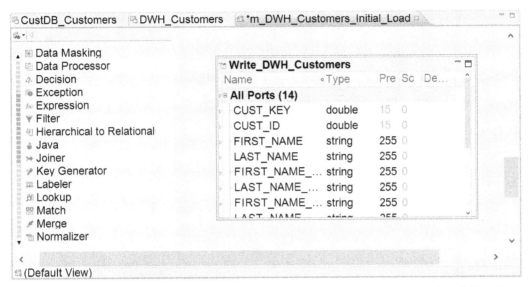

From the **Read_CustDB_Customers** data object connect the following
columns to the **Write_DWH_Customers** data object

Read_CustDB_Customers	*Write_DWH_Customers*
CUST_ID	CUST_KEY
	CUST_ID
FIRST_NAME	FIRST_NAME
	FIRST_NAME_ORIG
LAST_NAME	LAST_NAME
	LAST_NAME_ORIG

Click the **Write** data object title bar. In the properties pane at the bottom
half, click **Advanced** and select the **Truncate target table** checkbox.

 The asterisk (*) on the title bar of the mapping window indicates
that you have unsaved changes.

Save the mapping by using **File** menu → **Save** or by pressing **<CTRL> + S**. Right click anywhere on the empty mapping canvas (where there are no transformations and data objects) and click **Validate**. Developer will respond that the mapping is valid.

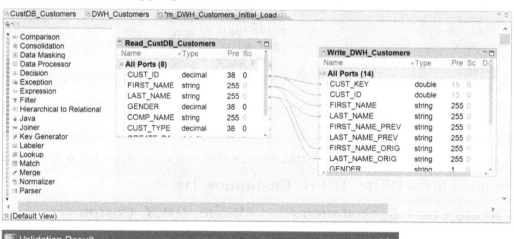

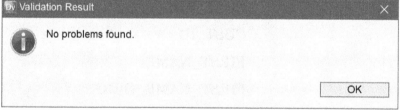

Executing the mapping

Now that you have a valid mapping, let us go ahead and execute it. But before you do that, you need to enable the Progress pane. Progress pane allows you to monitor jobs that you started from the Developer tool. To do so, go to Window menu → Show View → Progress. Progress pane will appear. You will notice that the progress pane will have the message "No operations to display at this time". Now, right click on the mapping canvas and click **Run mapping**. A progress window will appear. While the mapping is executing you will notice that the progress is displayed both in the progress pane as well as on the progress dialog box. Once the mapping is complete, the progress pane will indicate the start time, end time and also the mapping status.

 You can click "**Run in the background**" button to let the current mapping run in the background to hide the progress dialog box. You can always monitor your current jobs in the Progress pane. To hide the progress dialog box always, check the box "**Always run in the background**".

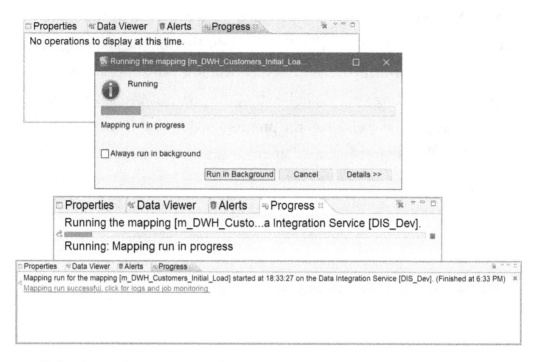

Validating the target data

Switch to the **DWH_Customers** data object in the workspace. In the bottom half, switch to the **Data Viewer** tab and click **Run**. You will now notice data in the **DWH_Customers** table:

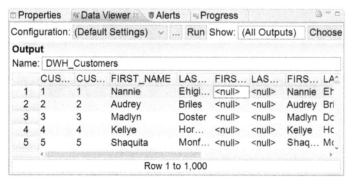

Chapter 6 – Architecture

Introduction

In this chapter you will take a look at various aspects of Informatica Platform architecture. Informatica Platform supports different Informatica products such as Informatica Data Quality and Informatica Big Data Management. In this chapter, you will only look at some of the fundamental concepts of architecture as they are applicable to Data Integration.

Informatica Services

Administrator	Metadata Manager	Analyst	Monitor		Repository Manager
Resource Manager	PowerExchange Services		Search Service		PC Designer
Scheduler	Web Services Hub		Content Management Service		Workflow Manager
Email	PC Integration Service		Data Integration Service		Workflow Monitor
License	PC Repository Service		Model Repository Service		
Informatica Core Services					Developer

As shown in the architecture diagram here, Informatica Platform can have many services hosted in the same domain. Some of them are mandatory and some are optional, and enabled by licenses and products you own. Some of them are system services and some of them are user-created.

Informatica core service

When you install Informatica on a multi-node environment, by default – you will have Informatica core service running on all the nodes with administrator console running on the master gateway node. You'll need Informatica core service running on each participating node. Core service interacts with the domain and lets the domain know the availability of the node for service execution as well as job execution. During system upgrades such as OS and database, you can stop the core service on a corresponding node, perform upgrades and start the services to let the node participate in the domain again.

 All nodes in an Informatica domain must be of the same Informatica software version.

System services

License service

When you install Informatica services on a node and create a domain, you are prompted for license key. A license service is automatically created based on the key you provide. You may have more than one license service created in a domain – each using a particular license key. You can have one or more license services in domain. Each license service can be assigned to one or more application services. The license services also lists various options that you are entitled for , such as GRID, High Availability, connectivity to certain databases, etc.

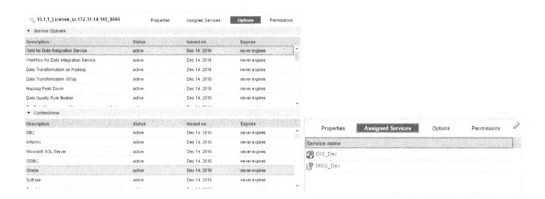

Scheduler service

Scheduler service allows you to create various schedules and execute jobs according to those schedules. Scheduler service is a system service and is created by default. However, it is enabled by users as needed. Once scheduler service is enabled, users can create various schedules and assign them to various jobs.

Email service

Email service is used to store the email related configuration that can be leveraged by workflows, to send email notifications based on the workflow orchestration,

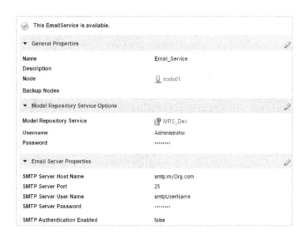

PowerCenter services

Informatica PowerCenter relies on PowerCenter Repository and PowerCenter Integration Services. PowerCenter Repository stores the metadata associated with the PowerCenter transformations, mappings and workflows. PowerCenter Repository Service manages the repository. PowerCenter Integration Service is the execution engine that runs the mappings and workflows. PowerCenter clients interact with these services:

PowerCenter Repository Manager, PowerCenter Designer, PowerCenter Workflow Manager, and PowerCenter Workflow Monitor.

Platform services

Now let us take a look at the services that form the core of this book: Model Repository Service (MRS) and Data Integration Service (DIS). Model repository service is used to store the metadata that you create using Developer tool or Analyst tool. This is the service that you interacted with as part of our Lab 1. DIS is the processing engine that processes the mappings and workflows. Mapping you created in Lab 1 is executed by a DIS. DIS is also used to execute data previews, profiles, and other executable objects in the MRS.

Connections

Connections are an important aspect of the Informatica Architecture. A connection stores information on how to connect to a particular data store. This includes attributes such as database name, database server, port, username and password. Creating a connection external to a mapping and workflow allows you to reuse the connections across various objects in various folders and projects. This helps maintain unified metadata on how to connect to a particular system. Connections can be of various types:

→ Databases: Oracle, DB2, SQL Server, ODBC, JDBC, etc.
→ Cloud: Salesforce, Workday, etc.
→ Cluster: Hadoop
→ Enterprise applications: SAP, Microsoft Dynamics CRM, etc.

→ File systems: Amazon S3, Azure Blob, Hadoop File System, etc.

→ Messaging: JMS, Kafka, etc.

→ NoSQL: MongoDB, Cassandra, HBase, etc.

→ Social Media: Facebook, LinkedIn, Twitter, etc.

→ Web: HTTP, OData, etc.

Security

Informatica Platform has comprehensive security features. Though detailed security configurations are out of the scope of this book, you will take a look at a high level overview of several security related features in the platform in this chapter.

Users

A user represents any person or application that intends to access Informatica Platform. A user authenticates with Informatica Platform by using a user name (login) and a password.

Groups

Users can be organized into groups to allow or deny access to certain systems at a group level instead of individual user level. You can create groups within groups (called sub groups) to have a hierarchical structure that you need to define the security and access levels of your choice.

Privileges and permissions

Privileges are the actions that a user can perform on certain domain objects. Privileges are predefined. For example, a user needs "Access Developer" privilege for a given MRS to access that MRS from the Developer tool.

Similarly, the user needs "Create, Edit and Delete Projects" privilege to create new projects inside that MRS.

While privileges define the actions a user can perform, permissions control the objects on which the user can perform these actions. For example, a user with "Create, Edit and Delete Projects" can edit any existing project in the MRS as long as the user has "Write" permission on the MRS. MRS projects have "Read", "Write" and "Grant" permissions. For a better understanding, let's take an example, say user 'X' has "Create, Edit and Delete Projects" privilege on a MRS. Now let us look at various permissions that user can have and what having those permissions mean to the user:

→ Read Permission: User can see the project in the developer tool, open them and see any mapping, workflow and other objects inside it.
→ Write permission: In addition to seeing the contents of the project, user can modify them and save the objects.
→ Grant permission: User can grant others read or write permissions on the project.

 Note that privileges are applied at service level such as MRS, DIS and permissions are applied at object level such as projects and connections.

Roles

A role is defined as a collection of privileges that you assign to users and/or groups. For example, you can define a collection of privileges that are needed for a user to monitor jobs in production and call them as "Operator role". You can now assign this operator role to various users and groups easily. Any time you add an extra privilege to this role, all the users and groups in that role will automatically inherit it.

Chapter 7 – Interacting with the client

This chapter aims at giving you several tips and tricks that allow you to work with the Developer client. These tricks will get you around the Developer UI.

Navigating in the MRS

Object Explorer

You can use Object Explorer pane to browse through the objects in the MRS.

If Object Explorer is not displayed by default, you can view it by clicking the Window menu → Preferences → Show view → Object Explorer. Expand the containers (such as Project or folder) or categories (such as Mapping, Workflows) to browse the child objects. You can open an object, rename an object, validate it, delete it, copy and paste it from the Object Explorer itself.

You can select multiple objects using SHIFT or CTRL key and perform bulk operations such as opening several objects in one gesture.

Object locations

You can have objects from various projects and folders open in the workspace at the same time. When you place your mouse on the window tab title, you will see the absolute path of the object that is currently open.

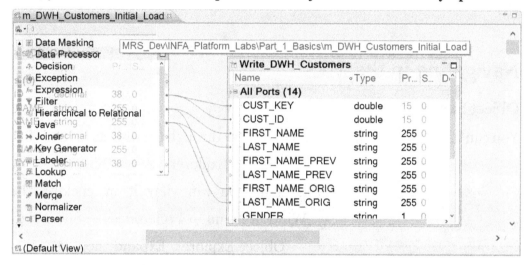

Opening the data object from inside a mapping

You can quickly access the data objects from inside the mapping. Go to the data object properties → Data Object sub tab and click the hyperlink. You can also hover over the hyperlink to see the full path of where the object is

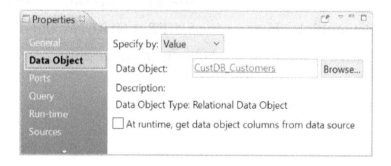

Navigating within mappings and workflows

Outline view

Outline view is extremely handy when you have large mappings and you need to get to a transformation. Just click on the transformation name in the outline view and focus will jump to that transformation in the mapping canvas.

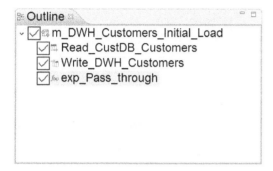

Quick outline

When you want to find a transformation or an object inside the mapping canvas, you can use Quick outline to search for it. To access quick outline, right click the mapping canvas and choose Quick outline or press <CTRL>+O. Quick outline is different from the outline view in the sense that it provides search capabilities. If you have no selection (of transformation), Quick outline lists all the transformations in a mapping. This allows you to quickly jump from one object to another without scrolling

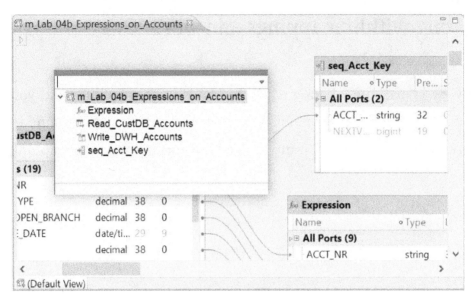

When you have an object selected, quick outline lists all the ports in the object. This allows you to quickly jump from one port to another

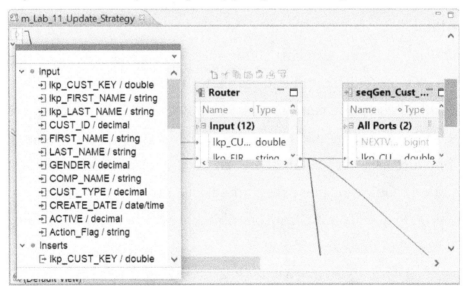

Searching for ports in a transformation

To search for ports in a transformation, go to the ports tab. On the top-right corner, use the text box to type a phrase or search string. As you type, a popup appears listing all the ports in the transformation that match your criteria

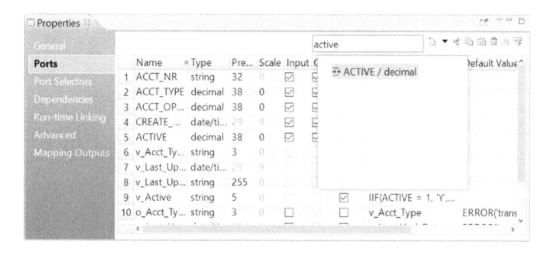

You can asterisk (*) wild card to find various patterns

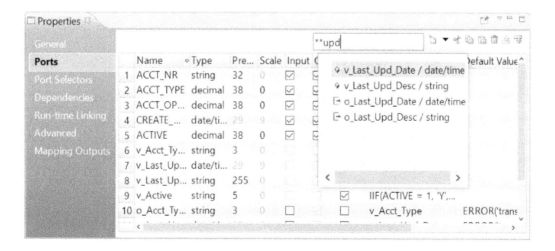

Productivity

Maximizing the workspace

The default view of the Informatica Developer keeps several panes visible. You can double click on the workspace tab to minimize all other panes and views and maximize the workspace view. Double click again to go back to previous view

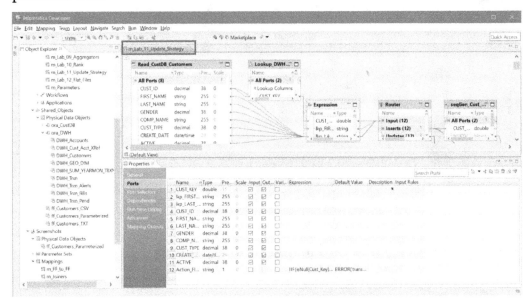

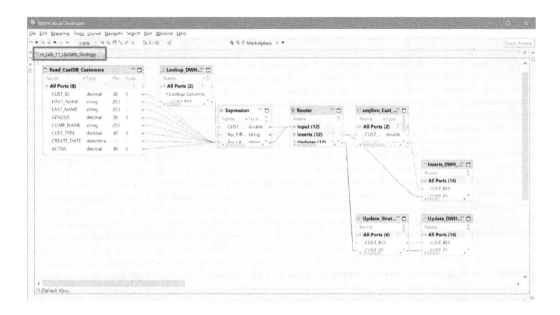

Analyzing dependencies of an expression port

When writing complex expressions, it is important to quickly analyze the dependencies of each expressions to understand the impact of changing something. To do this, you go to the expression properties → Dependencies tab. Select a variable port or output port to see all the ports it depends on

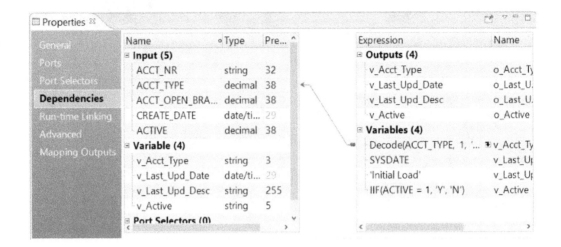

Similarly, select an input port to see all the variable and/or output ports it affects

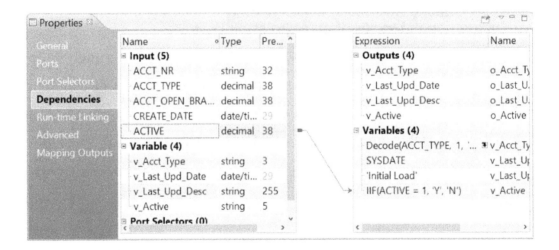

 Dependencies tab is available in expression transformation only

Debugging and execution

Validating a mapping

Right click a mapping and choose Validate. Developer tool validates the mappings and shows you the warnings and the errors associated with the mapping. To validate the mapping, right click on the mapping canvas and click Validate. A message box appears indicating the validity of the mapping. If the mapping is invalid go to the validation log pane to see the details. If this is not visible already, you can enable it by clicking on the Window menu → Show view → Other → Informatica → Validation log.

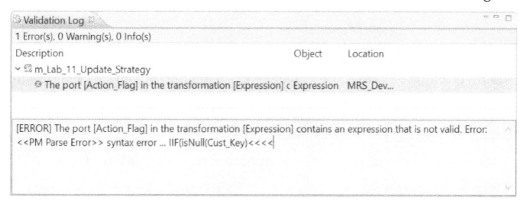

Setting up a default DIS

As seen in the first lab, we first need to select a DIS to execute the mappings. This DIS is configured as default DIS for that Developer instance. You can configure a different default DIS for each installation of Developer tool.

To configure default DIS, go to Window → Preferences → Informatica → Data Integration Services → Expand the domain that has the DIS you want to choose as default → Select the DIS and click Set as Default

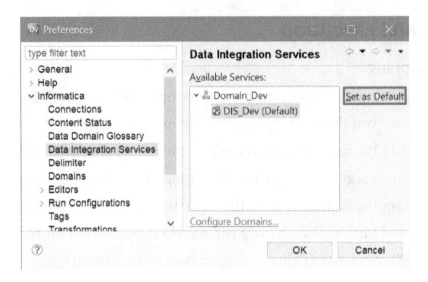

Evaluating expressions

When building expressions, you can use the Evaluate expression functionality to quickly evaluate the results of variable and output ports by passing sample input values. To evaluate expressions, go to expression editor in variable / output ports in supported transformations. Click on the "Test >>" button on the top right corner. Expression editor expands to show all the input and variable values used in the expression. Type in a value next to each port and click evaluate. The result is displayed at the bottom

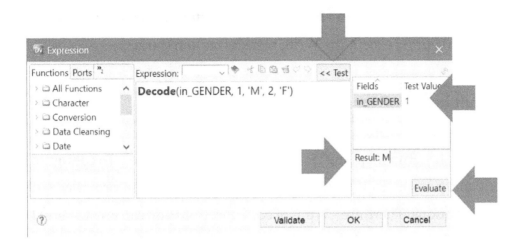

Viewing the midstream data

Viewing the output of a transformation is a very important aspect of

debugging. You can preview the output of a transformation by simply right clicking the transformation and clicking Run Data Viewer. Data viewer executes the mapping till the current (selected) transformation and displays the results in the Data Viewer pane. You can also run the data preview by switching to the Data Viewer pane and click Run button

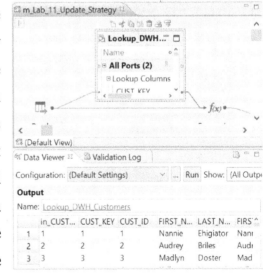

You can run data viewer on any transformation including Read (source) except the Write transformation (target)

Default Run configurations

You can define several run configurations that you can use with Data Viewer and also the "Run mapping" feature in the Developer tool. To configure run configurations go to Window menu → Preferences → Informatica → Run configurations. There are 3 types of configurations you can create here: Data Viewer, Mapping and Web Service. In these configurations, you can configure the number of rows to read (for example, when data previewing the default is 1,000 rows. You can adjust that value here), tracing levels, sort order and optimizer levels

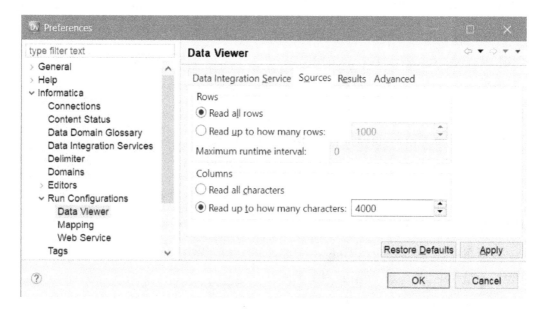

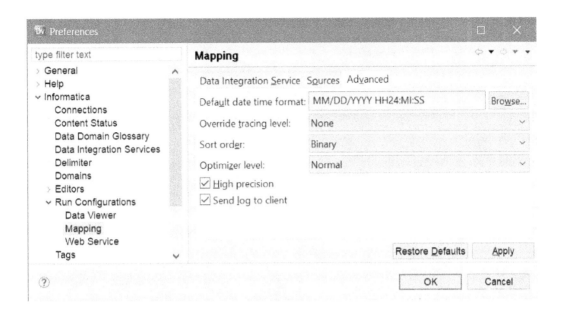

Custom Data Viewer run configuration

To use a Data Viewer configuration, go to the Data Viewer tab and choose the configuration in the drop down box. Click the ellipsis (...) button to open the configurations dialog box. Here you can create a new configuration.

Once a configuration is created, choose it in the drop down and click Run. The data viewer will now use the configuration selected

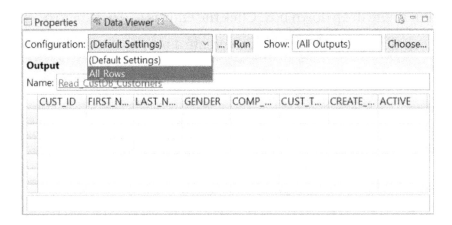

Custom Mapping run configuration

To access mapping run configurations, right click on the mapping canvas and choose "Run mapping using advanced options". A dialog box appears where you can choose the configurations. Choose "New configuration..." to create a new mapping configuration and use it

Viewing optimized mapping

When a mapping is executed DIS applies several optimizations to ensure the mapping executes with high performance. As part of this process, DIS may add some transformations, move some transformation logic (either by introducing other transformations or by using other functionality in existing transformations) to achieve the same result in a more optimized way. For example, take a look at this mapping below

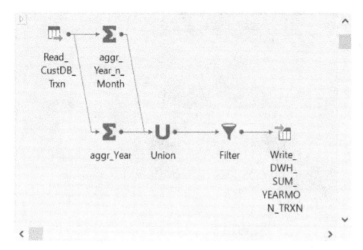

In this mapping, there is a filter that is applied after aggregating the data. For demonstration purposes, this filter condition is set to Year = 2016. This mapping can definitely run faster and achieve the same result if this filter is pushed down to the source database. The DIS evaluates the mapping and optimizes such filter. In this scenario, the mapping will be at runtime re-written as shown here. Notice that the filter transformation is removed in this optimized mapping. It is now moved to the source properties as a filter condition. You can view the optimized mapping that DIS creates in the Developer itself. Right click the mapping and click "Show optimized mapping" a new sub tab opens inside the mapping canvas that shows you the optimized mapping

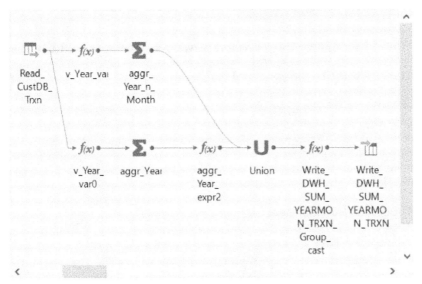

Data types

Informatica platform has native data types known as Universal data types.

These are different (though compatible) from the database types. When you open a data object in the workspace, you will see the database data types. When you use the data object in a mapping you will see the universal data types. As you can see in the screenshots

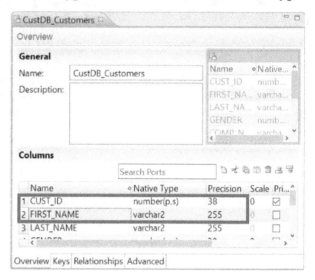

below, CUST_ID is number(p,s) in Oracle and translated to decimal (38,0) in the mapping canvas. Similarly, varchar2 is translated into string.

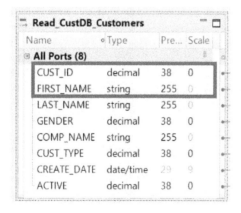

Chapter 8 – Core Transformations

This chapter introduces several core transformations. Each section of the chapter introduces you to one core transformation and discusses it to a certain detail. Each section starts with discussing a transformation and ends with an example/exercise based on the bank use case study discussed in the earlier chapter.

Transformations

A transformation is an object that processes and transforms the data provided to it in a very specific way. A transformation is not responsible for reading data from a data store (such as a table or file) or writing to it. That is the responsibility of the data objects. A transformation receives data from a data object, or another transformation. On receiving the data, the transformation transforms the incoming data as defined/configured by the user, and then passes it onto next transformation or data object. Each transformation, as you will learn in the upcoming chapters, has a unique way of transforming the data. Typically, you use a combination of transformations to modify the data as desired.

Transformation types

Depending on the functionality offered by a transformation, they can be categorized in many ways.

Based on their effect on rows:

Some transformations impact the order of the rows or the amount of the rows or change the row type (insert / update / delete / ...). These transformations are categorized as **Active transformations**. The transformations that do not impact these rows are known as **Passive transformations**.

Based on the connectivity in the mapping:

Some transformations require their inputs and outputs to be "linked" to other transformations/objects. These are known as **Connected transformations**. Some transformations can remain not connected to any transformation in a mapping and just remain as independent objects. These transformations are called **Unconnected transformations**. Unconnected transformations can be invoked from other transformations via specific function calls in transformation language.

Based on the ability to cache:

Some transformations can cache the data passed on to them and use it for further processing. Example is the "lookup" transformation. Lookup transformation can read a source, cache the data and compare it with the incoming data. Such transformations are called **Cached transformations**. Transformations such as expressions do not need any cache and work on the rows independently. These are known as **Un-cached transformations**. You can configure some cached transformations to run in an un-cached mode.

Active/ Passive transformations

An active transformation affects the row type or transaction boundaries. A passive transformation does not change the row type and doesn't impact the transaction boundaries. So, passive transformations do not require that all columns through them. For example, when working with an expression transformation, you can only pass the columns that you intend to modify or the column values that you need to perform calculations into it. Other columns can bypass the expression and merge / concatenate in the subsequent transformation. Since active transformations either impact the transaction boundaries or row type, you cannot merge columns from two active transformations without a Joiner.

 Note that this does not mean you will have to pass all columns through all transformations. You can always choose only a subset of columns to move from one transformation to another (regardless of their type). You can merge / concatenate data from two passive transformations into one transformation. But you cannot merge / concatenate data from an active transformation and active/passive transformation without joining them first.

Active transformations typically have one or more of the following impact on the rows that pass through them:

a. Transaction boundaries: Informatica processes data in blocks of rows. Typically, all the data in a data block gets committed together. However, some transformations may perform actions that may cause some data in the block to commit at a different interval than the rest. This may be intentional and needed. For example, you may have a requirement to commit data only once for every department. So, you may want to first group the data by department, and issue a commit only after each last row of the grouped data. In this example you are intentionally changing the transaction boundaries.

b. The order of rows: Transformations like Sorter change the order in which the rows pass through them and thus indirectly affect the transaction boundaries.

c. The row type: All rows by default passing through a mapping are treated as "Inserts". You can mark rows as Update or Delete using Update Strategy transformation. In this case, though you are not moving the transaction boundaries, this is considered an active transformation.

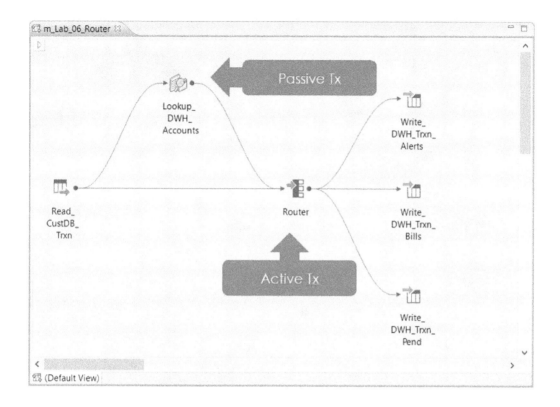

Connected / Unconnected transformations

A mapping typically contains one or more sources, targets, and a bunch of transformations connected to each other as a pipeline. The transformations that are connected to each other to take inputs or provide outputs, are called connected transformations. Connected transformations require at least one input port and one output port connected to other objects. Some special transformations can remain in the mapping without being connected to the pipeline at all. Some examples are lookup and stored procedure. In the unconnected scenario, these transformations are used as function calls, from other transformations through transformation language reference.

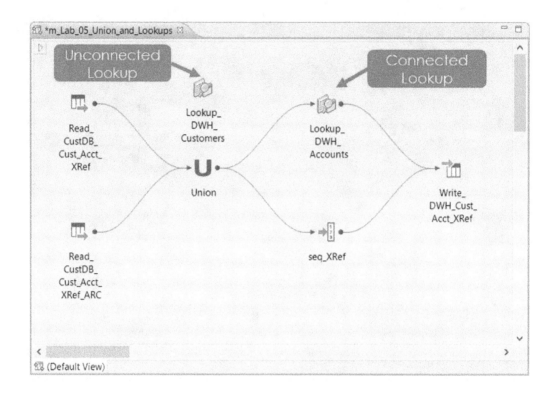

Filter transformation

Filter is an active transformation used to determine whether or not certain rows are allowed to continue in the data flow. This decision is made by evaluating a condition provided by the user. All rows that pass the condition or evaluate as true, will be allowed to pass onto the subsequent transformations. All rows that evaluate as false will be dropped from further processing.

Filter condition

Filter condition is the property where you can define the condition that needs to be evaluated for each row to determine whether it will be dropped or continued past the transformation.

Sequence Generator transformation

Sequence Generator is analogous to the sequences in the databases. It provides unique incremental values that can be used for primary and surrogate keys, or any column that requires unique numbers.

NEXTVAL

NEXTVAL is a pre-defined port in the Sequence Generator that provides you the next value in the sequence.

Start value

You can set the start value of the Sequence Generator using this property. You can choose the sequence values to start from a specific number. By default, this value is zero (0).

Incremental value

This is the step value. Sequence Generator adds the incremental value to the Start value to derive the NEXTVAL. Then it will continue to add the incremental value to derive the new values for the NEXTVAL. By default, this value is one (1).

End Value

This is the max value that the Sequence Generator will reach to before it resets or cycles back. By default, this value is 9,223,372,036,854,775,807.

Reset

You can enable the Sequence Generator to reset the sequence values every time a mapping runs. You can use this property in conjunction with other properties such as Start Value to determine the final values that come out of the Sequence Generator.

Cycle

If you enable cycling, Sequence Generator will automatically start with Start Value when it reaches the end value.

> Cycle differs from the Reset based on the fact that when cycle is selected, Sequence Generator will start with the Start Value only when it hits the End Value. When Reset is selected, Sequence Generator will always start with the Start Value every time the mapping is restarted – regardless of whether the mapping reached the end value or not in the last run.

Lab 2 – Using Filter, Sequence Generator

Use case

The bank has two types of customers: personal (individual) and business (enterprise) customers. Bank wants to load all the personal (individual) customers into the Data Warehouse. Architects at the bank prefer to have non-data related keys in the Data Warehouse. They prefer to have surrogate keys for every dimension in the Data Warehouse.

Challenges

→ Not all data needs to be loaded. Some data should be filtered out.

→ Surrogate key (unique numbers) needs to be generated for both customers and accounts.

Technical solution

In the previous chapters, you have created a mapping to load the table in to the Data Warehouse. For personal customers, first name and last name need to be loaded. For enterprise customers, company name needs to be loaded. You will also leverage the Sequence Generator transformation to generate unique keys for customers and accounts.

Steps for solution

a. Connect to the MRS/folder

    a. Launch Informatica Developer and connect to the Model Repository (**MRS_Dev**) by double clicking on the Model Repository Service and providing username and password.

    b. Double click your project (**INFA_Platform_Labs**) to open it.

    c. Double click the folder (**Part_1_Basics**) to open it.

b. Create a mapping and add data objects

    a. Right click the folder (**Part_1_Basics**) and click → **New** → **Mapping**.

    b. Name the mapping as **m_Lab_02_Filter_SeqGen**.

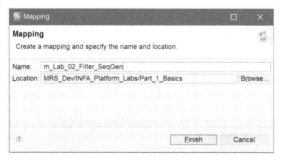

c. Expand the folder **Shared_Objects → Physical Data Objects → ora_CustDB**.

d. Drag the **CustDB_Customers** into the mapping canvas.

e. Choose **Read → As Independent Data Object(s)** and click **OK**.

f. **Read** data object appears in the mapping.

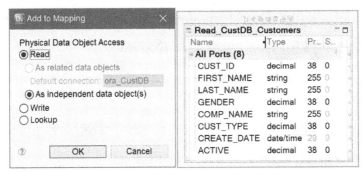

g. Expand the folder **Shared_Objects → Physical Data Objects → ora_DWH**.

h. Drag the **DWH_Customers** into the mapping canvas.

i. **Write** data object appears in the mapping.

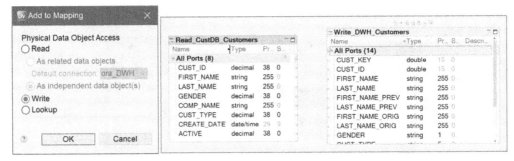

j. Select the **Write** data object and go to the properties pane. In the advanced pane, check the **Truncate target** table option.

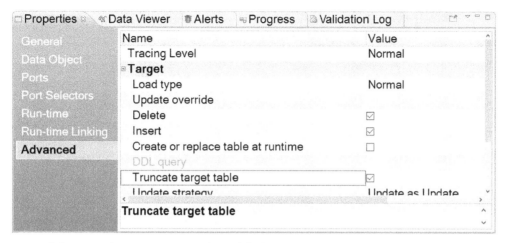

c. Add Transformations and build the pipeline

    a. Right click on the empty mapping canvas (not on any object) and choose **Add Transformation**.

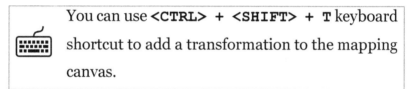

You can use **<CTRL> + <SHIFT> + T** keyboard shortcut to add a transformation to the mapping canvas.

    b. Choose **Filter** in the dialog box and click **OK**.

    c. **Filter** transformation is added to the mapping canvas.

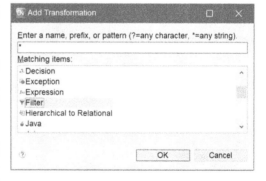

    d. Drag the following columns from the read data object (**Read_CustDB_Customers**) to the Filter transformation (**Filter**): **CUST_ID, FIRST_NAME, LAST_NAME, GENDER, ACTIVE**.

e. From the Filter transformation connect the columns to the write data object as follows:

Filter	Write_DWH_Customers
CUST_ID	CUST_ID
FIRST_NAME	FIRST_NAME
	FIRST_NAME_ORIG
LAST_NAME	LAST_NAME
	LAST_NAME_ORIG
GENDER	GENDER
CUST_TYPE	CUST_TYPE
ACTIVE	ACTIVE

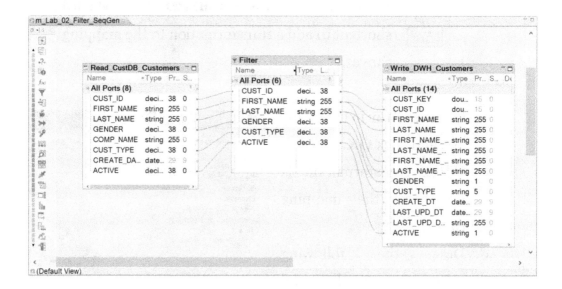

f. Right click on the empty mapping canvas and choose **Add Transformation**.

g. Choose **Sequence Generator** in the dialog box and click **OK**.

h. Name the Sequence Generator as **seqGen_Cust_Key** and click **Next**.

i. We will leave the configuration values as defaults and click **Finish**.

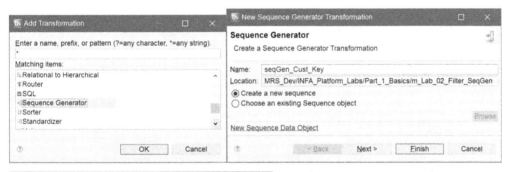

j. Drag the **CUST_ID** from the Filter transformation (**Filter**) into the Sequence Generator.

k. From the Sequence Generator, drag the **NEXTVAL** into the Write object (**Write_DWH_Customers**) → **CUST_KEY** field.

l. Validate the mapping now. You will get the No Problems found message.

m. Save the mapping by clicking **File** menu → **Save**.

You can use <CTRL> + S keyboard shortcut to save the currently active object in the workspace.

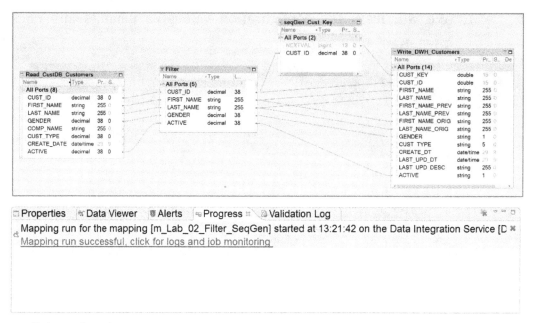

☐ Properties   ⏱ Data Viewer   🗑 Alerts   ⟲ Progress ⊠   📄 Validation Log

Mapping run for the mapping [m_Lab_02_Filter_SeqGen] started at 13:21:42 on the Data Integration Service [D ✖
Mapping run successful, click for logs and job monitoring

Validate the data

We can do the data preview on the object DWH Customers to validate the data loaded. You can also use an external tool like SQL Developer and query the database to check the data. You will notice that the CUST_TYPE is only 1 – just as you applied the filter.

☐ Properties   Data Viewer   🗑 Alerts   Progress   Validation Log

Configuration: (Default Settings) ⌄ … Run   Show: (All Outputs) Choose…

Output

Name: DWH_Customers

	CUST...	CUST...	FIRS...	LAST...	FIRS...	LAST...	FIRS...	LAST...	GEN.	CUST_TYPE	CRE...	LAST...	LAST...	ACTI...
1	44049	9966	Jalee...	Harling	<null>	<null>	Jalee...	Harling	0	1	<null>	<null>	<null>	1
2	44050	9968	Yolan...	Mcguf...	<null>	<null>	Yolan...	Mcguf...	1	1	<null>	<null>	<null>	1
3	44051	9969	Noma	Feeling	<null>	<null>	Noma	Feeling	0	1	<null>	<null>	<null>	0
4	44052	9972	Buffy	Germ...	<null>	<null>	Buffy	Germ...	2	1	<null>	<null>	<null>	1
5	44053	9977	Ona	Loch	<null>	<null>	Ona	Loch	2	1	<null>	<null>	<null>	1
6	44054	9978	Caleb	Bader...	<null>	<null>	Caleb	Bader...	0	1	<null>	<null>	<null>	1
7	44055	9979	Delin...	Grosh...	<null>	<null>	Delin...	Grosh...	1	1	<null>	<null>	<null>	1
8	44056	9980	Kylie	Amous	<null>	<null>	Kylie	Amous	2	1	<null>	<null>	<null>	1
9	44057	9981	Clinton	Corsey	<null>	<null>	Clinton	Corsey	2	1	<null>	<null>	<null>	1

Row 1 to 1,000

Chapter 9 – Working with Relational Data Objects

When you drag a data object into the mapping, you can choose the operation that you want to apply on the data object. Some examples of operations of a relational data object are: Read, Write, and Lookup. Similarly, if you are using a Social Media data object, you will notice additional operations such as Get Friends, Read posts, etc. There are several properties that you can configure for the operation inside the data object. You have already looked at one such option **"Truncate target table"** for the Write operation of the **DWH_Customers**. Now, let us take a look at some of the properties in the **Read** operation of the CustDB Customers data object. you will begin by looking at each tab of the Read operation of a data object. The Read operation has the following tabs: General, Data Object, Query, Run-time, Sources, Run-time Linking, and Advanced.

> We will refer to the Data Object operations as transformation. So, a Read transformation means Read operation for a data object and a Write transformation means Write operation for the data object.

Relational Data Object properties

When you open a relational data object in the workspace, you can work with the relational data object properties. It has several tabs at the bottom of the tab. In each of these tabs, you will be able to configure various properties

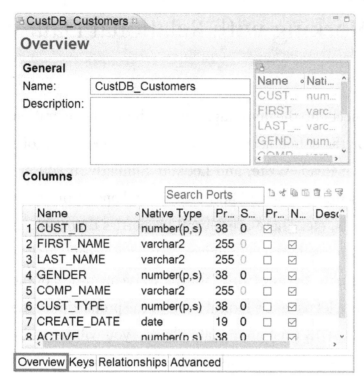

related to the data object. In the **overview** tab, you can edit the data object name here. Changing the data object name doesn't change the table name or underlying resource name. You can also work with the ports/columns associated with this data object. You can add new columns; edit existing columns' data types and precision/scale.

 If the metadata in the Informatica is out of sync with the underlying database metadata, it could yield in runtime errors/failures of the mapping.

In the keys tab, you can add/edit the referential integrity. You can add primary / foreign keys in this tab. When you import the table definitions from the database, Informatica developer also imports primary and foreign keys automatically. If you want to create additional constraints to let Informatica know the integrity of the tables, you can create them here. Creating a primary / foreign key in the Informatica developer does not create the constraints in the database underneath. These constraints will be applicable to the tables during the loads from Informatica only. If you want to create a primary key, click the **Add** button. In the New Key section, you can choose the columns that are part of the constraint.

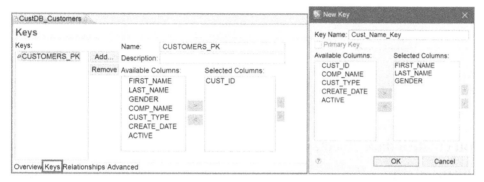

When you have multiple data objects, you can create foreign keys to define

the referential integrity between various data objects. If you want to create a new foreign key, in the relationships tab, click **Add** and a New Relationship appears. In this dialog box, expand any data object from any project/folder and choose the Primary Key associated with it and click OK. This will create a

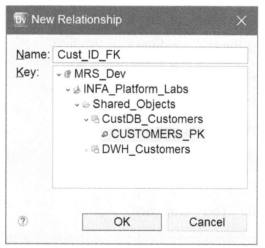

foreign key reference to the selected data object/ primary key. Once you create the reference, you can choose the columns that participate in the foreign key relationship.

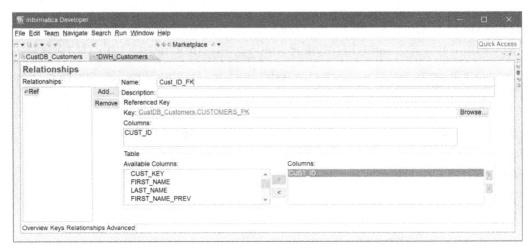

Once you create a data object, you can also use the advanced tab to change some advanced properties such as changing the connection associated with

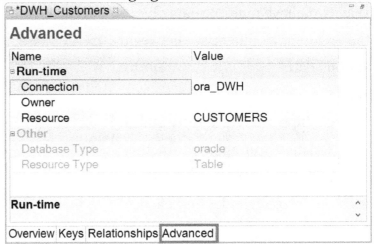

it. If the table you imported is in a different schema other than the one in the connection name, you can use the owner name property to define it. You can also rename the object name in the resource property.

 The data object name and table name are independent properties. In Informatica, you can name the data object in Informatica anything you want. To change the physical table name, change the resource property in the advanced tab.

Read operation/transformation

General tab

Property	Description
Name	This is name of the operation. By default, it will be <operation>_<data object>. For example, Read_CustDB_Customers.
Description	You can provide a description about the operation here.
When column metadata changes	By default, it is set to Synchronized Output Ports. This determines whether the object metadata should be synchronized with the source. Dynamic mappings are out of scope for this book.

Ports tab

This tab lists all the ports/columns in the data object that are exposed in this operation. You will learn more about ports in the next chapter.

Query tab

You can customize several properties related to relational databases here. There are two options available in this tab: Simple and Advanced. When you choose **Simple** you can customize several individual components related to SQL such as WHERE clause, ORDER BY clause, and database specific HINTS.

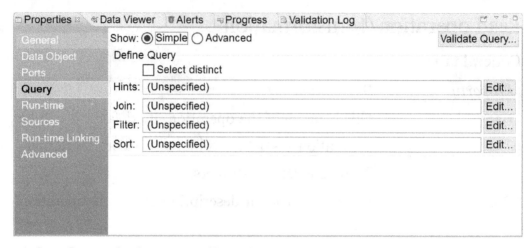

In the advanced tab, user is allowed to provide a complete custom query. In the advanced mode, user is responsible for providing the custom query, and confirming that the output of the query matches the metadata definition of the data object.

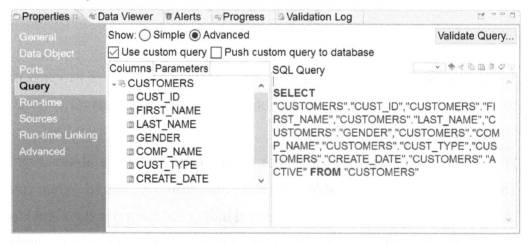

Let's take a quick look at the properties available in the simple option:

Property	Description
Select distinct checkbox	If this box is checked, Informatica will add a "DISTINCT" clause when it generates the SQL query to read the data.
Hints	You can provide the database specific hints here. These hints are applied after SELECT. Informatica does not validate the hints provided. It is user's responsibility.
Join condition	A data object can have more than one source associated with it. When more than one source is associated with it, you can use this property to define a join condition.
Filter	You can specify the where clause. The keyword WHERE is not needed in the property.
Sort	This is where you can specify an order by clause.

When these properties are applied, you have to ensure that the values are valid at the database level. For example, when providing a hint, it has to be relevant and understandable by the underlying database. Similarly, any filter condition or join condition must match the underlying database syntax. Now, let's apply these properties to the Read_CustDB_Customers operation in the mapping. See the screenshot below on the properties that are set:

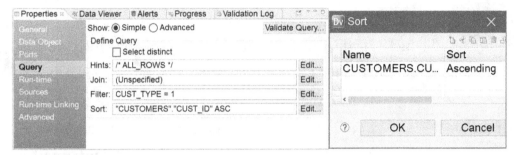

These properties will generate the following query at runtime. You can see the runtime query in the mapping log:

```
SELECT /* ALL_ROWS */"CUSTOMERS"."CUST_ID",
"CUSTOMERS"."FIRST_NAME", "CUSTOMERS"."LAST_NAME",
"CUSTOMERS"."GENDER", "CUSTOMERS"."CUST_TYPE",
"CUSTOMERS"."ACTIVE" FROM "CUSTOMERS" WHERE CUST_TYPE = 1
ORDER BY "CUSTOMERS"."CUST_ID" ASC
```

> If you are a PowerCenter user, you will notice that the Informatica Platform does not have a concept of source qualifier. You can directly customize the read operation itself.

Filtering the source data

Now that you understand the properties in the query tab, let's drill down into some of them – beginning with filtering the data. As you have just seen, you can apply a filter condition in the query tab of the data object inside a mapping. This expression needs to be a valid SQL expression as it will be evaluated by the database to which the object will connect to. You can also write a query / filter condition that is ANSI SQL standard and applies to all databases. At runtime, DIS will use these values to build the runtime SQL query and execute it at the database level. Some examples of such filter condition are:

Source filter value	Query generated at runtime
CREATE_DATE > SYSDATE – 10	SELECT … FROM … WHERE CREATE_DATE > SYSDATE – 10
ACTIVE IS NOT NULL	SELECT … FROM … WHERE ACTIVE IS NOT null
DEPT_NO IN (SELECT DEPT_NO FROM DEPT)	SELECT … FROM … WHERE DEPT_NO IN (SELECT DEPT_NO FROM DEPT)

If you don't want to filter the number of rows but are interested in only some columns to be fetched from the source database, just connect the columns that you need from the source data object. The columns that you connect from the read operation of a data object to a subsequent transformation in the mapping directly impacts the runtime query generated. See the screenshot below:

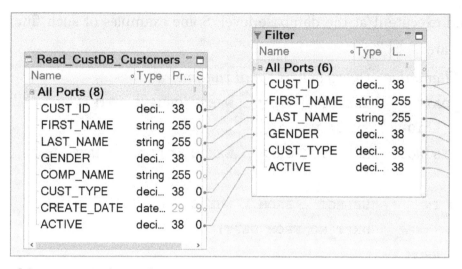

This screen is from the mapping you built as part of Lab 2. Now notice the query generated for this read operation in the mapping log. You will notice that the COMP_NAME and CREATE_DATE fields are not retrieved as part of the select query.

```
SELECT"CUSTOMERS"."CUST_ID", "CUSTOMERS"."FIRST_NAME",
"CUSTOMERS"."LAST_NAME", "CUSTOMERS"."GENDER",
"CUSTOMERS"."CUST_TYPE", "CUSTOMERS"."ACTIVE" FROM
"CUSTOMERS"
```

Runtime tab

In the runtime tab, you can set the connection, owner and the resource name associated with this data object operation. Sometimes you have tables in different schemas / databases that are of same structure. Typically, in such cases you want to apply similar transformations on them too before loading to your target database/datawarehouse systems. You can use the connection property to point the data object to a different connection.

When you change the connection in the data object operation inside a mapping, it does not change the connection that data object is associated with.

If the table that you are accessing via a data object operation is not in the default schema, you can overwrite it in the Owner name property in the runtime tab. This is very handy when you have two sets of tables maintained in your database – one used for your metadata import purposes and every developer has access to it, and the other one contains the real data that only system/application accounts have access to. In this case, you can provide the schema name in the Owner name property of the data object to point it to a different schema when the mapping runs.

In the traditional Data Integration world, it is not uncommon to read data from synonyms instead of tables. In such scenarios, you may want to import the metadata from tables so that you can import the referential integrity as well. But during runtime you only want to query the synonyms. In these scenarios, you can specify the **Resource** name in the runtime tab. Informatica will use this as the table name when generating the queries.

Advanced tab

Advanced tab contains the PreSQL and PostSQL properties. You can provide valid SQL queries in these properties. A PreSQL is executed just before executing the SQL query generated for this read operation. A PostSQL is executed after the last row is fetched from the source. For example, when you want to rebuild indexes on the table before querying it, you can place the command to rebuild an index in the PreSQL. Similarly, if you are reading off a staging table and want to clear it automatically after you read it, you can add a Truncate Table command in the PostSQL.

 You can execute more than one SQL command in the PreSQL and PostSQL properties. To execute more than one command separate them by a semi-colon (;).

Write operation/transformation

Write operation of the relational data object allows you to write to the physical table. Many of the write operation properties are the same or very similar to the read operation itself. In this section, you will look at properties that are unique to the write operation.

Run-time tab

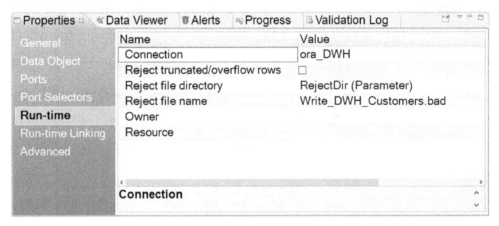

In this tab – just as in the read operation, you can set the Connection, Owner and Resource for the physical object. Additionally, you can also configure the reject properties as well for a write operation. By checking the Reject truncate/overflow rows, whenever a string value is getting truncated or a numeric value is overflown (i.e. the value you are trying to write is larger than the maximum value the database type can hold), the records will be rejected. In those scenarios, the rows that were meant to be written to the table will now be written to a Reject file in a directory – both configurable by Reject file name and Reject directory respectively.

Advanced tab

There are many properties in the advanced tab that you can configure to control in the advanced tab of the write operation.

Property	Description
Load type	This is by default set to Normal. When set to Bulk, DIS will try to load the data into a staging file and then invoke an external loader such as Oracle SQL* Loader to load the data.
Update Override	You can use this property to override the default UPDATE clause. By default, DIS generates an UPDATE query syntax for the records that you mark as update in your mapping. This property allows you to provide a different query (including different WHERE clause) for these updates.
Delete	When checked (which is the default), this write transformation will allow rows to be deleted.
Insert	When checked (which is the default), this write transformation will allow rows to be inserted.
Create or replace table at runtime	When this option is checked, another property named DDL query will be enabled. You can provide

Property	Description
	a DDL query in that property. Before DIS loads data to this target, it will execute this DDL query. You can use these to create tables just before loading the table.
Truncate target table	When this is checked, table will be emptied just before data is loaded. When this option is used, DIS issues a Truncate Table command to delete the data. If you prefer to use a DELETE statement to empty the table, use PreSQL.
Update Strategy	There are 3 possible values for this property: Update as Update: This is the default, for every row marked as Update, DIS issues updates in the target database. Update as Insert: When this option is selected. DIS issues INSERT queries for every row marked as updates. Updates as Inserts can be used to solve the Slowly Changing Dimensions (Type 2) Update else Insert: When this option is selected, DIS attempts to issue updates for every row marked as update. If the UPDATE fails for lack of row in the target table, it then issues INSERT queries. It is important to note that this option takes longer to execute as it has to wait for the command to execute,

Property	Description
	check the failure and then run another INSERT query.
PreSQL	Provide a query that you can execute just before loading the data to the target. You can use this property to issue queries such as disabling the index on the table before data loads.
PostSQL	You can use this property to execute one or more SQL statements that will be executed after the last row is loaded to the database. You can use this property to issue queries such as rebuilding the indexes, refreshing the materialized views, etc.

Lab 3 – Working with relational data objects

Use case

The customers table in the source contains both personal (individual) and business customers. The accounts table contains accounts held by both kinds of customers. Bank would like to load only personal customers and their associated information into the Data Warehouse. Hence you need to load accounts associated only with personal customers. A customer may hold more than one account at the bank. Customers can also have shared savings accounts meaning each account can belong to more than one customer. This complex "many to many relationship" is maintained in a customer-account cross reference table. The process that loads accounts table must take cross reference table into account to ensure that only accounts associated with personal customers are loaded.

Steps for solution

Import Relational Data Objects:

In this step, you will import multiple data objects. To do so, instead of using the New Data Object route, you will use Connection Explorer.

1. Import Source Data Objects
    a. Go to **Window** menu → **Show view** → **Connection Explorer**.
    b. **Connection Explorer** pane will popup
    c. Click **Select Connection.**
    d. **Select Connection** dialog box appears.
    e. Expand **Domain_Dev** → **Database** → **Oracle** → **ora_CustDB** and click > button.
    f. **Ora_CustDB** connection will now appear in the right side pane and click **OK**.
    g. In the connection explorer, expand the **Domain_Dev** → **ora_CustDB** → **CUST_DB** → **Tables**.
    h. Select **ACCOUNTS** and **CUST_ACCT_XREF**. You can use **SHIFT** key to select multiple tables at the same time.
    i. Right click the objects and choose "**Add to project...**"
    j. In the **Add to Project** dialog box, choose "**Create a data object for each resource**" and click **OK**.
    k. You will be prompted for the location where these objects need to be imported. Choose **Shared_Objects** folder and click **OK**.
    l. Both the tables will now be imported.

m. Right click the **ACCOUNTS** data object and click **Rename**. Rename it as **CustDB_Accounts**.

n. Right click the **CUST_ACCT_XREF** data object and click **Rename**. Rename it as **CustDB_Cust_Acct_XRef**.

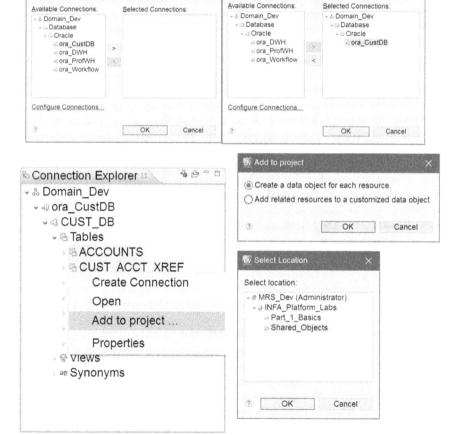

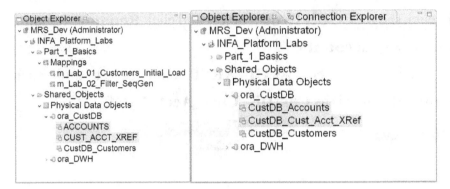

2. Create the mapping and use source data objects:

   a. Right click the folder **Part_1_Basics** and click **New →
      Mapping**.

   b. Name it as **m_Lab_03_Relational_Data_Objects** and click
      OK.

   c. Drag the **CustDB_Accounts** data object into the mapping and
      choose **Read → As Independent Data Object(s)** and click
      OK.

   d. Read transformation is now added to the mapping.

   e. Choose the Read transformation and in the **Properties** pane go
      to **Sources** tab and click **Add** button.

   f. Choose   **CustDB_Customers**   and
      CustDB_Cust_Acct_XRef objects. You can depress SHIFT
      key to select multiple objects. Click **OK** to confirm.

   g. The data object will now show 19 ports (from all the 3 tables)

   h. In the **Query** tab, **Join** property click **Edit**.

   i. Type the following condition:

   ```
   "CUSTOMERS"."CUST_ID" =
   "CUST_ACCT_XREF"."CUST_ID"AND
   ```

```
"ACCOUNTS"."ACCT_NR" = "CUST_ACCT_XREF"."ACCT_NR"
```

j.   Click **OK** to confirm.

k.   In the **Query** tab, **Filter** property click **Edit**.

l.   Type the following condition:

```
"CUSTOMERS"."CUST_TYPE" = 1
```

m.   Click **OK** to confirm.

n.   Now you have defined how to join these 3 data objects and what
     filters to apply on them.

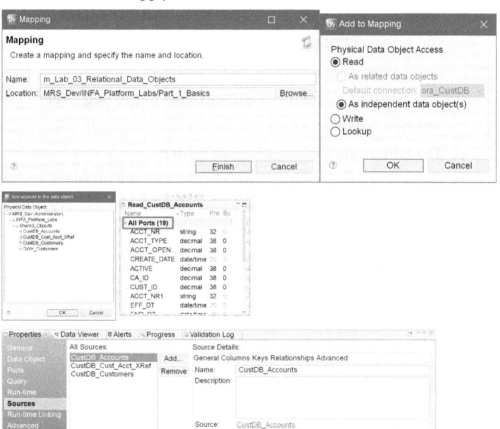

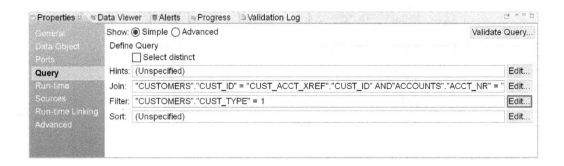

3. Create Sequence Generator for surrogate keys:

    a. Right click the mapping canvas and click **Add Transformation** (or press **<CTRL> + <SHIFT> + T**). Select **Sequence Generator** transformation and click **OK**.

    b. In the wizard, name the Sequence Generator as **seq_Acct_key** and click **Next**.

    c. Leave the default values and click **Finish**.

    d. Sequence Generator will appear in the mapping canvas.

    e. Drag the **ACCT_NR** from the read transformation to Sequence Generator **seq_Acct_key**.

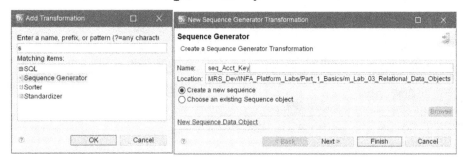

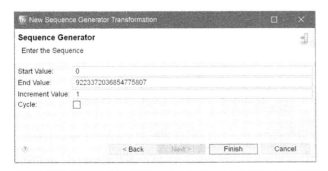

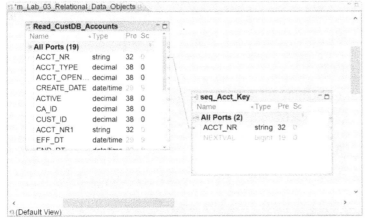

4. Import and use target data object:

    a. Now, let's switch to the connection explorer.

    b. Click the **Select Connections** icon.

    c. Expand the domain (**Domain_Dev**) → **Database** → **Oracle** and select **ora_DWH**.

    d. Click the > icon.

    e. **ora_DWH** will now appear in the selected connections.

    f. Click **OK** to close the Select Connection dialog box.

    g. Expand the **domain** → **ora_DWH** connection → **DWH** schema → **Tables**.

h. Select   the   following   objects: **ACCOUNTS, CUST_ACCT_XREF**. Use **SHIFT** key to select more than one object.

i. Right click them all and click **Add to Project...**

j. Choose "Create a data object for each resource" and click **OK**.

k. In the Select Location dialog box, choose **Shared_Objects** folder and click **OK**.

l. Your objects will now be imported and you can see them in the **Object Explorer**.

m. Right click each of these object and rename them to add a prefix of **DWH_** You will now have **DWH_Accounts** and **DWH_Cust_Acct_XRef**.

n. From the object explorer, drag the **DWH_Accounts** table into the mapping canvas and choose **Write**.

o. Connect the columns as follows:

From Transformation	From Port	To port in Target
Seq_Acct_Key	NEXTVAL	ACCT_KEY
Read_CustDB_Accounts	ACCT_NR	ACCT_NR
Read_CustDB_Accounts	ACCT_TYPE	ACCT_TYPE
Read_CustDB_Accounts	ACCT_OPEN_BRANCH	ACCT_OPEN_BRANCH
Read_CustDB_Accounts	CREATE_DATE	CREATE_DATE

From Transformation	From Port	To port in Target
<< No link >>	<< No link >>	LAST_UPD_DT
<< No link >>	<< No link >>	LAST_UPD_DESC
Read_CustDB_Accounts	ACTIVE	ACTIVE

    p. Validate the mapping and run it.

    q. You will notice that the first ACCT_KEY is Zero (0) – since you have used the Sequence Generator defaults. You can customize the initial value of the Sequence Generator as needed.

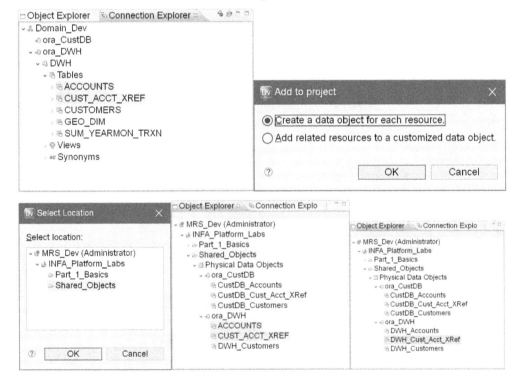

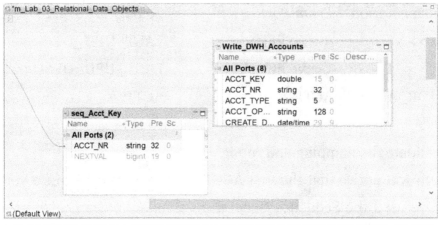

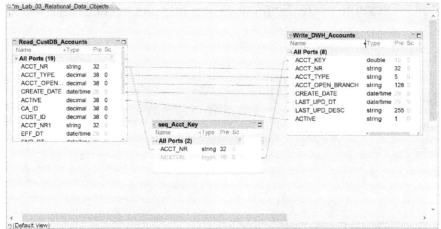

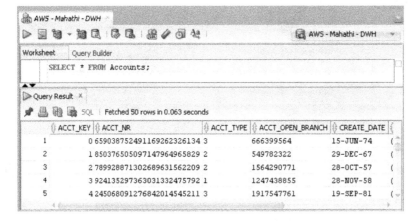

Chapter 10 – Expressions

Ports

Port is a term used to define the columns in the transformations. Port can also be defined as a data attribute that makes up a row. The difference between a port and column derives from the fact that ports have Informatica native data types while columns are database/data store specific. For example, Oracle's varchar2 and SQL Server's varchar data types are represented in their corresponding data object type as their native data types; but when these columns are converted into Informatica universal data types upon read. The first screenshot below represents how the object represents database native data types – number (38,0) and varchar2 (255), while the second screenshot represents the same data object when used in a mapping as Read transformation (Source). In the Read transformation, you will notice that Informatica universal data types are represented – decimal (38) and string (255) respectively.

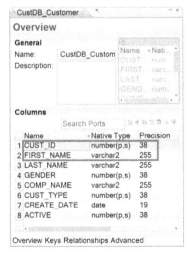
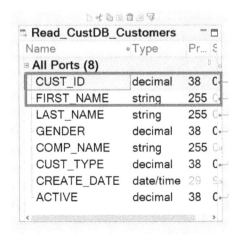

In a transformation, a port represents data that is flowing into, out of, and through the transformation. Based on their usage, ports can be categorized in many different ways:

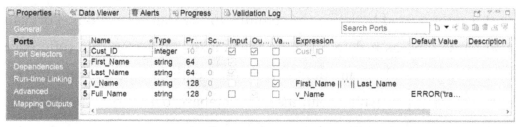

→ Input port: Brings data into the transformation. This port cannot be connected to the subsequent transformation.

→ Output port: This is a port whose value is derived in the current transformation. Hence it does not have a link from any previous transformations. The value in this port can be a static value or a value derived from other input or input/output ports.

→ Input / Output Port: This is a pass through port. The value that is brought in to the transformation is passed out as-is without any changes.

→ Variable port: This port is created inside the current transformation. Its value is used for computations and is not available outside the scope of this transformation. Value of Input port in a transformation is always the value it received from previous transformation for the current row. Whereas, for variable ports you can build an expression such that it can retain value computed in the previous row or re-compute the value based on values from the input ports and variable ports

→ Special ports: These ports are available only in specific transformations, and are unique to those transformations. Unlike other types of ports, a special port can also be of input or input/output port. For example, you can categorize an input port as "Sort key" in Sorter. In this case, the input port is also acting as a sort key port. Similarly, Aggregator has group by ports and lookup transformation has lookup ports. You will learn more about these along with the corresponding transformations.

When a transformation has many ports, the order of evaluation is always as follows:

   a. Input ports
   b. Input Output Ports
   c. Variable ports (in the order they appear in the transformation)
   d. Output ports

Organizing the ports

The order of ports is very important as they impact how values of variable ports are computed. In this section let us look at how to rearrange the ports once they are created. There are two ways you can quickly interact with the ports:

Inline editing

You can add / edit ports in the mapping canvas in the transformation objects directly. When you select a port in a transformation, the port is highlighted in green background. You will notice a mini toolbar appear right above the transformation that allows you to perform basic operations on the ports in the transformation. The toolbar has the following icons in this order: New port, cut port, copy port, paste port, delete port, move port up, and move port down. Similarly, if you double click on the whitespace after the last port in the transformation, it creates a new port and instantly lets you edit the new port you created. The new port will by default be of type String with a length of 10 characters.

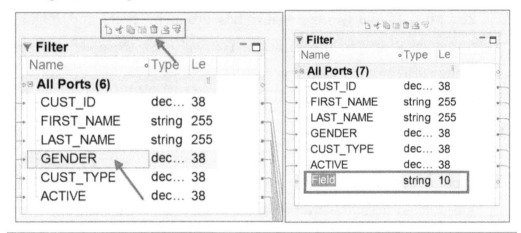

 You cannot change the port type (Input, Output, Variable...) in the mapping canvas. To do so, use the ports tab in properties pane.

 Variable ports are not displayed in the mapping canvas and can be edited only in the ports tab.

Ports tab

Every transformation has a ports tab in its properties pane. This tab allows you to add, edit, move, organize and delete ports. The ports tab has more functionality on organizing your ports than the inline editing in the mapping canvas. If you have selected a transformation such as Expression or Editor, you can also create different types of ports such as variable ports and output ports. To create a variable port, you can create a port just as you would normally do, and check the checkbox in the "Variable" column. To make it an input port you would check the "Input" column and to make it an output port, you would check the "Output" column. If you check both Input and Output port for a port, it will become Input / Output port – also known as a pass through port. Expression attribute will be automatically disabled for the Input / Output ports. Since the ports are pass through, you cannot change their value. Expression is also not available for Input only ports (where Input column is checked and variable and output columns are unchecked).

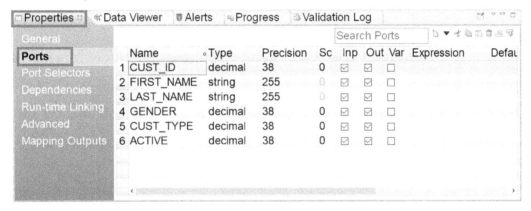

Searching for ports

When working across various transformations and large mappings with complex transformation logic, it is often hard to get to the port you want to work with. You can search for a port in the current transformation or the entire mapping. To search for a port in the current transformation, first go to the ports tab in the properties pane. Start typing in the text box on the top left corner of this pane as shown in the screenshot. You can use simple regular expressions to search for the ports. By default, the search box will look for all ports that begin with the letters you type. You can use a wild card such as "*" to search for all ports that contain the phrase or end with it, as shown in the screenshot here:

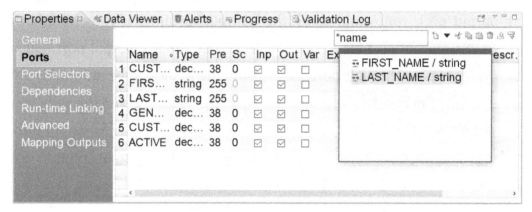

To search for ports across various transformations and in the current mapping, go to Edit menu → Find / Replace or press <CTRL>+F. the search pane will appear. Type your search phrase and hit <ENTER>. You can use the Options drop down and choose highlight all to see all matching results:

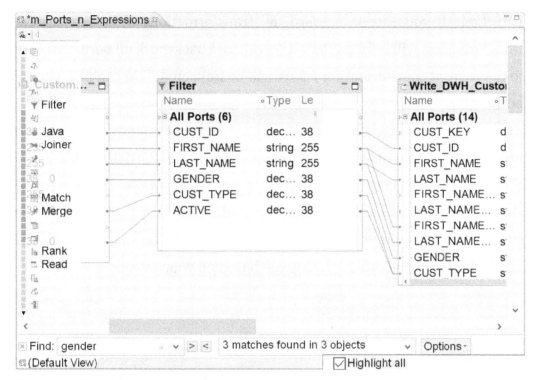

Propagating changes made to a port

Imagine you changed the data type or name of a port in the mapping and want to apply that change to the port across all the transformations it goes through. It is painful to do that manually. You will have to go to each transformation, go to its properties pane, ports tab, change the data type of the port, and validate the mapping. This process is not just tedious but also highly error prone. Thankfully, Informatica Developer is equipped to handle such scenarios. All you have to do is change the port in one of the transformations. Then in the mapping canvas, right click the port and choose **Propagate Attributes**. Propagate attributes dialog box will appear. Here you can choose several options such as:

Direction: If you choose forward, all transformations following current transformation will be impacted. If you choose backward, all ports that lead to the current transformation / port will be impacted. You can also choose both.

Attributes to propagate: You can choose what attributes you want to propagate – the default is only to propagate name and the datatype. You can also optionally choose precision, scale and description. If you choose "Include expression and conditional dependencies", any ports that use the current port in their transformation logic will also be updated with the name, data type and other attributes – based on your selection.

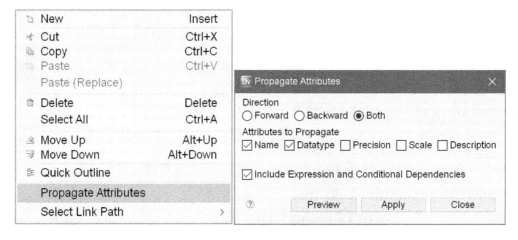

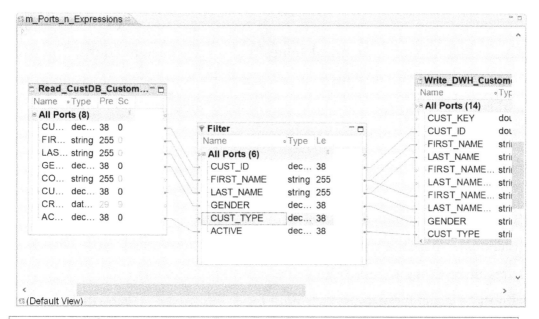

When propagation happens, the ports affected are highlighted in yellow color. In low contrast modes, these lines may not be clearly visible.

Data types

Each port is of a specific data type. There are many data types supported by the Informatica Platform. A data type defines the type of the data in the port. Data types can be of numerical values such as integers and decimals or string values containing text or date values or binary where Informatica will not attempt to interpret the text but passes them as is. When assigning or comparing values between different ports, they must be "compatible" types. A data type mismatch can cause a runtime error or in some cases data truncation. Let's look at some of the data types supported by Informatica Platform:

Integer

This is used to store numerical values that do not have fractions. You can use both signed and unsigned values. This data type uses a precision of 10 and scale of 0. An integer data type occupies about 4 bytes of memory to store the value. Integer values can range from -2,147,483,648 to 2,147,483,647.

Bigint

Bigint is another data type to store whole numbers (that do not have any fractions). This data type uses a precision of 19 and a scale of 0. It uses 8 bytes of memory to store the value and hence can store values that are almost twice as large as Integer data type. Bigint values can range from -9,223,372,036,854,775,808 to 9,223,372,036,854,775,807.

Decimal

Decimals can store fractional values. When high precision is enabled, they can support precision up to 38 digits. While a precision can range from 1 to 38 digits, scale can range from 0 to 38 digits. Decimal data type occupies 8 to 24 bytes depending on the precision values.

Double

Double data type can also store fractional values. It takes up to 8 digits of storage and can take precisions up to 15 digits.

 Rounding methods for double data types varies based on the runtime systems. Please refer to Informatica documentation for details.

String / text

Both string and text data types store character values and support the same precision of 1 to 104,857,600 characters. In Unicode mode, they take up almost twice the storage capacity as compared to ASCII mode. The difference between String and text is due to the differences in the various database systems. Typically, in any transformation that does not interact with a database (i.e. except, read, write, lookups and stored procedures), you can use the string and text interchangeably. When working with databases, use String for Char, Varchar, and NVarchar data types and use Text data type for Text, Long and Long Varchar data types.

Date / Time

This data type is used for date and time values. This data type has a fixed precision of 29 digits with a scale of 9. In this data type, you can store values ranging from Jan 1, 0001 A.D. to Dec 31, 9999 A.D. This data type takes 16 bytes of storage and can store date / time values up to nano seconds.

Timestamp With TZ

Timestamp with Time zone values are extensions of date data types. They take up to 40 bytes of storage and have a precision of 36 and a scale of 9. They can also store the value up to nano seconds. However, their value ranges are much shorter and range between Aug. 1, 1947 A.D and Dec. 31, 2040 A.D. -12:00 to +14:00.

Operators

Informatica Platform has many operators – some of which, you will see in this section. Operators are special symbols that perform specific operations on one or more operands and then return a result. Based on their usage, they can be classified as:

→ Arithmetic operators

→ String operators

→ Comparison operators

→ Logical operators

 When more than one operator is used, DIS will evaluate them in the order listed above.

Arithmetic operators

Operator	Description	Usage example
+	Add	BaseSalary + Bonus + PerDiem
-	Subtract	GrossSalary – Tax
*	Multiply	BaseSalary * 12
/	Division	MonthlySalary/4
%	Remainder of the division	MonthlySalary % Tax

String operators

There is only one String operator: Concatenation. Concatenation appends one string to another. You can use this operator multiple times to concatenate multiple values.

Operator	Description	Usage example
||	Concatenate	FirstName || ' ' || LastName

Comparison operators

Operator	Description	Usage example
=	Equals to	IIF(Port1 = Port2, 'Same')
>	Greater than	IIF(Port1 > Port2, 'More')
>=	Greater than or equals to	IIF(Port1 >=Port2, 'More or same')
<	Less than	IIF(Port1 <Port2, 'Less')
<=	Less than or equals to	IIF(Port1 <=Port2, 'Less or same')
<>or != or ^=	Not equals to	IIF(Port1 != Port2, 'Not equals to')

Logical operators

Logical operators are extensions of comparison operators as they operate on one or two Boolean expressions and return TRUE or FALSE.

Operator	Description	Usage example
AND	Returns TRUE if both the conditions are TRUE	IIF(tax >= valueA AND tax <valueB, bracketA, bracketB)

Operator	Description	Usage example
OR	Returns TRUE if any one of the condition evaluates to TRUE	IIF(baseSalary<= valueA OR tax <valueB, taxExempted, notExempted)
NOT	Negates the boolean expression value. TRUE becomes FALSE and FALSE becomes TRUE	IIF(NOT IsNull(bonus), noTax)

 Any operation involving NULL always evaluates to NULL. Any operator or function in transformation language returns NULL if one or more of its input is NULL.

Expression editor

An expression editor is where you write expressions. You open an expression editor when you try to add/edit an expression. For example, when you try to edit variable / output ports, you open the expression editor. Expression editor is also used in various transformations. You have already used expression transformation when writing filter condition in the Filter transformation usage in Chapter – Core Transformations

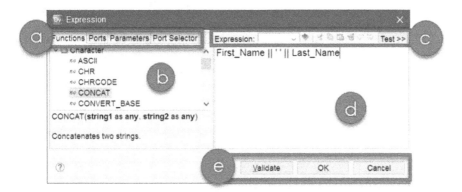

Let us look at the screenshot above. These are few areas of expression editor that you should get familiarized with:

a. **Function tabs**: There are many tabs here, each tab changes the function explorer.

b. **Function explorer**: This tab shows all functions available in the transformation language by default. When ports tab is selected, it will show all available ports in the current transformation. When parameters tab is selected, this explorer shows all system defined and user defined parameters that can be used in the current expression.

c. **Tool** menu: There are several tools available here for editing in this order: Search within expression (text box and the binoculars icon), cut, copy, paste and clear (the brush icon) and the Test function. See below for the test expression.

d. **Expression**: This is where you build/write the expression.

e. Action buttons: There are 3 action buttons:

  a. **Validate**: Validates the expression and indicates whether the expression is syntactically valid

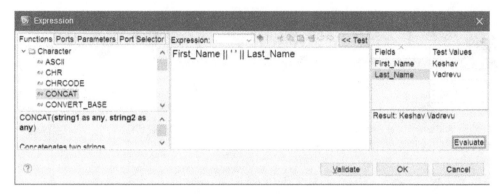

b. **OK**: Validates and saves the expression. This will close the dialog box.

c. **Cancel**: Ignores all changes made since the expression editor popped up and reverts the expression back to what it was before the dialog box was opened.

Testing out an expression

When you build/write an expression, you can test it instantaneously with the test function. When you click the **"Test >>"** button, the expression editor shows an extension of the dialog box. You will now see every port used in the expression listed in a grid. You can double click on the empty cells next to each port and provide some sample values. Once you have provided all values, click **Evaluate**. The result will be displayed right above the **Evaluate** button.

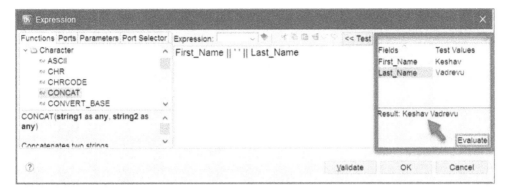

Transformation language

Transformation language is used to express logic in a predefined syntax using several inbuilt functions and operators. There are many transformations that allow you to write expressions. Expressions rely on the Informatica's transformation language syntax. This language contains many functions, operators and data types. You have already learned about operators and data types in the previous sections. Now, let us take a look at writing some expressions using functions.

Expression transformation

Expression transformation is probably the most widely used transformation in Informatica Platform. This transformation allows users to write expressions and calculations. These expressions can be used to compute various types of values inside a mapping execution. While transformation language can be used in several transformations, expression transformation can be used to build complex expressions and perform computations. Tasks like concatenating first name and last name to form full name, calculate numerical values like bonus based on base salary and more complex tasks can all be performed using expression transformations. Expression is a passive transformation; you can split your calculations / process them into various expression transformations and execute them in parallel. It is not possible to understand the usage of the expression transformation without understanding the transformation language reference. As you have seen in the previous sections, transformation language contains various operators such as addition and subtraction, and functions that allow various operations to be performed on strings, numbers and dates and other data types. You can use outputs of one or more calculations in another expression / ports.

Lab 4 – Expression transformation and transformation language

Use case

In the Initial Load lab that you built earlier, you have loaded the customers dimension in the Data Warehouse from the customers table in the Customer DB. You will now extend the same lab to add various expressions to it. In this lab, you plan to create two mappings – one for customers and one for accounts. Here's a list of expression changes you plan to do for customers table:

Column in target	Data in source is of type...	Transformation requirement
Gender	Numeric	Convert input values as follows: - 0 to U (Unknown) - 1 to M (Male) - 2 to F (Female)

Column in target	Data in source is of type...	Transformation requirement
Customer type	Numeric	Convert input values as follows: - 1 to P (Personal) - 2 to B (Business)
Last update date	N/A	Set it to the date of the mapping run
Last update Desc	N/A	Set it to a static value of "Initial Load"
Active	Numeric	Convert 1 to 'Y' (Active) and everything else to 'N' (Not active)

Changes to accounts table:

Column in target	Data in source is of type...	Transformation requirement
Account type	Numeric	Convert input values as follows: - 1 to SAV (Savings account) - 2 to CHK (Checking account) - 3 to CRD (Credit card)
Last update date	N/A	Set it to the date of the mapping run
Last update Description	N/A	Set it to a static value of "Initial Load"
Active	Numeric	Convert 1 to 'Y' (Active) and everything else to 'N' (Not active)

Lab 4a – Expressions on Customers table

1. Create mapping and import source, targets

    a. Right click the **Part_1_Basics** folder → Click New → Mapping.

    b. Type   the   mapping   name   as
        m_Lab_04a_Expressions_on_Customers and click **OK**.

    c. Drag the CustDB_Customers table from the object explorer into
        the mapping canvas and choose Read → as Independent data
        object(s) and click **OK**.

    d. Drag the DWH_Customers table from object explorer into the
        mapping canvas and choose Write and click **OK**.

    e. In the write transformation properties → Advanced tab → check
        the Truncate target table option.

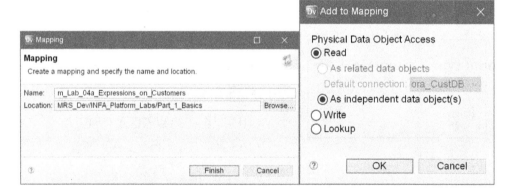

2. Add Sequence Generator transformation

   a. Right click mapping canvas and choose Add Transformation or press `<CTRL> + <SHIFT> + T`.

   b. Choose Sequence Generator and click **OK**.

   c. Name the Sequence Generator as "seq_Cust_Key" and click **Next**.

   d. Set the start value as 1 and click **Finish**.

   e. Drag the customer ID (CUST_ID) into the Sequence Generator transformation.

   f. Drag the NEXTVAL from the Sequence Generator and connect to the write transformation CUST_KEY port.

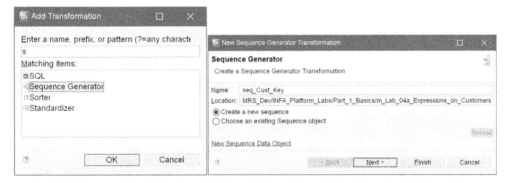

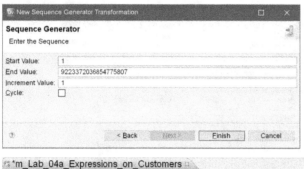

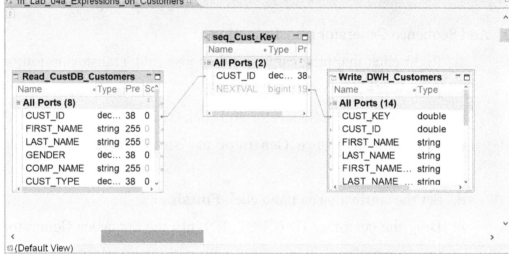

3. Add expression transformation

   a. Right click mapping canvas and choose Add Transformation or press **<CTRL>** + **<SHIFT>** + **T**.

   b. Choose Expression and click **OK**.

   c. Drag all the columns from the Read transformation into the expression.

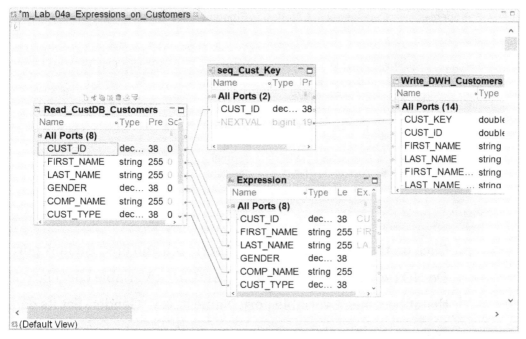

d. In the properties pane, go to ports tab.

e. Rename the following ports as shown below. To rename, you can double click the port name.

Column name	Rename it to...
GENDER	in_GENDER
CUST_TYPE	in_CUST_TYPE
ACTIVE	in_ACTIVE

f. Now remove the Output checkbox for these ports so that they become input only. You will notice that the input check boxes will be grayed out making these ports input only.

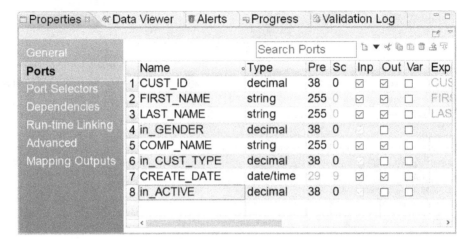

g. Click on the new port icon in the ports tab and create a new port. Do NOT choose New Dynamic Port. Check Variable checkbox so that it becomes a variable port. Name it as v_Gender. Set its data type as String and precision as 1. You will notice that the expression column will be enabled and will, by default, be set to the same as port name.

h. In the expression column, click on the down arrow icon to edit the expression. Set its value to as below and click **Validate**

Decode`(in_Gender, 1, 'M', 2, 'F')`.

i. "Expression is valid" message will be displayed. Click **OK** to close the message. Click OK again to close the expression editor

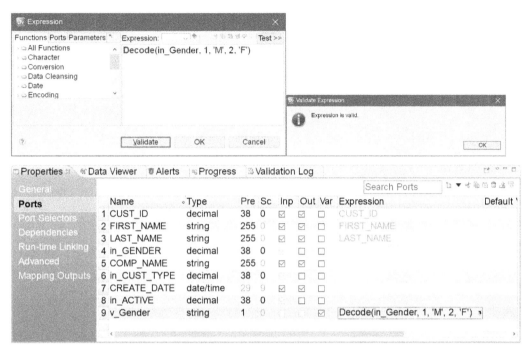

j. Similarly create the following variable ports:

Port name	Type	Precision	Expression
v_Cust_Type	String	1	IIF(in_CUST_TYPE = 1, 'P', 'B')
v_Last_Upd_Date	Date / Time		SYSDATE
v_Last_Upd_Desc	String	255	'Initial Load'
v_Active	String	1	IIF(in_Active = 'Y', 'N')

k. Variable ports are used to only compute values and hence variables cannot be directly linked to next transformations. To do so, you need output ports. Let's create output ports as shown below:

Port name	Type	Precision	Expression
o_Gender	String	1	v_Gender
o_Cust_Type	String	1	v_Cust_Type
o_Last_Upd_Date	Date / Time		v_Last_Upd_Date
o_Last_Upd_Desc	String	255	v_Last_Upd_Desc
o_Active	String	1	V_Active

l. Your expression will now look like this:

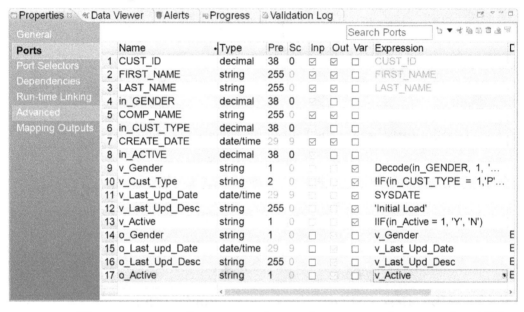

m. Now connect the ports from the expression to the Write transformation as follows:

Port in Expression	Port in Write transformation
CUST_ID	CUST_ID
FIRST_NAME	FIRST_NAME, FIRST_NAME_ORIG
LAST_NAME	LAST_NAME, LAST_NAME_ORIG

Port in Expression	Port in Write transformation
o_Gender	GENDER
o_Cust_Type	CUST_TYPE
o_Last_Upd_Date	CREATE_DATE, LAST_UPD_DT
o_Last_Upd_Des	LAST_UPD_DESC
o_Active	ACTIVE

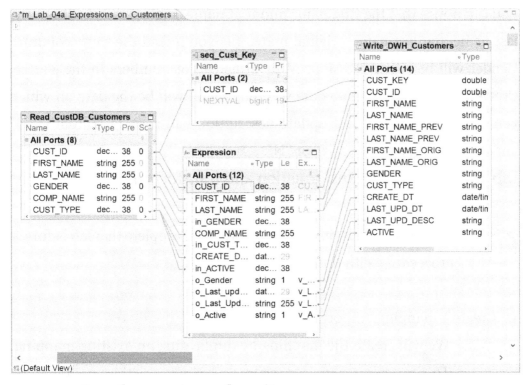

n. Save the mapping and run it.

You can notice that the first name and first name original match. Similarly, last name and last name original match (as you linked the same column). Gender will be either NULL or M or F instead of numbers in the source. Create date and last update date will match and will be the date on which you run the mapping. Last update description will contain "Initial Load" and active will have values "Y" or "N".

Lab 4b – Expression transformation and transformation language

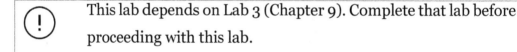

> (!) This lab depends on Lab 3 (Chapter 9). Complete that lab before proceeding with this lab.

1. Create a mapping, import source and targets:

    1. We will create the mapping by duplicating an existing mapping. To do so, right click the mapping "m_Lab_03_Relational_Data_Objects" and click **Copy**.

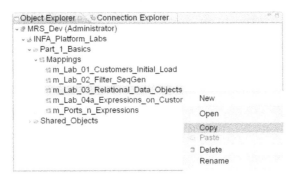

2. Now right click on the folder "Part_1_Basics" and click **Paste**.

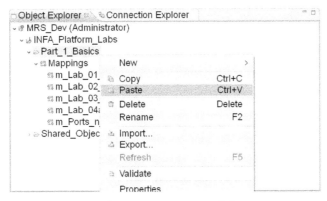

3. When prompted, choose to Reuse object.

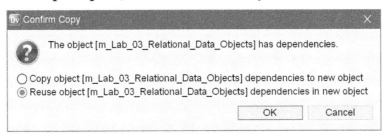

4. A   mapping   called "CopyOf_m_Lab_03_Relational_Data_Objects"   is   created. Right   click   it   and   click   Rename.   Rename   it   as "m_Lab_04b_Expressions_on_Accounts".

5. Right click the mapping and click **Open**.

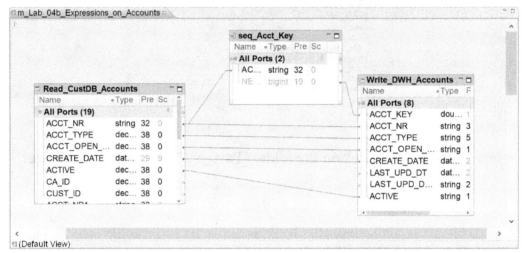

6. Delete the links from the read transformation to the write transformation.

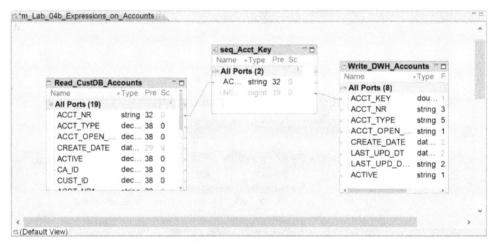

2. Add expression transformation to the mapping.

    a. Right click on the mapping canvas and click **Add Transformation** or press <CTRL> + <SHIFT> + T.

    b. Select expression transformation and click **OK**.

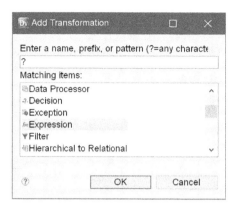

c. Drag the following ports from the Read transformation into an expression: ACCT_NR, ACCT_TYPE, ACCT_OPEN_BRANCH into the expression transformation.

d. Add the following variable ports:

Port name	Data type	precision	Expression
v_Acct_Type	String	3	Decode (ACCT_TYPE, 1, 'SAV', 2, 'CHK', 3, 'CRD', 'UNK')
v_Last_Upd_Date	Date / time		SYSDATE
v_Last_Upd_Desc	String	255	'Initial Load'
v_Active	String	5	IIF(ACTIVE = 1, 'Y', 'N')

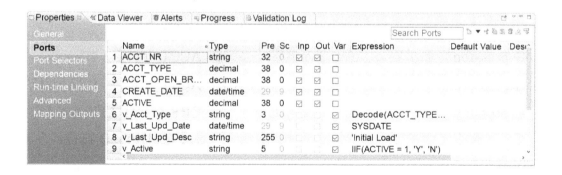

e. Create the corresponding output ports as follows:

Port name	Data type	precision	Expression
o_Acct_Type	String	3	v_Acct_Type
o_Last_Upd_Date	Date / time		v_Last_Upd_Date
o_Last_Upd_Desc	String	255	v_Last_Upd_Desc
o_Active	String	5	v_Active

Properties	Data Viewer	Alerts	Progress	Validation Log							

Search Ports

	Name	Type	Pre	Sc	Inp	Out	Var	Expression	Default Value	Descr
1	ACCT_NR	string	32	0	☑	☑	☐			
2	ACCT_TYPE	decimal	38	0	☑	☑	☐			
3	ACCT_OPEN_BR...	decimal	38	0	☑	☑	☐			
4	CREATE_DATE	date/time	29	9	☑	☑	☐			
5	ACTIVE	decimal	38	0	☑	☑	☐			
6	v_Acct_Type	string	3	0			☑	Decode(ACCT_TYPE...		
7	v_Last_Upd_Date	date/time	29	9			☑	SYSDATE		
8	v_Last_Upd_Desc	string	255	0			☑	'Initial Load'		
9	v_Active	string	5	0			☑	IIF(ACTIVE = 1, 'Y', 'N')		
10	o_Acct_Type	string	3	0	☐	☐		v_Acct_Type	ERROR('tra...	
11	o_Last_Upd_Date	date/time	29	9	☐	☐		v_Last_Upd_Date	ERROR('tra...	
12	o_Last_Upd_Desc	string	255	0	☐	☐		v_Last_Upd_Desc	ERROR('tra...	
13	o_Active	string	5	0	☐	☐		v_Active	ERROR('tra...	

General
Ports
Port Selectors
Dependencies
Run-time Linking
Advanced
Mapping Outputs

f. Now connect the following columns to the write transformation:

From Transformation	From port	Write transformation port
Seq_Acct_Key	NEXTVAL	ACCT_KEY
Expression	Acct_nr	ACCT_NR
Expression	o_Acct_Type	ACCT_TYPE
Expression	ACCT_OPEN_BRANCH	ACCT_OPEN_BRANCH
Expression	o_Last_Upd_Date	CREATE_DATE, LAST_UPD_DATE

From Transformation	From port	Write transformation port
Expression	o_Last_Upd_Desc	LAST_UPD_DESC
Expression	o_Active	ACTIVE

3. Validate and run the mapping:

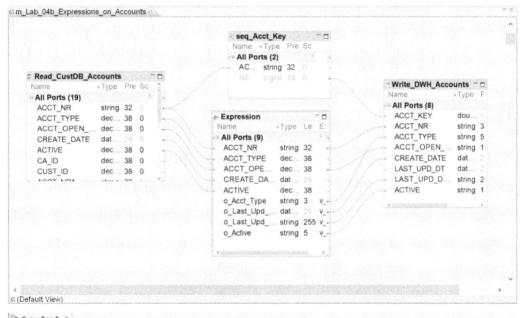

Chapter 11 – Core transformations continued

Union transformation

Sometimes similar data is stored in different physical tables. This could be for various reasons including performance. For example, it is common to partition the data in large size tables. When partitioned, the data is physically distributed across various data stores. At times, there is a need to bring this data back together to apply certain business rules. Union operation is defined as bringing two or more result sets together into a single result set of all the rows. A union transformation can have two or more input groups. All the input groups are expected to have the same / similar data structure. The transformation then appends the data and sends them all out in a single group. The DIS processes the data of all input groups in parallel and hence the order of the output of union transformation is not guaranteed.

Lookup transformation

Lookup transformation looks up a value in a table/file and returns a corresponding value. Lookup transformation is also capable of returning more than one value, in fact a full row for the corresponding value. One of the most common use cases for a lookup is to identify the presence of a record. For example, before you load data into a table, you would like to know if a copy of this record already exists in the target table. Hence lookup is widely used in insert-else-update processes. Lookup is also extensively used to resolve reference data. For example, while loading customers address information, you might want to resolve a zip code to the city / state codes or names.

Let us take an example to understand this better. Say, you are loading customers table from source (CustDB) to customers' dimension of Data Warehouse. The primary key in the customers table is the CUST_ID column. While this column exists in the customers dimension in Data Warehouse, it uses CUST_KEY (a surrogate key) as its primary key. When customer information in the source changes, it will be updated in the customers table in the source (replacing the original value). However, the Data Warehouse stores all changes as independent records. Thus there can be more than one row for the same CUST_ID value – with different CUST_KEY values. This is a relatively easy problem to solve as you just have to insert any new records or perform updates. The real challenge kicks in when you have to associate the customers to their accounts. When a customer adds a new account, the customer-account cross reference table in the source has CUST_ID and ACCT_NR associations. The table in the Data Warehouse on the other hand has CUST_KEY and ACCT_KEY. So, when the loads of this table happen you have the CUST_ID coming from the source that needs to be associated with its corresponding latest CUST_KEY first. To solve this problem, you will have to first "lookup" CUST_KEY in the "Customers" dimension for a given CUST_ID in the source and then pass it along to the cross reference table.

Lookup properties

Lookup receives values via input ports and returns the results via return ports. Lookup needs at least 1 input port and at least 1 output ports. You can also specify a lookup filter. When you apply a filter condition, the data retrieved from the lookup table is first filtered and then the input values are looked up in the remaining result set. For the lookup to be able to understand how to map the input data to the lookup dataset, you need to define a lookup condition. With this condition, the lookup transformation will be able to join the input data to lookup data.

 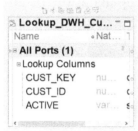 Let us apply this to the example you just talked about and see how it can be applied. When you drag the Customer dimension into the mapping instead of choosing Read or Write, choose Lookup operation and define the filter condition. Lookup transformation will filter the data based on the condition provided in the properties pane → query tab. In this example, you are filtering it by the active customers only.

Now, you go to columns tab and choose the return column. You can choose more than one return column. Though in this example, you are only choosing one column as return column – CUST_KEY.

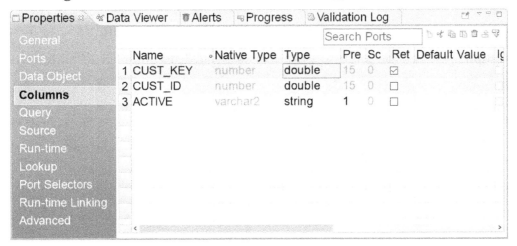

Then, you drag in the source columns into the lookup transformation. If the column names are the same as that in the lookup table, the input columns will be suffixed with 1 to resolve duplicate column names (notice the CUST_ID from the source linked as CUST_ID1 in the lookup transformation).

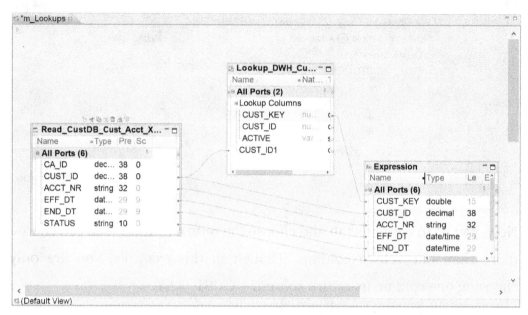

Now you complete the process by adding the lookup condition. In this example, you set the lookup condition as Input Customer ID to match the DWH Customers CUST_ID as follows:

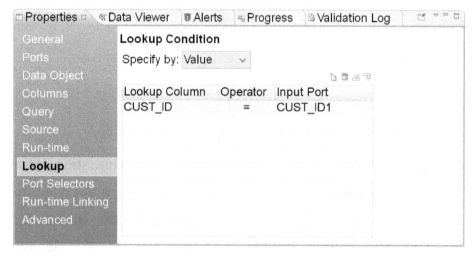

The input column names don't have to match the name with the database column names. But the lookup ports MUST exactly match the column names in the database. DIS will generate a lookup query based on the column names.

Lookup caches

Properties	Data Viewer	Alerts	Progress	Validation Log		

	Name	Value
Data Object	Lookup	
Columns	Lookup caching enabled	☑
Query	Lookup data cache size	Auto
Source	Lookup index cache size	Auto
Run-time	Cache file name prefix	
Lookup	Pre-build lookup cache	Auto
Port Selectors	Lookup cache directory name	CacheDir (Parameter)
Run-time Linking	Re-cache from lookup source	
Advanced		
	Lookup	

Lookup transformation can be cached or un-cached. When cached, lookup transformation will cache the lookup table data at the beginning of the mapping run. This cache is stored in the memory and will be spilled to disk as needed. When un-cached, lookup will query the underlying database for every input row. This is useful when underlying database changes too often and caching may produce incorrect results. However, there is a performance penalty in querying large lookup tables for every input row. Lookup caching can be enabled or disabled by checking / unchecking the "Lookup caching enabled" checkbox. When lookup caching is enabled, you can also configure the size of the cache. For larger caches, you may also want to configure the index cache size. By default, both of these cache sizes are set to "**Auto**". You can configure the values in KB, MB and GB. Some examples are "512 KB",

"64 MB", "4 GB". You can also choose to pre-build lookup caches. When lookup cache is pre-built, DIS will build the cache regardless of the input data. When pre-built option is disabled, DIS will build the cache only when the first input row is read from the source. This is very helpful when filter conditions are applied on the source data, which may at times lead to no data being read. In these cases, if the lookup size is large, you will end up building the cache and then not using it at all. This situation can be avoided by setting it to "Auto" so that DIS can automatically determine building the cache.

Static and dynamic caches

Lookup cache is by default static, i.e. the cache is built at the beginning of the mapping execution. Lookup cache can also be made dynamic. When lookup is enabled to be dynamic, if the lookup row is not found

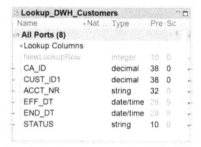

in the cache, it will be added in to the cache during the mapping execution itself. If the cache is updated, lookup will mark the rows accordingly by using the system defined **NewLookupRow** port. The NewLookupRow port is available only when dynamic cache is enabled.

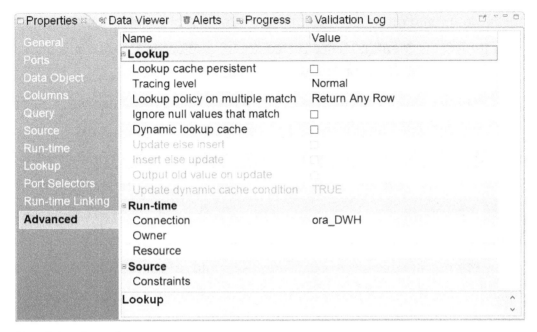

Persistent caches

In many cases, lookup caches are huge in size. So, rebuilding them for every mapping execution is not practical. In cases where the underlying table doesn't change that often or is guaranteed to be in sync with lookup (using dynamic caches), you can make the lookup cache to be persistent. When persistent cache is enabled, lookup cache that is built for the mapping is saved at the end of the mapping run. When the mapping runs next time, the DIS identifies that the prebuilt cache exists and uses it again instead of rebuilding it from the start.

Lab 5 – Union and Lookup

Use-case

Previously you have discussed the customers and accounts tables. These tables share "many to many"relationships. A customer can have more than one account and an account can have more than one customer associated with it (Joint accounts). Hence the customer and account tables are linked via a cross referenced table: Cust_Acct_XRef. This table has a reference to the Customer ID and Account Number and active status. Inactive records are present in another table of the same structure named Cust_Acct_XRef_ARC (archive). A similar table exists both in source and DataWarehouse. However, the Customer and Account dimensions in the Data Warehouse use surrogate keys. So, instead of referencing the relationship via Customer ID and Account Number, the Data Warehouse cross reference table uses Customer Key and Account Key. So, when updating the cross reference table in Data Warehouse from the source database, you need to resolve these surrogate keys by performing lookups on the DataWarehouse table. For streamlined processing, you will union the source cross reference table and its archive table first before looking up the IDs in the Data Warehouse table.

Challenges

a. The cross reference data is stored in two tables: Active table and archive table. Data from both these tables need to be merged and loaded to Data Warehouse.

b. The cross reference table contains Customer ID and Account number to identify relationships. However, Data Warehouse uses surrogate keys. You need to resolve these before loading target table.

Steps for the solution

1. Import the data objects:

a. Go to the connection explorer. If it is not open already, you can open it by clicking the Window menu → Show View → Connection Explorer.

b. Click Select connections. Select connections dialog box.

c. On the left hand side expand Domain_Dev → Databases → Oracle → ora_CustDB and click ">" icon. If the ora_CustDB is already available on the right hand side, just click OK to close the select connections dialog box.

d. In the connection explorer go to Domain_Dev → ora_CustDB (Connection) → CUST_DB (Schema) → Tables → CUST_ACCT_XREF_ARC.

e. Right click the data object and choose Add to project...

f. Choose "Create a data object for each resource" and click OK.

g. New Relational Data Object appears. Name the object as "CustDB_Cust_Acct_XRef_ARC".

h. Click Browse next to location.

i. Choose Project (INFA_Platform_Labs) → Folder (Shared_Objects) and click OK.

j. Click Finish in the New Relational data object.

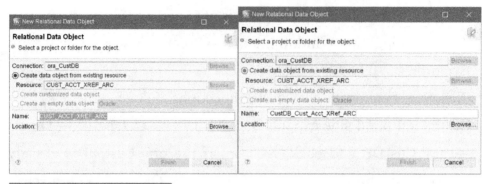

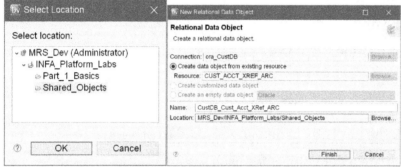

2. Create a mapping and add sources:

   a. Right click the folder Part_1_Basics and click New → Mapping.

   b. Name the mapping as "m_Lab_05_Union_and_Lookups" and click OK.

   c. Drag the CustDB_Cust_Acct_XRef data object into the mapping and choose the Read operation and click OK.

   d. Drag the CustDB_Cust_Acct_XRef_ARC into the mapping and choose Read and click OK.

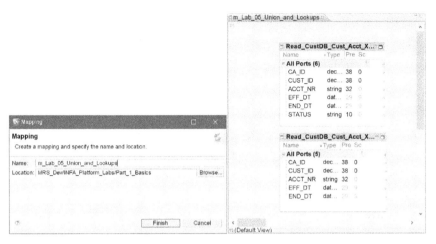

3. Union the sources:

   a. Add a union transformation by right clicking the mapping canvas and choosing Add Transformation.

   b. Choose Union and click OK.

   c. Drag all columns from the Read_CustDB_Cust_Acct_XRef on the Input Group of the Union transformation.

   d. In the union transformation properties tab, go to Groups tab.

   e. Rename the INPUT group as "Active" by double clicking on the name.

   f. Click New icon and add another group. Name it as "Archive".

   g. In the mapping canvas, drag all ports from the "Read_CustDB_Cust_Acct_XRef_ARC" on to the "Archive" group. You will notice that the Status column of the Archive group will remain unconnected.

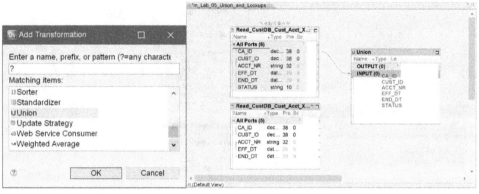

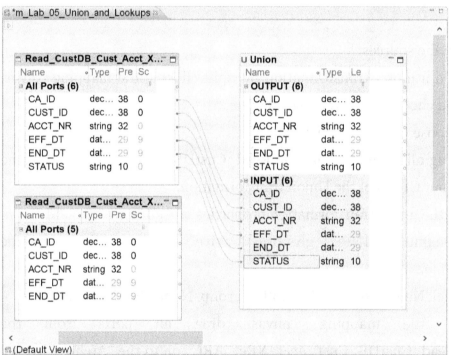

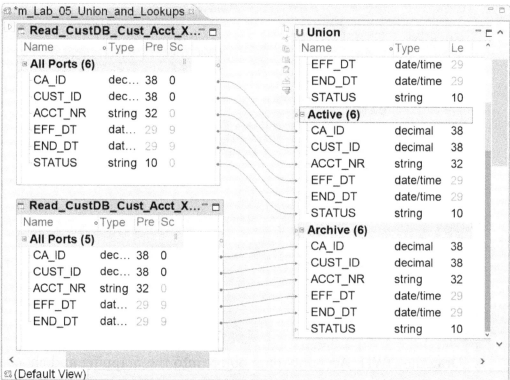

4. Lookup the surrogate keys:

    a. Drag the DWH_Customers data object into the mapping and choose "Lookup" and click OK.

    b. From the Output group of the union transformation, drag the Cust_ID into the lookup.

c. In the lookup properties, go to Columns tab. Remove all columns except CUST_ID and CUST_KEY. Choose the CUST_KEY column as return column.

d. In the lookup tab of Lookup properties, add new condition and set it to CUST_ID = CUST_ID1.

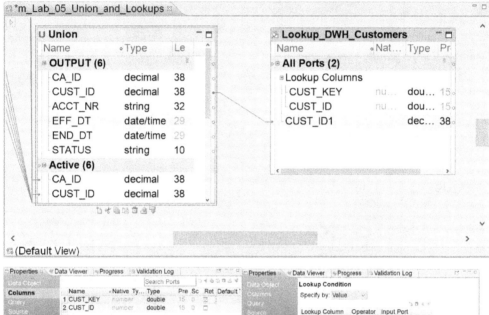

e. Drag the DWH_Accounts data object into the mapping and choose "Lookup" and click OK.

f. From the output group of the union transformation, drag the ACCT_NR into the lookup Lookup_DWH_Accounts.

g. In the lookup properties, go to Columns Tab. Remove all columns except ACCT_NR and ACCT_KEY. Choose the ACCT_KEY column as return column.

h. In the lookup tab of lookup properties, add new condition and set it as ACCT_NR = ACCR_NR1.

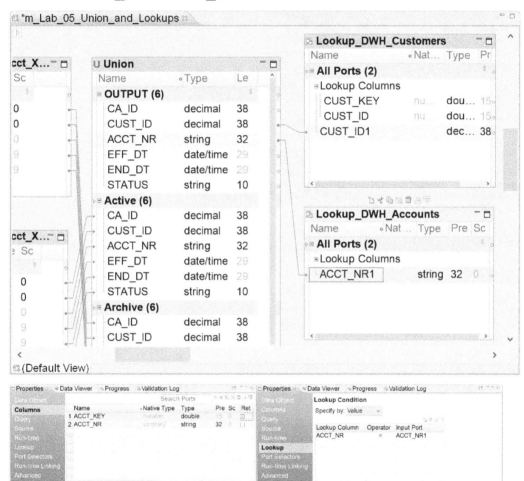

5. Add Sequence Generator:

   a. Add a new transformation by pressing CTRL + SHIFT + T and choose Sequence Generator and click OK.

   b. Name the Sequence Generator as seq_XRef and click Next.

   c. Change the start value as 1 and click Finish.

d. From the Output group of the union transformation, drag the EFF_DT , END_DT and STATUS into the Sequence Generator.

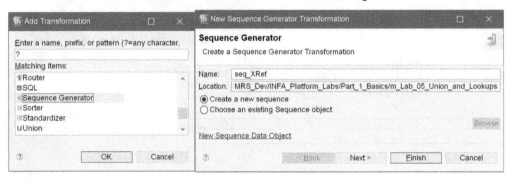

6. Add the target and complete the mapping:

a. Drag the DWH_Cust_Acct_XRef data object into the mapping and choose "Write".

b. In the properties tab, go to Advanced tab and check the Truncate Target Table option.

c. From the Sequence Generator (seq_XRef), connect the NEXTVAL to Write transformation CA_KEY.

d. From the Sequence Generator (seq_XRef) connect the EFF_DT, END_DT and STATUS to the corresponding columns in the Write transformation.

e. From the lookup Lookup_DWH_Customers, connect the CUST_KEY to CUST_KEY in Write transformation.

f. From the lookup Lookup_DWH_Accounts, connect the ACCT_KEY to ACCT_KEY in Write transformation.

Exercise

Try doing the following on your own:

a. Add an expression transformation before the Write transformation.

b. This expression should provide current date as the Last Update Date.

c. This expression should also receive CUST_KEY and ACCT_KEY from the corresponding lookup transformations. If either of them are NULL, set the ACTIVE status in the Write transformation to "I" for Inactive.

Router transformation

Router transformation is an advanced Filter transformation. In a typical programming world, filter can be compared to IF condition and Router transformation can be compared to the Switch-Case statement. In other words, Router transformation can be used when you have to deal with multiple IF statements. A Router takes one input group and routes and provides several output groups – each with a condition. When data matches a particular condition, the data is routed through the corresponding group. If data does not match any group, it will be automatically directed to the "default" group. Let us consider an example: while copying the transactions to the Data Warehouse, a bank wants to direct all On-Hold transactions and any transactions that are larger than $5000 to alerts table for fraud prevention processing. All other transactions will also be copied over to the main transactions table. In this example, a router transformation can be used to define a group for the fraud prevention processing. This will group will have a condition such as Amount >= 5000. Output of this group is connected to fraud prevention table and the default group is connected to main transactions table.

Lab 6 – Router transformation

Use-case

This use-case has 3 requirements:

1. Load all transactions that are greater than $5000 into the alerts table for anti-fraud processing.
2. Load all Bill Pay transactions to Bill Pay table so that Bill Pay system can pick these up and process them.
3. Load all pending transactions to another table so that customers can look at pending transactions easily.
4. Read the data from the source system as fewer times as possible so as not to overload it.

Steps for the solution

1. Import the target data objects:
    a. Go to Connection explorer. Expand the Domain → ora_DWH → DWH → Tables.
    b. Select the TRXN_BILLS, TRXN_ALERTS, TRXN_PEND tables. You can use SHIFT key to select more than one object.
    c. Right click all the three tables and choose Add to project.
    d. Choose Create a data object for each resource and click OK.
    e. When prompted for location, choose INFA_Platform_Labs project → Shared_Objects and click OK.
    f. In the object explorer, you will now see the 3 new tables.

g. Right click each of this table, choose Rename and Add "DWH_" prefix to them.

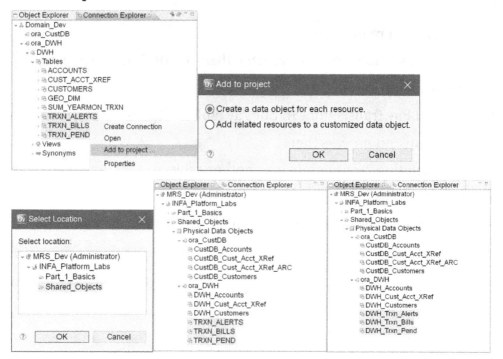

h. Now, switch to the Connection explorer.

i. Expand Domain_Dev → ora_CustDB → CUST_DB → Tables.

j. Select the TRXN table, right click and choose Add to project.

k. Choose Create a data object for each resource.

l. Name the object as "CustDB_Trxn" and choose the location as the Shared_Objects folder and click Finish.

m. Object will now appear in the Object Explorer.

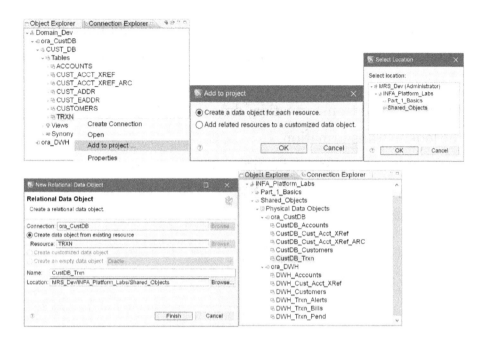

2. Create mapping, sources and targets:

   a. In the object explorer, right click the folder Part_1_Basics folder and choose New → Mapping.

   b. Name the mapping as "Lab_06_Router" and click OK.

   c. Drag the CustDB_Trxn data object into the mapping and choose Read operation and click OK.

   d. Drag the DWH_Trxn_Alerts, DWH_Trxn_Bills and DWH_Trxn_Pend data objects into the mapping and choose Write as operation and click OK.

   e. Drag the DWH_Accounts data object into the mapping and choose Lookup operation and click OK.

f. In the properties pane, Columns tab, delete all columns except ACCT_NR and ACCT_KEY and choose ACCT_KEY as Return port.

g. From the Read transformation, drag the ACCT_NR column into the lookup transformation.

h. In the lookup transformation properties, lookup tab, create a new condition and set it as ACCT_NR = ACCT_NR1.

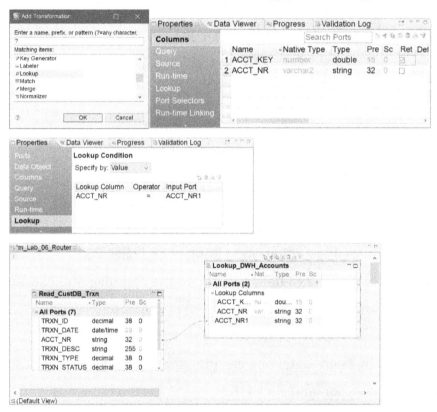

3. Add Router and route the data:

a. Add a transformation – choose Router and click OK.

b. From the Read transformation, drag the TRXN_ID and TRXN_DATE into the Router.

c. Then drag the ACCT_KEY from the lookup into the Router.

d. Then drag the following columns from Read transformation into the Router: TRXN_DESC, TRXN_TYPE, TRXN_STATUS, TRXN_AMOUNT.

e. In the Router properties, go to groups tab.

f. Create the following groups: Alert_Trxn, Bill_Pay_Trxn, Pending_Trxn

g. Set the filter conditions as:

    i. Alert_Trxn → Trxn_Amount > 500

    ii. Bill_Pay → Trxn Trxn_Type = 3

    iii. Pending_Trxn → Trxn_Status = 3

h. From the Alert_Trxn group connect all columns to the DWH_Trxn_Alerts by matching column name.

i. From the Pending_Trxn group connect all columns to the DWH_Trxn_Pend by matching column name.

j. From the Bill_Pay_Trxn group connect all columns to the DWH_Trxn_Bills by matching column name. Additionally, connect Trxn_Date to Billed_Date in the Write transformation.

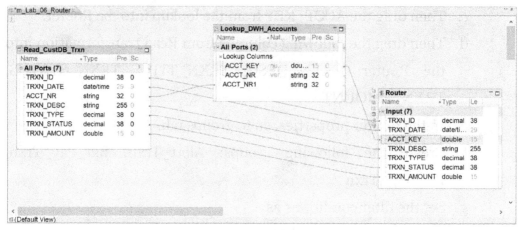

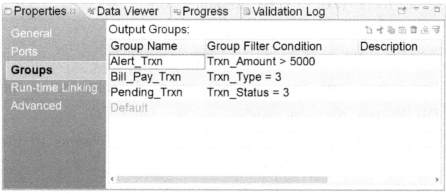

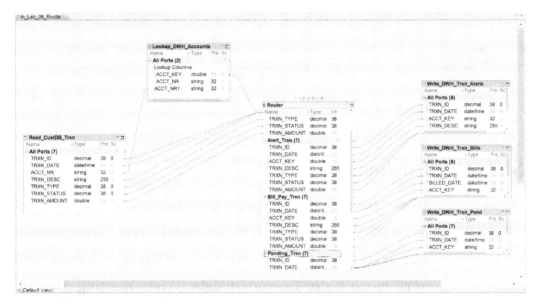

4. Validate and run the mapping:

Trxn_Alerts will have records only with Trxn Amount greater than $5000.

	TRXN_ID	TRXN_DATE	ACCT_KEY	TRXN_DESC	TRXN_TYPE	TRXN_STATUS	ALERT_REASON	TRXN_AMOUNT
1	2	19-NOV-01	5704	Nabors Industries Ltd. Executive	6	4	(null)	7558.42
2	4	14-NOV-00	4870	CNF Inc. Executive	5	1	(null)	8401.65
3	5	23-OCT-04	559	Duke Energy Research and Development	7	1	(null)	6726.15
4	7	11-JUN-03	5838	Schlumberger Ltd. Human Resources	3	1	(null)	9029.46
5	9	30-OCT-00	5316	Capital One Financial Corp. Accounting	1	4	(null)	8432.97
6	10	04-OCT-03	3883	Constellation Brands Information Technologies	5	1	(null)	7021.6
7	11	05-DEC-01	(null)	Pulte Homes, Inc. Human Resources	8	4	(null)	8801.6
8	17	16-DEC-04	3440	Deere and Co. Human Resources	3	5	(null)	9049.93

Trxn_Bills will have data only with Trxn_Type as 3.

	TRXN_ID	TRXN_DATE	BILLED_DATE	ACCT_KEY	TRXN_DESC	TRXN_TYPE	TRXN_STATUS	TRXN_AMOUNT
1	7	11-JUN-03	(null)	5838	Schlumberger Ltd. Human Resources	3	1	9029.46
2	12	13-JAN-02	(null)	373	Interpublic Group of Cos. Inc. Manufacturing	3	5	957.55
3	17	16-DEC-04	(null)	3440	Deere and Co. Human Resources	3	5	9049.93
4	20	15-OCT-01	(null)	5261	Sonic Automotive Research and Development	3	1	2616.65
5	49	29-OCT-06	(null)	(null)	Dow Jones and Co. Customer Support	3	5	755.14
6	50	29-SEP-01	(null)	(null)	Best Buy Co., Inc. Executive	3	3	8656.03
7	54	23-AUG-08	(null)	(null)	Johnson and Johnson Customer Support	3	3	5664.31
8	60	10-NOV-03	(null)	3875	Alltel Corp. Consulting	3	2	9645.64
9	72	26-MAY-11	(null)	1378	Bausch and Lomb Manufacturing	3	2	7031.6

Trxn_Pend will have data with Trxn_Status as 3.

	TRXN_ID	TRXN_DATE	ACCT_KEY	TRXN_DESC	TRXN_TYPE	TRXN_STATUS	TRXN_AMOUNT
1	23	07-NOV-01	900	Alltel Corp. Consulting	1	3	542.39
2	24	15-MAY-01	3730	International Business Machines Corp. Facilities	4	3	2698.05
3	28	14-DEC-03	(null)	Goodyear Tire and Rubber Co. Information Technologies	1	3	9317.94
4	32	29-OCT-01	(null)	Fannie Mae Accounting	10	3	6626.61
5	36	23-MAY-03	4912	Allstate Corp. Accounting	9	3	3610.06
6	42	10-APR-10	919	American Family Ins. Group Human Resources	8	3	8891.11
7	43	27-OCT-04	978	Boeing Company Customer Support	7	3	7085.23
8	44	04-SEP-11	5183	Apple Computer Inc. Sales	9	3	9663.69
9	50	29-SEP-01	(null)	Best Buy Co., Inc. Executive	3	3	8656.03

Fetched 50 rows in 0.021 seconds

Sorter transformation

Sorter is used to sort the data in stream. Sorter can be used when we need sorted output written to tables / files. It is also widely used in conjunction with joiners and aggregators to improve their efficiency. Joiners and aggregations work much faster on sorted data. When creating a sorter transformation, you will have to define the "Sort keys" the columns on which the data needs to be sorted. You also define the order of the sorting such as Ascending / Descending – for each column. To choose the Sort Keys, go to the "Sort" tab in the sorter properties and click Choose. You can then select the sort keys. You can then assign the order by double clicking the Ascending or descending text in the Sort tab. Deduplication can be performed in the Sorter transformation by choosing "Distinct rows only" option

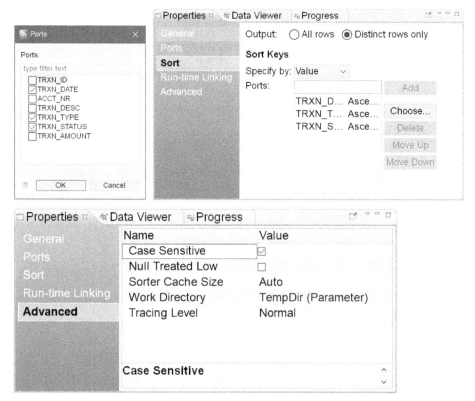

Sorter is by default case sensitive. You can turn this off in the "Advanced" tab by unchecking the "Case Sensitive" checkbox. Sorter performs the sorts in the memory by building a cache. You can customize the sort size – but by default the size is automatic as determined by the DIS. You can also additionally configure a working directory. When working with large datasets, if the entire data set cannot fit in the memory, the DIS will use the Work Directory to spill the Sort operations to disk.

Lab 7 – Sorter transformation

1. Import the target:

    a. Switch to connection explorer.

    b. Expand the Domain_Dev → ora_DWH → DWH → Tables.

   c. Right click TRXN and click Add to project.

   d. Choose Create a data object for each resource.

   e. Then name the data object as "DWH_Trxn" and choose the location as "Shared_Objects".

   f. Click Finish to complete.

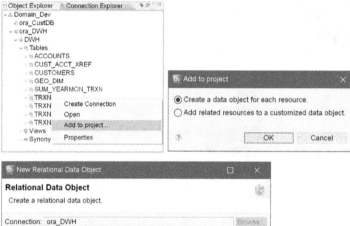

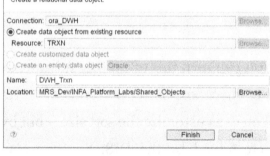

2. Create a new mapping:

   a. Right click the folder Part_1_Basics and choose New → Mapping.

   b. Drag the CustDB_Trxn into the mapping and choose Read and click OK.

   c. Right click mapping canvas, click Add Transformation and choose Sorter and click OK.

   d. Drag all columns from the source into the Sorter.

e. In the Sorter properties, go to the Sort tab.

f. Click Choose and check the TRXN_DATE and click OK.

g. Double click on "Ascending" and choose "Descending".

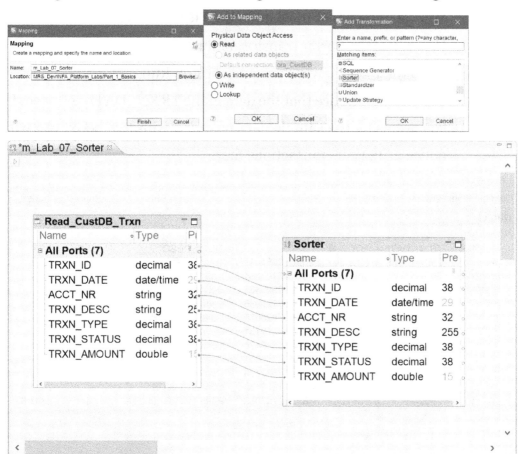

3. Verify the data:

    a. Select the Read transformation.

    b. Go to the Data Viewer pane and click on Run.

    c. You will notice that the data in the TRXN_DATE is not sorted.

    d. Now select the Sorter transformation.

    e. Go to the Data Viewer pane and click on Run.

    f. You will now notice that the data in the TRXN_DATE is sorted. If you are using the sample data provided with this book, you will notice 2013 year transactions first.

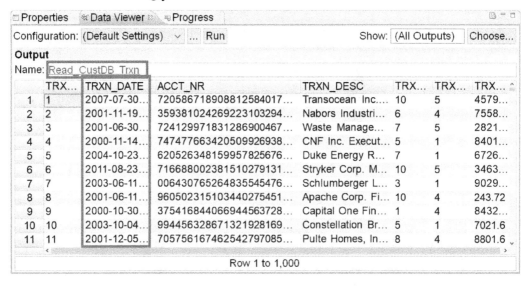

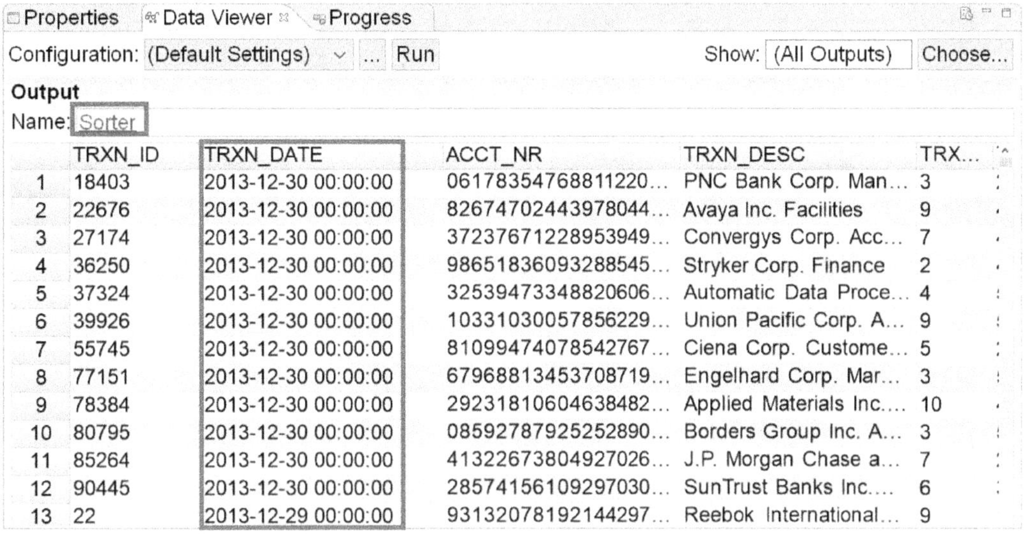

			Properties		Data Viewer ※		Progress									

Configuration: (Default Settings) ∨ ... Run   Show: (All Outputs) | Choose...

Output

Name: Sorter

	TRXN_ID	TRXN_DATE	ACCT_NR	TRXN_DESC	TRX...
1	18403	2013-12-30 00:00:00	06178354768811220...	PNC Bank Corp. Man...	3
2	22676	2013-12-30 00:00:00	82674702443978044...	Avaya Inc. Facilities	9
3	27174	2013-12-30 00:00:00	37237671228953949...	Convergys Corp. Acc...	7
4	36250	2013-12-30 00:00:00	98651836093288545...	Stryker Corp. Finance	2
5	37324	2013-12-30 00:00:00	32539473348820606...	Automatic Data Proce...	4
6	39926	2013-12-30 00:00:00	10331030057856229...	Union Pacific Corp. A...	9
7	55745	2013-12-30 00:00:00	81099474078542767...	Ciena Corp. Custome...	5
8	77151	2013-12-30 00:00:00	67968813453708719...	Engelhard Corp. Mar...	3
9	78384	2013-12-30 00:00:00	29231810604638482...	Applied Materials Inc....	10
10	80795	2013-12-30 00:00:00	08592787925252890...	Borders Group Inc. A...	3
11	85264	2013-12-30 00:00:00	41322673804927026...	J.P. Morgan Chase a...	7
12	90445	2013-12-30 00:00:00	28574156109297030...	SunTrust Banks Inc....	6
13	22	2013-12-29 00:00:00	93132078192144297...	Reebok International...	9

4. Connect the target:

    a. Drag the DWH_Trxn into the mapping.

    b. Connect all columns from Sorter into the Write transformation.

> (!) When you run a SELECT query on a database table, the data is not guaranteed to return exactly how it is stored. Hence if you run a SELECT query on the DWH_Trxn table after running the above mapping, you may not necessarily see the data sorted. This is why, you executed a data preview to confirm the data sort.

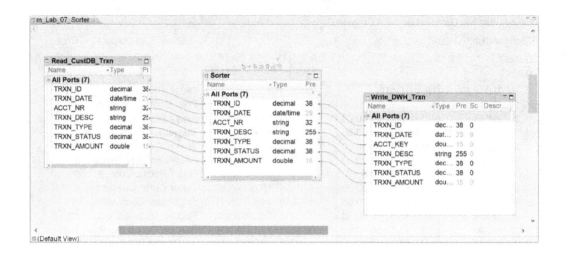

Joiner transformation

In relational databases and data warehouses, it is very common to have to

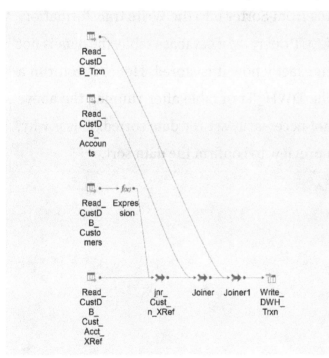

join the data from various tables. At times, it is also required to join data from various types of objects – not just various objects of the same type. When you want to join two tables from the schema/database, you can specify the join condition between these data objects in the

"Read" transformation. The joins and filters specified in the "Read" transformation are pushed down to the database level. When you want to join the data of heterogeneous data sources, you cannot specify it in the "Read" transformation because it will not be possible to push the join to the database. For example, when you want to join the data between Oracle and flat file, Oracle is not aware of metadata of flat files. So pushing down the join logic to database is not possible. This is where the Joiner transformation comes in handy. You can use Joiner transformation to join the data from any two data sources regardless of the type. You can also join the data from various pipelines. In the latter case, you are typically applying several transformations before you want to join the data from various sources. Joiner transformation can join the data only from two sources/pipelines. If you need to join more sources than that, you need to use more Joiner transformations. So, to join "n" transformations – you will need "n-1" Joiner transformations. Unlike read transformation, Joiner transformation does not get pushed down to the database. It by default, gets executed within the DIS context. In various cases, DIS does apply performance optimizations which include partial processing to be pushed to databases.

Master and detail

A Joiner transformation joins data from two streams: Master and Detail – as designated by the user. A master is typically the dataset that has a unique set of values for a given join key. Detail typically has more than one value for the same join key. For example, when joining managers and employees based on the "Manager ID" in both tables, managers table is the master table as the Manager ID is unique in it. Employees table will have repetitive and non-unique values for Manager ID and hence will be a detailed table. Master dataset is also relatively smaller in size. Hence, DIS caches the master dataset (and spills over to the disk as needed) so that it can perform in memory joins.

Types of joins

There are various kinds of joins that you can perform with Joiner transformation: Normal join, master outer join, detail outer join, and full outer join. Each type defines how the data between the master and detail datasets is joined together. In a normal join, DIS keeps the data that matches the join condition on both sides. In a master outer join, you keep all rows from the detail table and the matching rows from the master. In a detail outer join, DIS keeps all rows from the master and matching rows from the detail. In a full outer join, DIS keeps rows from both master and detail – even if they don't have corresponding matching rows. The Venn diagram below helps you understand the various types of the joins:

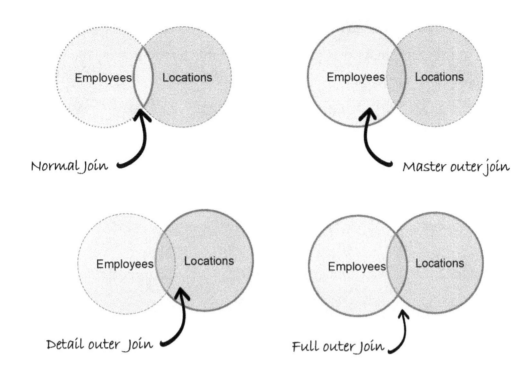

The red bordered zones represent the result set. In the 1st type of join (normal join), you are only fetching the data that is common between both the datasets/tables. In the master outer join, you are keeping all the detailed rows. i.e. all rows from employees and matching rows from the locations table. *Vice versa* happens in the detail outer join scenario. In a full outer join, you keep all data from both the tables. In relational world, these joins are also referred as Normal joins, left outer join, right outer join and full outer join. When using this terminology depending on which table you place to the left of the join clause, your definition of left outer join and right outer join will vary.

Let's take a look at the various types of join using a sample dataset as listed below. In this sample, you regard locations table as the master dataset and employees table as the detail:

Emp ID	Emp Name	Loc ID
1	John Doe	101
2	Jane Doe	101
3	John Roe	102
4	John Smith	

Loc ID	Location name	Country
101	San Francisco, CA	USA
102	New York, NY	USA
103	Bangalore, KA	India

Normal join

In a normal join, data that matches the join condition in both master and detailed dataset is retained. All other data is discarded. So, for above datasets when you join them by the location ID, you get the following result dataset:

Emp. ID	Emp. Name	Loc ID	Location name	Country
1	John Doe	101	San Francisco, CA	USA
2	Jane Doe	101	San Francisco, CA	USA
3	John Roe	102	New York, NY	USA

You will notice here that the employee ID #4 (John Smith) and the location ID #103 (Bangalore, KA) are not present in the result set because they don't have matching records in the corresponding table.

Master outer join

When the same datasets are joined together via a "master outer join", you see the following result:

Emp. ID	Emp. Name	Loc. ID	Location name	Country
1	John Doe	101	San Francisco, CA	USA
2	Jane Doe	101	San Francisco, CA	USA
3	John Roe	102	New York, NY	USA
4	John Smith			

Detail outer join

When the same datasets are joined together via a "detail outer join", you retain all rows from master table and the matching rows from the detail table. So, the end result will look like this:

Emp. ID	Emp. Name	Loc. ID	Location name	Country
1	John Doe	101	San Francisco, CA	USA
2	Jane Doe	101	San Francisco, CA	USA
3	John Roe	102	New York, NY	USA
		103	Bangalore, KA	India

Full outer join

When a full outer join is applied, data from both the tables are retrieved even if there are no corresponding matches. Hence the result set will look like:

Emp. ID	Emp. Name	Loc. ID	Location name	Country
1	John Doe	101	San Francisco, CA	USA
2	Jane Doe	101	San Francisco, CA	USA
3	John Roe	102	New York, NY	USA
4	John Smith			
		103	Bangalore, KA	India

Note that he unmatched rows are filled with NULL values where matching values are not present.

Lab 8 – Joiner transformation

Use-case

We have 3 geography tables in the data source. You are going to de-normalize this information by joining them together and load into a de-normalized geography dimension.

Challenges

a. Data from multiple tables need to be flattened out with losing any data attributes.

b. City information is mandatory but states' information is available only for United States at this time. If the state for any given city is not available, the record should still be retained.

Steps for the solution

1. Import source geography tables:

    a. In the developer, switch to connection explorer.

    b. Expand the domain (Domain_Dev) → connection (ora_CustDB) → Schema (CUST_DB) → Tables.

    c. Select the GEO_CITIES, GEO_STATES, GEO_COUNTRIES. You can use SHIFT key to select multiple values.

    d. Right click the tables and choose Add to project...

    e. Choose "Create a data object for each resource" and click OK.

    f. In the "Select Connection" dialog box, choose MRS (MRS_Dev) → Project (INFA_Platform_Labs) → Folder (Shared_Objects) and click OK.

    g. Data objects will be imported. You can see them in the object explorer.

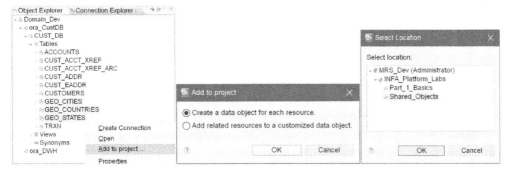

```
Object Explorer    Connection Explorer
MRS_Dev (Administrator)
  INFA_Platform_Labs
    Part_1_Basics
    Shared_Objects
      Physical Data Objects
        ora_CustDB
          CustDB_Accounts
          CustDB_Cust_Acct_XRef
          CustDB_Cust_Acct_XRef_ARC
          CustDB_Customers
          CustDB_Trxn
          GEO_CITIES
          GEO_COUNTRIES
          GEO_STATES
        ora_DWH
```

2. Import target geography dimension:

   a. In the developer, switch to the connection explorer.

   b. Expand the domain (Domain_Dev) → connection (ora_DWH) → Schema (DWH) → Tables. Select the GEO_DIM.

   c. Right click the table and choose Add to project...

   d. Choose "Create a data object for each resource..." and click OK.

   e. In the "New Relational Data Object" dialog box, name the object as "DWH_GEO_DIM".

   f. In the location, click Browse...

   g. Choose MRS (MRS_Dev) → Project (INFA_Platform_Labs) → Folder (Shared_Objects) and click OK.

   h. In the New Relational Data Object dialog box, click Finish.

   i. Data object is now imported. You can see them in the object explorer.

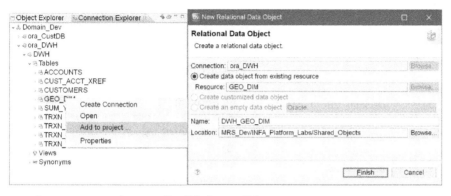

3. Create mapping and add data objects:

    a. Right click the folder Part_1_Basics and choose New → Mapping.

    b. Name the mapping as "Lab_08_Joiners" and click OK.

    c. Drag the GEO_CITIES, GEO_STATES, GEO_COUNTRIES objects from the object explorer into the mapping and choose "Read" → as Independent data object(s) and click OK.

    d. Data objects are added to the mapping canvas.

    e. From the object explorer, choose DWH_GEO_DIM data object in the object explorer and drag it into the mapping canvas.

    f. Choose "Write" and click OK.

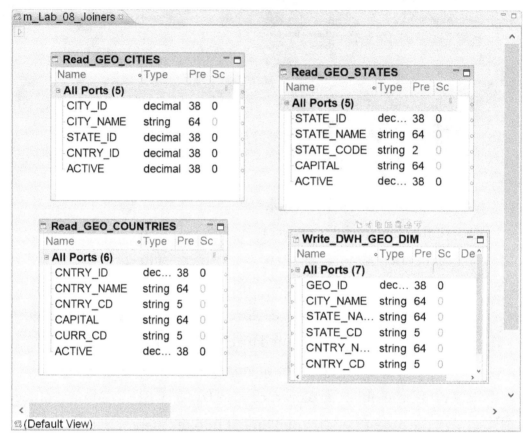

4. Add Joiners and complete the mapping:

   a. Press <CTRL> + <SHIFT> + T to add transformation.

   b. Choose Joiner transformation and click OK.

   c. Double click the title and rename it as jnr_City_n_Countries.

   d. Drag all columns from "Read_GEO_CITIES" to the detail group of the Joiner.

   e. Drag all columns from "Read_GEO_COUNTRIES" to the master group of the Joiner.

   f. In the Joiner properties → Join sub tab → add a new condition and set it as "CNTRY_ID1 = CNTRY_ID".

g. Set the join type as "Normal".

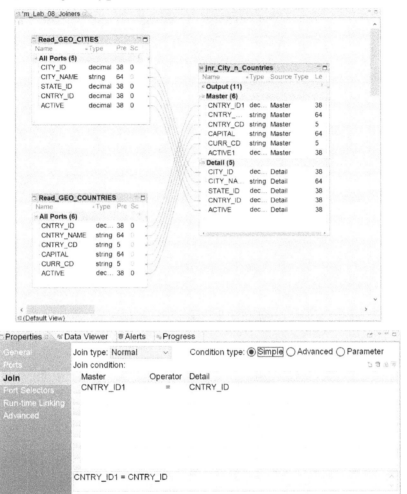

h. Add another Joiner transformation into the mapping canvas and name it as "jnr_CityCountry_n_States".

i. From the Joiner "jnr_City_n_Countries" drag all output group columns (11) into "jnr_CityCountry_n_States" detail group.

j. From the "Read_GEO_STATES" data object drag all columns into the "jnr_CityCountry_n_States" master group.

k. In the Joiner properties set the join condition as "STATE_ID = STATE_ID1". Set the join type as "Master outer" join.

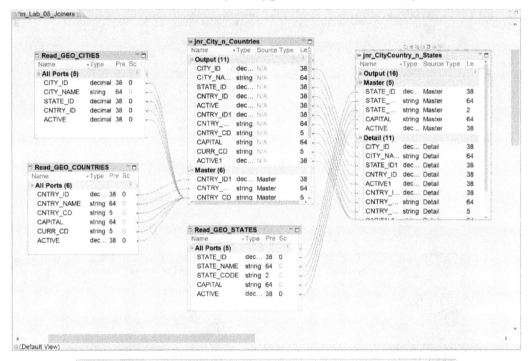

l. Connect the columns from the Joiner "jnr_CityStates_n_Countries" to the "Write_DWH_GEO_DIM" as below:

Jnr_CityCountry_n_States	Write_DWH_GEO_DIM
CITY_ID	GEO_ID
CITY_NAME	CITY_NAME
STATE_NAME	STATE_NAME
STATE_CODE	STATE_CD
CNTRY_NAME	CNTRY_NAME
CNTRY_CD	CNTRY_CD
CURR_CD	CURR_CD

m. Select the Write_DWH_GEO_DIM data object.

n. In the properties tab → advanced sub tab → check the "Truncate target table" checkbox.

o. Validate the mapping and save it.

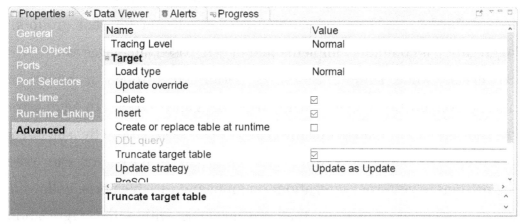

5. Run the mapping and validate the data:

    a. Right click the mapping and choose "Run Mapping".

    b. Open the data object DWH_GEO_DIM and run the Data Viewer.

    c. You will notice 1232 records with NULL values for the state attributes. For non US records you will notice that the State code will be empty (NULL), but the record still flows through the mapping due to the master outer join between cities and states.

Properties	Data Viewer	Alerts	Progress	Validation Log			

Configuration: All_Rows   ...   Run   Show: (All Outputs)   Choose...

Output

Name: DWH_GEO_DIM

	GEO_ID	CITY_NAME	STATE_NAME	STATE_CD	CNTRY_NAME	CNTRY_CD	CURR_CD
1	319	Coral Springs	Florida	FL	United States	USA	USD
2	320	Corby	<null>	<null>	United Kingdom	GBR	GBP
3	321	Corona	California	CA	United States	USA	USD
4	322	Corona del Mar	California	CA	United States	USA	USD
5	323	Coronado Island	California	CA	United States	USA	USD
6	324	Corpus Christi	Texas	TX	United States	USA	USD
7	325	Costa Mesa	California	CA	United States	USA	USD
8	326	Coventry	<null>	<null>	United Kingdom	GBR	GBP

Row 1 to 1,232

Aggregator transformation

Aggregator transformation is used to group the data in the pipeline by a user-defined group key and summarize information for that group(s). Aggregation is commonly implemented in SQL based languages as GROUP BY clause while summarization is performed through a bunch of aggregation functions such as SUM, MIN, MAX and COUNT. In Aggregator transformation, you can define the group by ports via "Group By" sub tab of the properties pane. Once you select the group by ports, you can write expressions to perform aggregations on input and variable ports. Following are the aggregate functions that are available within the aggregation transformation:

a. AVG

b. COUNT

c. FIRST

d. LAST

e. MAX

f. MEDIAN

g. MIN

h. PERCENTILE

i. STDDEV

j. SUM

k. VARIANCE

An expression returns the results row by row, whereas the aggregator performs calculations on groups of data. You can use single-level or multi-level aggregate functions, but you cannot include both in the same transformation. Several aggregate functions such as SUM can be used with conditional clauses. Computation of the expression occurs only for the rows that evaluate for the clause as true. For example, SUM(Trxn, Trxn >0) can be used to calculate the sum separately for debit and credit transactions. You can have more than one group by port in an aggregator. When more than one group by port is defined, the order in which they appear. The port order can affect the aggregator results

Lab 9 – Aggregator transformation

Use-case

The transactions table contains transactions of various timelines. You want to summarize the transactions by year and month and load them to a data warehouse table.

Challenges

a. Data must be aggregated at two levels: years and month

b. An additional row must be inserted that represents the whole year

c. Process only cleared transactions

Steps for solution

1. Import the data objects:

    a. Switch to the connection explorer.

    b. Choose Domain (Domain_Dev) → connection (ora_DWH) → Schema (DWH) → Tables → SUM_YEARMON_TRXN.

    c. Right click the table and choose Add to project.

    d. Choose "Create a data object for each resource" and click OK.

    e. Prefix the data object with "DWH_" and choose location as "Shared_Objects" and click Finish.

    f. Data object is imported into the MRS.

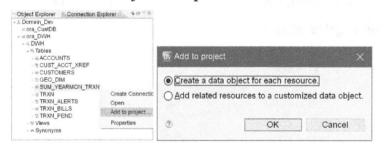

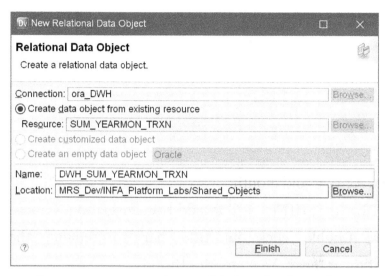

2. Create a new mapping and bring the data objects in:

   a. Right click the folder "Part_1_Basics" and choose New → Mapping.

   b. Name the mapping as "m_Lab_09_Aggregators" and click Finish.

   c. Drag the CustDB_Trxn object from the MRS (MRS_Dev) → Project (INFA_Platform_Labs) → Folder (Shared_Objects) → Physical Data Objects → Connection (ora_CustDB) → CustDB_Trxn into the mapping canvas and choose Read and click OK.

   d. Similarly, drag the DWH_SUM_YEARMON_TRXN table into the mapping canvas and choose "Write" and click OK.

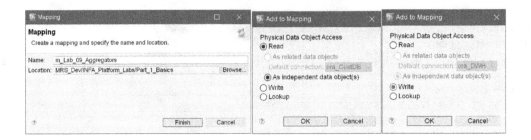

3. Aggregate the data for year and month:

   a. Press <CTRL> + <SHIFT> + T to add transformation. Choose Aggregator. Double click its title bar to rename the transformation as "aggr_Year_n_Month".

   b. Drag the TRXN_DATE, TRXN_TYPE, TRXN_AMOUNT ports from the read data object into the Aggregator.

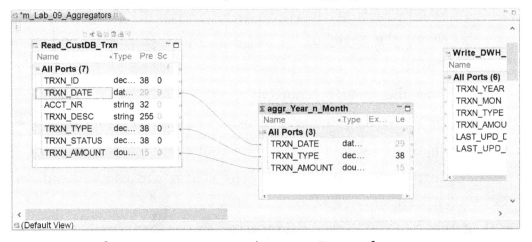

   c. In the Aggregator properties, go to Ports tab.

   d. Click on the New Port icon and add the 2 variable ports and 1 output ports.

Port name	Type	Data type	Expression

v_Year	Variable	Integer	To_Integer(To_Char(TRXN_DATE, 'YYYY'))
v_Month	Variable	Integer	To_Integer(To_Char(TRXN_DATE, 'MM'))
Year	Output	Integer	v_Year
Month	Output	Integer	v_Month
SUM_TRXN		double	SUM(TRXN_AMOUNT)

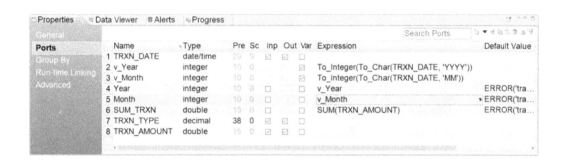

e. In the Aggregator properties, Group by sub tab → click Choose.

f. Check v_Year and v_Month and click OK.

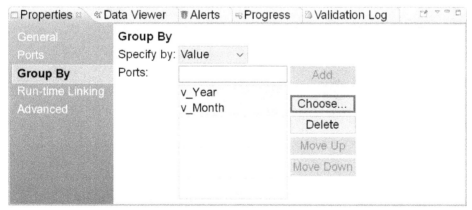

4. Aggregate the data for year only:

a. Press <CTRL> + <SHIFT> + T to add transformation. Choose Aggregator. Double click its title bar to rename the transformation as "aggr_Year".

b. Drag the TRXN_DATE, TRXN_TYPE, TRXN_AMOUNT ports from the read data object into the Aggregator.

c. Click on the New Port icon and add the 1 variable port and 1 output ports.

Port name	Type	Data type	Expression
v_Year	Variable	Integer	To_Integer(To_Char(TRXN_DATE, 'YYYY'))
Year	Output	Integer	v_Year
Month	Output	Integer	0
SUM_TRXN	Output	double	SUM(TRXN_AMOUNT)

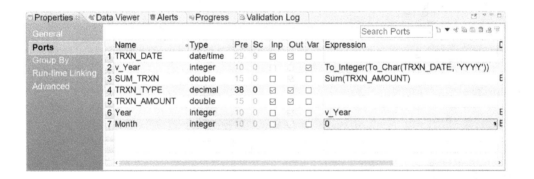

d. In the Aggregator properties, Group by sub tab → click Choose.

e. Check v_Year and click OK.

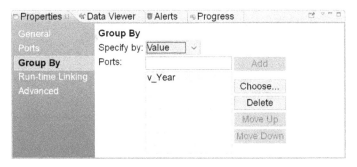

5. Union the data from two levels of aggregations:

    a. Create a union transformation <CTRL> + <SHIFT> + T.

    b. In the groups tab, create two groups: Year, Year_n_Month.

    c. From aggr_Year drag Year, Month, TRXN_TYPE, SUM_TRXN into the year group.

    d. From the aggr_Year_n_Month connect the Year, Month, TRXN_TYPE, SUM_TRXN.

    e. From the union transformation output group connect the following ports to write transformation as follows:

Union output group	Write transformation
Year	Trxn_Year
Month	Trxn_Mon
Trxn_Type	Trxn_Type
SUM_TRXN	Trxn_Amount

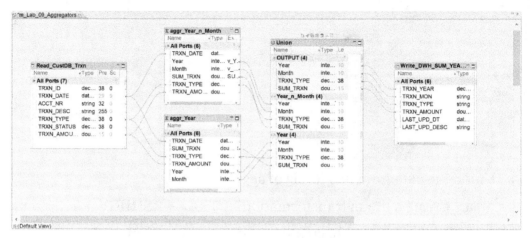

6. Validate, save and run the mapping. The results show 1 record per every year and month and one additional record with month as Zero (0).

□ Properties ◊ Data Viewer ☒ ☱ Alerts ꞊ Progress ◷ Validation Log

Configuration: (Default Settings) ∨ ... Run   Show: (All Outputs) Choose...

Output

Name: DWH_SUM_YEARMON_TRXN

	TRXN_YEAR	TRXN_MON	TRXN_TYPE	TRXN_AMOUNT	LAST^
1	2000	0	6	35734455.56	<nul
2	2000	1	3	3025883.73	<nul
3	2000	2	7	2992692.83	<nul
4	2000	3	4	3123578.05	<nul
5	2000	4	1	3092467.67	<nul
6	2000	5	9	2896843.83	<nul
7	2000	6	4	3058520.94	<nul
8	2000	7	4	2819614.9	<nul
9	2000	8	3	3122552.57	<nul
10	2000	9	7	2975704.93	<nul
11	2000	10	6	3020938.2	<nul
12	2000	11	7	2902107.38	<nul
13	2000	12	6	2703550.5300000003	<nul
14	2001	0	3	34748255.3199999	<nul

Row 1 to 182

Rank transformation

Rank transformation is used to select top or bottom 'n' records such as top 5 customers by transaction amount, top 10 employees by salary, etc. Rank transformation is usually applied with a sort. Rank transformation's performance can be greatly improved by providing sorted input. A Sorter can be added just before the Rank transformation to sort the data on the rank columns. Rank can then be configured with "Sorted Input" checkbox to expect its input data pre-sorted. Let's take a look at the Rank transformation practically:

Lab 10 – Rank transformation

1. Create a new mapping and name it "m_Lab_10_Rank" and click OK.
2. Drag the CustDB_Trxn data object into the mapping canvas and choose "Read" and click OK.
3. Press <CTRL> + <SHIFT> + T to add a transformation and choose "Rank" and click OK.
4. Drag all ports from the read object into rank transformation.

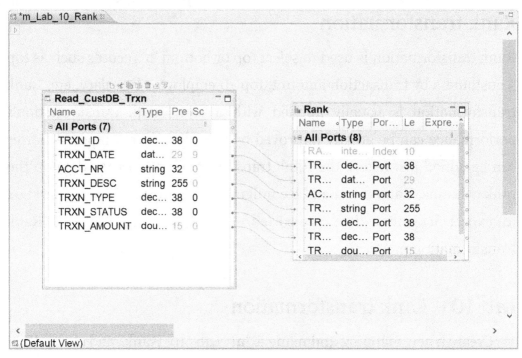

5. Go to the Rank properties tab, go to Rank sub tab.

6. In the group by section, click choose. Check ACCT_NR and click OK.

7. In the Rank section, click "Browse..." and choose TRXN_AMOUNT and click OK.

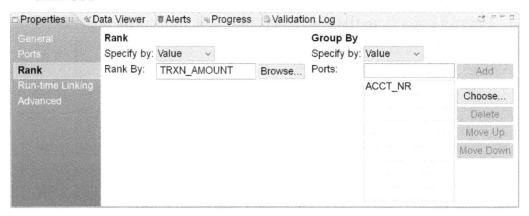

8. In the advanced tab, set Number of Ranks to 5.

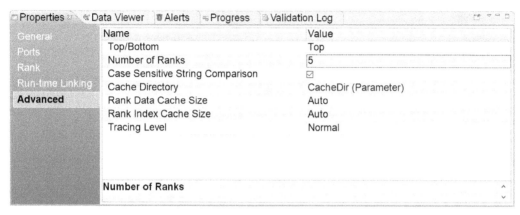

9. Drag the DWH_Trxn in to the mapping canvas and choose "Write".

10. Connect all columns from rank to the Write_DWH_Trxn.

11. Right click the Rank transformation and run Data preview.

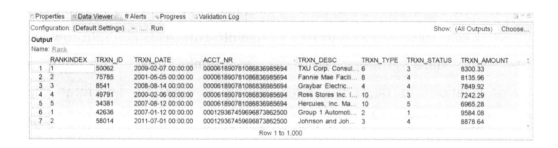

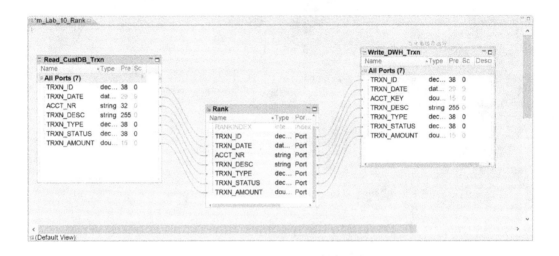

Update Strategy transformation

Update Strategy transformation is used to mark the rows in a pipelines as insert, update, delete or as rejected. By default, DIS treats all input rows as Inserts. Update Strategy is most commonly used with lookup transformation. In these use-cases, lookup is used to determine the presence of the record in the target database, and Update Strategy is then used to mark the records as insert / update / delete accordingly. You can mark a record reject if you do not want it to be loaded to target database. Reject records are logged into a reject file. You can use the reserved words DD_INSERT, DD_UPDATE, DD_DELETE and DD_REJECT to mark a row as Insert, Update, Delete or Reject respectively. It is important not to use active transformation after an update strategy as it changes the transaction boundaries. In other words, you should use Update Strategy transformation as close to the target as possible. Let us consider an example to understand this more. Imagine you have used the update strategy condition as follows

```
IIF(isNull(lkpCust_ID), DD_Insert, DD_Update)
```

In this example, Update strategy is preceded by a lookup that is querying the target table. If the target table has a Customer ID, it is returned via lkpCust_ID. NULL value indicates the row is present in the input stream but there is no row with that customer ID in the target table and hence it should be marked as an insert (DD_Insert). If the row already exists in the target, lookup is returning the row's primary key via lkpCust_ID. So, the presence of the value means we have to update the row in the target. So, we set the row marker to update (DD_Update). Now, if your update strategies are followed by the target / write transformation, the DIS looks at the corresponding row indicators and issues the relevant query to the database i.e. either INSERT or UPDATE.

If an active transformation such as aggregator is used in between the update strategy and target, the aggregator groups several rows into one. Since some of these rows may be marked as insert and some as update, DIS will reset the row markers and default them all to Insert. So, the Update Strategy is practically rendered useless.

 All rows by default are treated as Inserts by the DIS unless marked otherwise by the Update Strategy

Lab 11 – Using Update Strategy to update rows

Use-case

The customers table in the CustDB schema receives incremental updates at regular intervals. We need to be able to process them and load the incremental data into the Customers table in the DWH.

Technical challenges

- Determine if a row is already present in the target schema and dynamically determine whether the row is to be inserted or updated
- When updating the rows in the DWH schema, preserve the old values for first name and last name columns

Steps for solution

Create the mapping with Source

- Create a new mapping and name it "m_Lab_11_Update_Strategy" and click Finish. From the "Shared_Objects" folder, drag the "CustDB_Customers" object into the mapping canvas. Choose Read → as Independent Object(s) and click OK. Read transformation is added to the mapping

Configure the lookup to check the row presence in the target

- Now drag the "DWH_Customers" object into the workspace and choose Lookup operation and click OK.
- Drag the CUST_ID port from the Read_CustDB_Customers into the Lookup_DWH_Customers and rename it (by double clicking on the port name) as in_Cust_ID. Change the data type to double
- In the lookup properties, set the lookup condition as

```
CUST_ID = in_CUST_ID
```

 Data types of the ports on either side of the lookup condition should be exactly matched. In our example, the data type of the CUST_ID in the CustDB schema and the DWH schema are different. Hence we changed the input port's data type to a compatible data type so that the lookup condition will validate

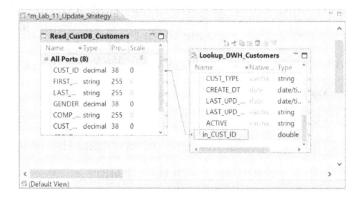

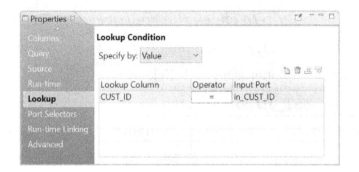

Use an expression to determine Insert / Update

- Create an expression transformation and drag the CUST_KEY, FIRST_NAME and LAST_NAME fields from lookup transformation into the expression. Then rename them to add a prefix of "lkp_". These ports will now be lkp_CUST_KEY, lkp_FIRST_NAME, lkp_LAST_NAME

- Create an expression transformation and drag the CUST_KEY, FIRST_NAME and LAST_NAME fields from lookup transformation into the expression. Then rename them to add a prefix of "lkp_". These ports will now be lkp_CUST_KEY, lkp_FIRST_NAME, lkp_LAST_NAME

 Lookup ports doesn't have to be renamed to be used. However, adding the lkp_ prefix helps us differentiate the input ports from the lookup ports further down the stream

- Now drag all the input ports from the read transformation into the expression.

- In the expression Properties pane → Ports tab, create a new output port named "Action_Flag" with data type as String(1) and set its expression as

$$IIF(isNull(lkp\_CUST\_KEY, `I', `U')$$

- With this expression, if the customer key in the lookup transformation returns a NULL value, we are marking each record as "I" for inserts. Otherwise, we are marking the records as "U" for updates. Note that simply creating an 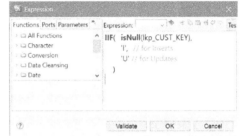 expression to mark the records as such do not affect the actual rows. We need to use Update Strategy transformation for that. But we are using this flag so that we can redirect inserts into a separate branch in the mapping pipeline.

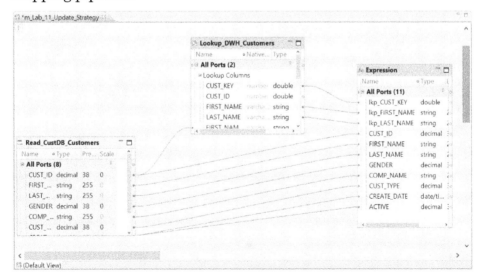

Create a router to separate insert pipeline from updates

- Create a Router transformation in the mapping now. Drag all the ports from the expression into the router's input group and create two output groups: Inserts and Updates.

- Set the Inserts group condition as:

$$Action\_Flag = `I'$$

- Set the Updates group condition as:

$$Action\_Flag = `U'$$

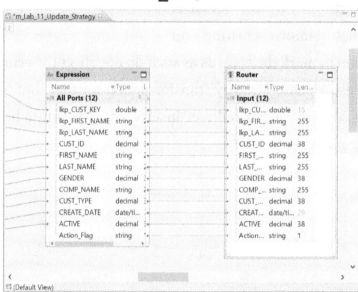

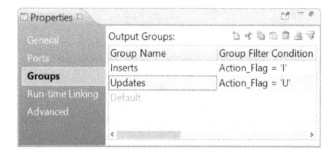

Complete the insert pipeline

- Create a sequence generator transformation with its name as **"seqGen_Cust_Key"** and **Start** value as **10001**. Drag the lkp_CUST_KEY from the Inserts output group of the router into the sequence generator

 In the sample data I used in these labs, I have 10,000 input rows. These are already loaded into the DWH. Depending on the sample data you are using update the sequence generator initial value such that you do not get primary key rejections when running the mapping

- Now drag the DWH Customers into the mapping and choose Write operation. Once the write transformation is added to the mapping rename the transformation (by double clicking on the transformation title) as "Insert_DWH_Customers"

 Changing the write operation name doesn't change the target table it writes to. Table name is a property that can be customized in the write transformation

- Connect sequence generator's nextval to the CUST_KEY in the Insert_DWH_Customers. Connect CUST_ID, FIRST_NAME, LAST_NAME form the routers "Insert" group to the Insert_DWH_Customers as shown here

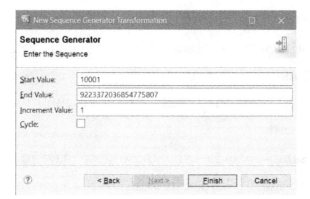

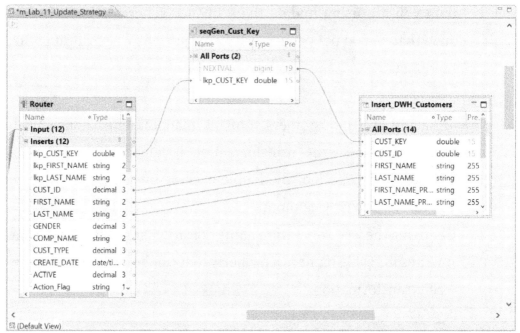

Complete the update pipeline

- Create an update strategy transformation drag all the ports in the "Updates" group of the router into it
- Set the update strategy expression as

```
IIF(
    lkp_FIRST_NAME = FIRST_NAME AND
    lkp_LAST_NAME = LAST_NAME,
    DD_Reject,
    DD_Update
    )
```

- We are comparing the input first name and last name values (from CustDB customers) with the lookup values (which is on our target – DWH Customers) to see if the values are the same. If they are, we reject the record (not load it to the target). If any one of them is different, we mark the record as update to the target

- Drag the DWH_Customers table again into the mapping and choose "Write" operation. Rename the operation as "Update_DWH_Customers"

- Connect the columns as follows

UPDATE_STRATEGY	UPDATE_DWH_CUSTOMERS
lkp_Cust_KEY	CUST_KEY
CUST_ID	CUST_ID
FIRST_NAME	FIRST_NAME
LAST_NAME	LAST_NAME
lkp_FIRST_NAME	FIRST_NAME_PREV
lkp_LAST_NAME	LAST_NAME_PREV

- By using this mapping, we are loading the value already in the target (which we brought in via lookup) into the _PREV columns and loading the new values we received in the input into the first and last name fields. We are also retaining the same CUST_KEY (which is needed for the updates work properly)

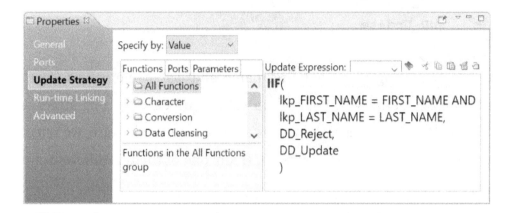

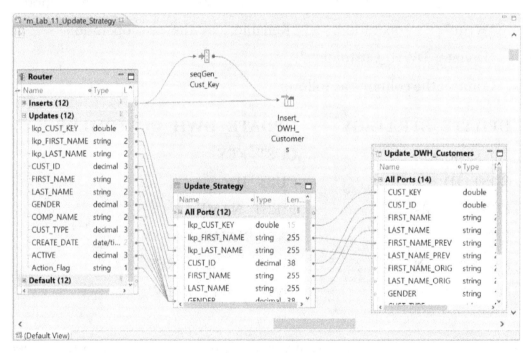

Validate and test the mapping

Your complete mapping will now look like this:

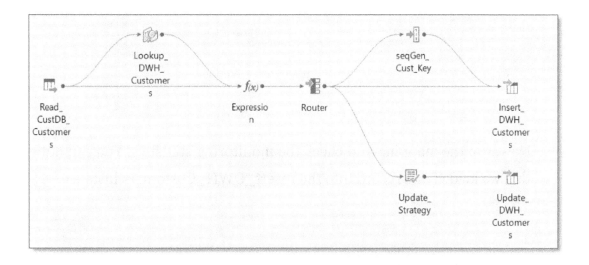

To check the results of the mapping, insert a row in the source (CustDB) customers table. For example,

```
Insert into Customers(Cust_ID, First_Name, Last_Name)
Values ((Select Max(Cust_ID) + 1 from Customers), 'New',
'Record');
Commit;
```

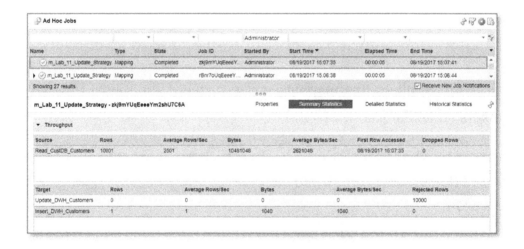

```
AWS - Mahathi - Cust DB

Worksheet    Query Builder

Insert into Customers(Cust_ID, First_Name, Last_Name)
Values (
    (Select Max(Cust_ID) + 1 from Customers),
    'New',
    'Record'
    );
Commit;
```

Now, run the mapping and check the monitoring statistics. You can notice that we loaded one record into the Insert_DWH_Customers instance.

Name	Type	State	Job ID	Started By	Start Time ▼		Elapsed Time	End Time	
m_Lab_11_Update_Strategy	Mapping	Completed	zkj9mYUqEeeeY...	Administrator	08/19/2017 15:07:35		00:00:05	08/19/2017 15:07:41	
m_Lab_11_Update_Strategy	Mapping	Completed	rBnr7oUqEeeeY...	Administrator	08/19/2017 15:06:38		00:00:05	08/19/2017 15:06:44	

Showing 27 results   ☑ Receive New Job Notifications

m_Lab_11_Update_Strategy - zkj9mYUqEeeeYm2shU7C6A   Properties   Summary Statistics   Detailed Statistics   Historical Statistics

▼ Throughput

Source	Rows	Average Rows/Sec	Bytes	Average Bytes/Sec	First Row Accessed	Dropped Rows
Read_CustDB_Customers	10001	2501	10481048	2621046	08/19/2017 15:07:35	0

Target	Rows	Average Rows/Sec	Bytes	Average Bytes/Sec	Rejected Rows
Update_DWH_Customers	0	0	0	0	10000
Insert_DWH_Customers	1	1	1040	1040	0

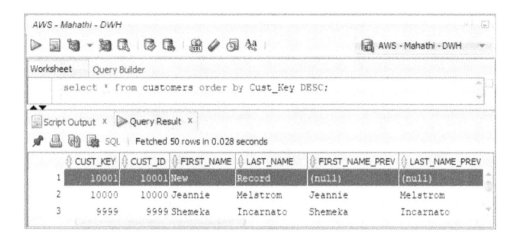

Notice that the _PREV values are NULL because we did not connect them in our mapping

Now, let us update one row in the input CustDB Customers table. For example,

```
Update Customers Set First_Name = 'Updated' where
First_Name = 'New';
Commit;
```

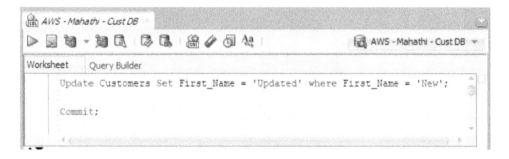

Rerun the mapping and you will notice the statistics as follows

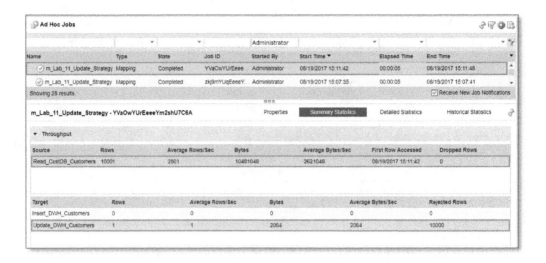

You will notice that we are reading 10,001 rows, but are updating one row. Notice the 10,000 rows that we marked as rejects because the first name and last name of the input data is exactly same as that in the target

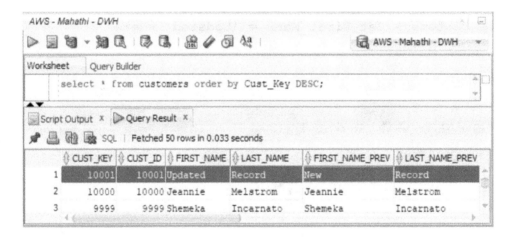

Notice that the previously first and last names are now present in the _PREV columns

Chapter 12– Flat file processing

Introduction

Flat files are directly stored on the operating system's file system. There are two types of flat files that are widely used for data storage and exchange:

a. Delimited Files

b. Fixed width files

In both the file formats, each row is represented by a line. Each line is separated by a line separator (CRLF – Carriage Return Line Feed on Windows and Line Feed on UNIX platforms). These line separators are invisible characters and can be added into a file by pressing the enter key (↵).

Delimited files

In delimited files, each row is divided into columns with a column separator in between. Most commonly used separators are comma (CSV file), tab (TSV file), and pipe.

A sample CSV (Comma Separated Values) file is as shown below:

```
CUST_ID, CITY, ZIP
1,Whitehall,18052
2,Redwood City,94065
```

Fixed width files

Fixed width files do not use a delimiter but instead use fixed positions to represent the start of each column. Data within the column is usually left aligned, but can also be right aligned in some cases. A sample fixed width file is as shown below with margins:

```
1             10            20            25     30
|---------|----------|----------|-----|
CUST_IDCITY                     ZIP
1Whitehall              18052
2Redwood City94065
```

Informatica Platform supports both the file formats. In terms of development, operating with flat files is very similar to operating with the databases. You follow the same steps as with the databases:

   a. Import the flat file structure

   b. Develop a mapping

   c. Run the mapping

Some notable differences when operating with flat files as compared to operating with databases are:

a. A relational connection is not needed since no database engine is required. However, the file name and its location must be specified. The location specified must be relative to the DIS.

b. Relational tables have truncate target table option, which allows you to empty the table before load. Files similarly have overwrite and append modes. In overwrite mode, the whole file is replaced with every session run. In append mode, the data is appended to the existing contents of the file.

c. Relational tables accept insert, update and delete operations. Files do not support these. Hence to perform these operations, you should read the file as an input, compare the changes and write the resultant to a new file.

d. Data integrity can be maintained in the tables with the help of referential integrity. With such files, integrity has to be explicitly maintained. DIS will not perform any integrity checks when reading from / writing to files.

Importing flat file definitions

Importing delimited flat files

Create a new data object by going to File menu and New menu. Choose

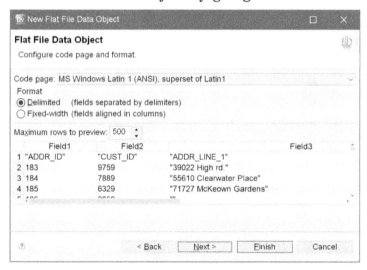

Physical Data Objects → Flat file data object and click Next. In the Flat File Data object properties, choose "Create from existing flat file". Click Browse next to it to browse and select a sample file. This sample file will be used to define the metadata /structure of the file. Define a name to this object and click Next. You will then define the structure of the file in the subsequent screens. You begin with defining the general properties such as whether the file is delimited or fixed-width. You will also define whether the string/text columns are enclosed in single/double quotes. In the next screen, you get to column level metadata. This is where you define data types of individual columns, their precision, and scale. For example, you can define the numeric columns and string columns in these screens. In this screen, you can also preview the sample rows in the same screen.

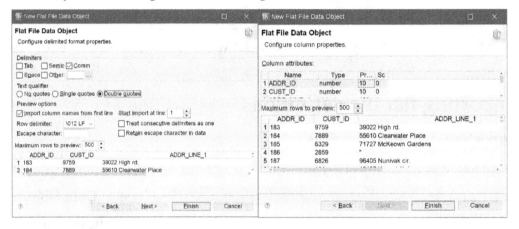

Importing fixed-width flat files

Create a new data object by going to File menu and New menu. Choose Physical Data Objects →

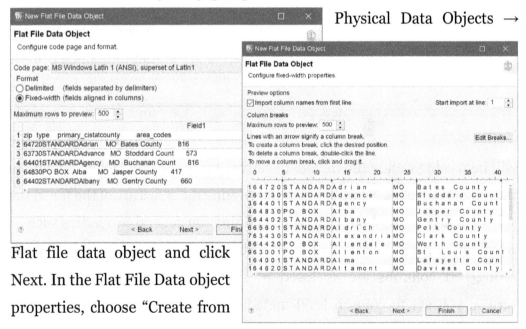

Flat file data object and click Next. In the Flat File Data object properties, choose "Create from

existing flat file". In the format, choose "Fixed-width". You will notice that the entire row data is displayed as a single column. In the next screen, you can choose whether the first row contains column names. Since you have chosen the fixed-width file format, you need to define where a column begins and ends. You do so by clicking in the data – between characters. Wherever you click, a line is displayed indicating separation of columns. You will notice that there is a ruler on the top indicating the character position. For example, in the picture below, you can notice that you have created breaks at 5, 13, 23, 41 columns. So, column 1 is defined as starting at 0 and is 5 characters long. Column 2 is defined as starting at character 6 and is 7 characters long and so on. Then you can preview the data in the final screen. Once Finish button is clicked, the data object is opened in the workspace. You can preview the data object here.

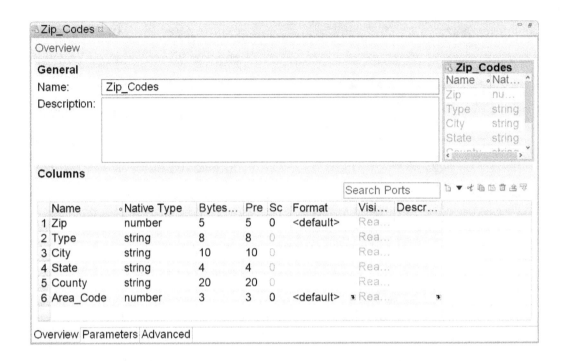

Advanced file handling

When you open a flat file data object, you can configure several additional properties. You can configure the flat file data object properties in the advanced tab. In this tab, you can configure delimited file properties, fixed-width properties, properties associated with reading flat files, and properties associated with writing flat files. In the format section (properties that apply

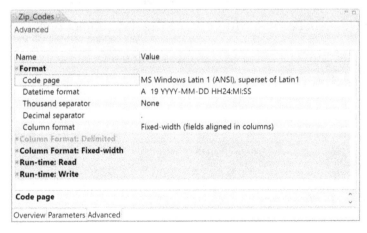

to both delimited and fixed width), you can configure the code page. Default code page is MS Windows Latin 1 (ANSI), superset of Latin 1. Date format is set to 19-byte format (YYYY-MM-DD HH24:MI:SS). There are other formats available to choose from and you can define your own custom format as well. In the same screen you can also define thousand separator operator and decimal separator operator. For example, in US decimal separator is "." whereas in some European countries, it is ",". You can also change the file type from delimited to fixed width or *vice-versa* here.

Delimited file properties

In addition to specifying the delimiter, you can configure several properties in this section. You can configure the text qualifier. Typically text qualifier is set to single quote or double quote. When flat files have delimiter as part of the string / values, a text qualifier is set and all text values are enclosed in these text qualifiers. This allows Informatica to recognize the beginning and ending of a string value and also to treat all characters inside the text qualifier, including the delimiter, as part of the text. Let's see the example file content below:

```
CUST_ID, ADDRESS, ZIP
1,Whitehall, PA,18052
2,Redwood City, CA,94065
```

In this example, the file has Customer ID, Address (including city and state) and the Zip field. The Address field contains names of city and state separated by a comma. But in the address field the comma is to be treated as data instead of column delimiter. There are two ways to solve this: a) using text qualifier b) using escape character. When text qualifier (such as double quote) is used, the content of the file will now look like this. Note that text qualifiers are applied only for string / text fields and not for other fields.

```
CUST_ID, ADDRESS, ZIP
1,"Whitehall, PA",18052
2,"Redwood City, CA",94065
```

Now by defining the text qualifier as double quote, DIS will be able to read the entire text Whitehall, PA (including the comma) as the text of the field. Another way to resolve this is by using an escape character. You can define an escape character such as \ to escape the delimiter. See example below:

```
CUST_ID, ADDRESS, ZIP
1,Whitehall\, PA,18052
2,Redwood City\, CA,94065
```

In this example, by defining the escape character as \, you are indicating to the DIS that whenever it sees the character \, it is to treat the next character (,) as part of data instead of as delimiter.

Fixed width file properties

When reading from / writing to fixed width files, the start positions of each column are assumed to be static. Columns are padded with spaces to ensure the start and end positions align. When a column data is NULL, you can choose to repeat the NULL characters to fill the length of the column. When the "Repeat NULL character" is checked, DIS treats all the NULL characters in the column as one.

Depending on whether the file is processed in Windows or Linux, the number of characters taken to represent the end of the line is different. In Windows, a Carriage Return + Line Feed is used to represent the end of the line. In Unix and Linux platforms, just a line feed is used to represent the end of the line. Hence you can configure this as needed in the "Number of bytes to skip between records". Default value is 2.

When working with fixed width data, DIS always goes with the positions and length of the columns. Hence all rows are expected to be of same length. However, sometimes some rows can be shorter. Look at this example below:

```
1          10          20          25   30          40          50
|---------|-----------|----------|-----|----------|-----------|
CUST_ID    ADDRESS                 CITY      ZIP
1833 Mickley Rd, Apt 1 Whitehall        18052
2900 Blair Ave,
Apt QRedwood City94065
3           700 Evelyn Rd, Unit 1 San Diego       22434
```

In the above example, new line character (Carriage return and/or line feed) is present in the second row's data. By default, with line sequential unchecked, DIS treats the newline character as part of the data. So, it will continue to read the Apt Q as part of the address field until the size of the field is reached. In the example above Address field is defined as 15 characters. Hence it will read the address for 15 bytes whether or not it has a newline character. If the line sequential checks, DIS will honor the new line character and will treat all subsequent columns as having NULL value. It will then continue to read the next line. So with the example above, "Apt Q Red" will become part of the CUST_ID of Row 3 and "wood City 94065" will become part of the ADDRESS field of Row 3 and CITY and ZIP fields will be NULL. The next line will continue to be read properly as the data is aligned properly.

So, for the input data shown above, output data will be as follows:

Line sequential is unchecked (default)

CUST_ID	ADDRESS	CITY	ZIP
1	833 Mickley Rd, Apt 1	Whitehall	18052
2	900 Blair Ave.↵ Apt Q	Redwood city	94065
3	700 Evelyn Rd Unit 1	San Diego	22434

 Note that the newline character shown here is only for visualization purposes and it will not be visible (though present) in the real data.

Line sequential is checked

CUST_ID	ADDRESS	CITY	ZIP
1	833 Mickley Rd, Apt 1	Whitehall	18052
2	900 Blair Ave	{NULL}	{NULL}
Apt Q Red	wood City 94065	{NULL}	{NULL}
3	700 Evelyn Rd Unit 1	San Diego	22434

 Note that the dataset you have used above is best suited for Line sequential to be turned off. There may be other use-cases where you want to turn on (check) the line sequential format.

When working with fixed width data, there is usually a lot of space at the end of the data that is padded to keep the file format structure in tact but may not be useful for the real processing you want to do. These spaces can be trimmed automatically by DIS by selecting the option "Strip trailing spaces".

Runtime processing of the files

So far you have seen the properties and the design-time interface of the flat file processing. However, it is very important to note that you are only importing the flat file definitions from the client so that the model repository (MRS) stores the structure of the flat files. Where you have stored the file on the client and imported is not relevant when you execute the mapping.

 The paths that you define in a flat file data object are relative to where your DIS is executing – not where you imported the file from.

 In the Informatica Platform, you can import a flat file as a data object and configure it differently for reading and writing.

Read properties

In the flat file data object, you can configure the properties for read and write. These properties (file paths, file names, etc.) can be different for read and write though the file format needs to be exactly the same (delimited / fixed width). You define the runtime file name in the "Source file name" or the "Output file name" property. You can choose the read the file content either from a flat file or from the output of a command. This is controlled by the "Input type" property. You can set its value as "File" or "Command". When the Input type is set as "Command", the command property will be enabled. You can provide any valid OS command here. If your DIS is running on windows, you can provide any batch command or batch script name (with path). If your DIS is running on UNIX / Linux, you can provide any shell command or shell script (with path). Either way, the output of the command is expected to adhere to the structure you defined while importing the flat file object (columns, data types, lengths, etc.).

Sometimes, you may have more than one file that complies to the same

Run-time: Read	
Input type	File
Source type	Direct
Source file name	cust_address_input.csv
Source file directory	/data/input/
Concurrent Read Partitioning	Optimize throughput
Connection Type	None
Command	
Truncate string null	☐
Line sequential buffer length	1024
Generate Run-time Column Names	From data file header (first line)
Control file name	
Control file directory	
Default Field Type	string
Default Precision	10
Default Scale	0
Constraints	

structure that needs to be processed. These files may be in the same directory or they could be in various different directories. At times, you may want to process the entire directory treating all files in the directory as split-files (parts of the same logical file) or sometimes you want to define a flat file that contains the names of the split-files that are to be processed. You can handle these scenarios by configuring the "Source type" and its relevant properties. By default, source type is set as "Direct". This means that DIS will process the file exactly as you indicated and there is only one physical file that you want to process. If you set the source type as "Indirect", DIS will open the file that you defined in "Source file name" and starts reading the content of the file. However, DIS will not treat each line of this file as a row / data, but treats it as a file name / path. It will then start processing each of those files in that order. You can list paths with absolute paths pointing to different directories/folders in the indirect file. Similarly, when you set the source type as "Directory", DIS expects only "Source file directory" to be set. It will then read all the files in the directory and process them accordingly. The order in which the files are read are not guaranteed. However, DIS will move on to next file only after processing the current file hence all contents of a file in the directory are processed together.

When working with large files you would ideally want the data to be partitioned. DIS can process partitioned data. When the data is partitioned, the relative order of rows is not maintained. You can control this at the data object level by changing the "Concurrent read partitioning" property. By default, it is set to "Optimize throughput". With this value, DIS will not preserve the road order. When you change it to "Keep relative order", the DIS will keep the row order for each partition. You can also set it to "Keep absolute order" if you want the row order to be preserved exactly as it is in the file – which leads to the lowest performance among the three.

Write properties

When writing data to flat files, the default DIS behavior is to overwrite any existing file. You can choose the "Append if exists" if you want to add to the existing file instead of overwriting it. You can configure the file name using the "Output file name" property and the output directory using the "Output file directory" property.

Just as you can read from files or commands, you can write the output to a file or to a command. All the data that you try to write from the mapping will be streamed to the command you specify using the "Command" option. To write output to a command instead of the flat file, choose the "Output type" as "Command" instead of "File". File is the default output type.

DIS by default assumes that the directory to which you want to write to already exists, if it doesn't or if you are not sure if it does, check the box "Create directory if does not exist" and the DIS will create the directory for you.

It is very common to create files with headers and footers. DIS allows you to define whether you want to create a header using the property "Header

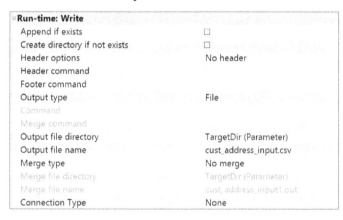

options". By default, the header options are set to "No header". With this value, DIS will not create any header row. You can alternatively set it to "Output field names" to ask the DIS to write the header names as available in the data object or set it to "Use header command option". With this option, DIS relies on the header command to print the header field names. You can define the header command in the "Header command". Similarly, you can define a footer command as well. When a header command or footer command is used, Informatica DIS will execute those commands at the OS level and accordingly place the output at the top of the file or at the bottom of the file.

When processing data in parallel using partitioning, DIS will create multiple output files – one for each partition. You can choose to merge these files into one using the property "Merge type". The default value for this property is "No merge". With this value, the DIS does not merge the partitioned files. Each partition will write the data to a different file. If you set it to "Sequential", DIS will merge all the files at the end of the mapping processing. Setting it to "Concurrent" will make DIS to write to a merged file as and when each partition has data to write. Since all data is being merged concurrently, order of rows will not be maintained in the "Concurrent" merge. You can also set it to "File list". File list mode is exactly same as the "Indirect" file mode – only on the write mode. In this mode, each partition will write data to a different file. In the end, DIS will create an indirect file containing list of paths and files that it just created.

 Please note that the flat file data objects also contain dynamic mapping and Hadoop related properties, which are not discussed in this book.

Lab 11 – Working with delimited files

Use-case

In this lab, you will read from a delimited file and write to a fixed width file of same format.

Steps for the solution

Import the delimited CSV flat file:

1. Create delimited file data object.

    a. Right click the folder Shared_Objects in the project INFA_Platform_Labs and choose New → Data Object.

    b. In the wizard that shows up, choose Flat file data object and click Next.

2. Set the general properties.

    a. Click "Choose from an existing flat file" and click Browse next to it.

    b. Choose the file customers.csv that you have stored previously on your computer.

    c. Name the object as ff_Customers_CSV and click Next.

3. Configure the code page and format.

    a. Leave the code page to default – MS Windows Latin 1 (ANSI), superset of Latin 1.

    b. Click Next.

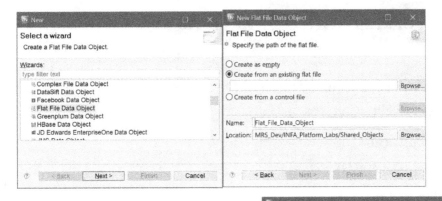

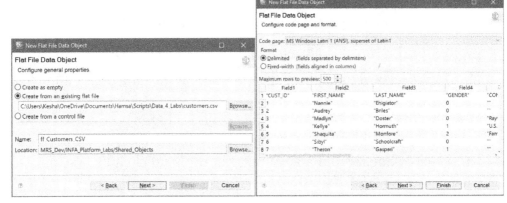

4. Configure the delimited format properties:

   a. Set the format as "Delimited" and click Next.

   b. Choose "Comma" as delimiters – should be selected by default.

   c. Set the text qualifier as "Double quotes" – should be selected by default.

   d. Check the box that is titled "Import column names from the first line". This will automatically set the "Start import at line" value to "1".

   e. Click Next to continue.

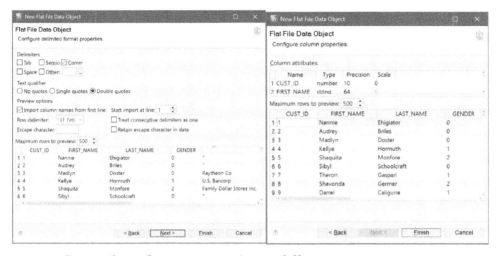

5. Configure the column properties as follows:

    a. Set the data types as shown in this table below:

Column name	Data type	Precision	Scale
CUST_ID	Number	10	
FIRST_NAME	String	64	
LAST_NAME	String	64	
GENDER	Number	8	
COMP_NAME	String	128	
CUST_TYPE	Number	8	
CREATE_DATE	Datetime	29	
ACTIVE	Number	8	

    b. Click Finish.

6. Edit the data object that opened in the workspace

    a. In the data object, you can see all the ports listed in order. Next to the CREATE_DATE field, set the format click the down arrow to edit the default format.

b. In the screen that popped up, choose custom format.

c. Set the format as "DD-MON-YY" and click OK.

d. Press CTRL + S to save the object.

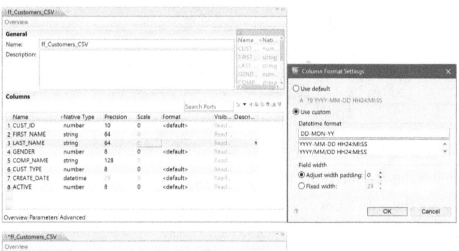

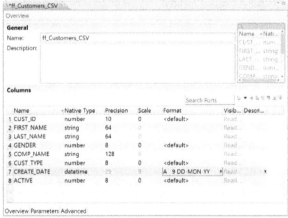

     e. Import the fixed width file into the Developer

7. Create a fixed-width data object:

     a. Right click the folder Shared_Objects in the project INFA_Platform_Labs and choose New → Data Object.

     b. In the wizard that shows up, choose Flat file data object and click Next.

8. Set the general properties:

     a. Click "Choose from an existing flat file" and click Browse next to it.

     b. Choose the file customers.txt that you have stored previously on your computer. Note that you previously imported .csv file (comma separated values files). Now you are importing a .txt file (text file).

     c. Name the object as ff_Customers_TXT and click Next.

9. Configure code page and format:

     a. Leave the code page to be default – MS Windows Latin 1 (ANSI), superset of Latin 1.

     b. Set the format to be fixed-width.

     c. You will see that the data is not aligned with the column names.

     d. Click Next.

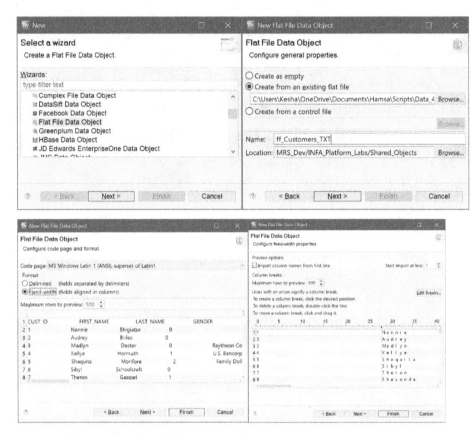

10. Configure fixed-width properties:

    a. Check the import column names from first line.

    b. Start import at line will be automatically set to 1.

    c. Add breakpoints at the following locations: You can add breakpoints by clicking in the UI at the location based on the ruler or click the Edit Breakpoints and add these locations: 8, 72, 136, 144, 272, 280, 309, 317.

    d. Click Next.

11. Set the column names and properties as follows:

Column name	Data type	Bytes to process	Precision
CUST_ID	Number	8	8
FIRST_NAME	String	64	64
LAST_NAME	String	64	64
GENDER	Number	8	8
COMP_NAME	String	128	128
CUST_TYPE	Number	8	8
CREATE_DATE	Datetime	29	29
ACTIVE	Number	8	8

12. Click finish

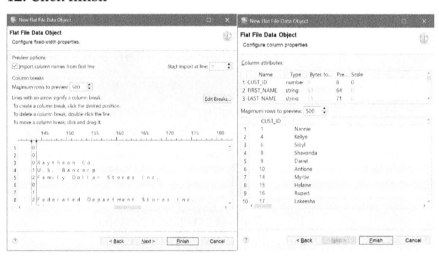

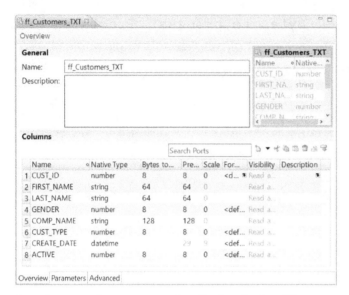

Set the runtime properties for both the files:

When you import the flat file definitions, developer will store the paths on the local machine. You need to change them to the DIS paths. When a mapping executes, it executes on DIS (server), so you need to define the path as relative to DIS. You will make this change in both the flat file definitions.

13. Open the ff_Customers_CSV (delimited file) by right clicking it in the object explorer and selecting Open. It should have already been opened when you imported the flat file in the first step of this lab.

14. Go to advanced sub-tab and scroll to the Run-time: Read section.

15. In the source file directory property, choose "Assign Parameter".

16. In the parameters dialog box, choose the sys: SourceDir and click OK.

17. Your data object will now look like as shown in the screenshot:

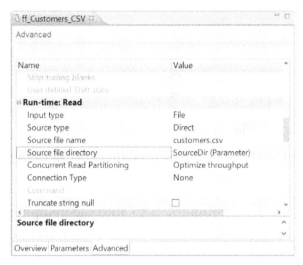

18. Open the ff_Customers_TXT (fixed-width file) by right clicking it in the object explorer and selecting Open. It should have already been opened when you imported the flat file in the previous step.

19. Go to advanced sub-tab and scroll to the Run-time: Write section. Note you are not updating the "Read" properties. You are updating the write properties only as you will use this as a target in our mapping.

20. Output file directory property should already be pre-populated with TargetDir (parameter). If not in the drop down, choose "Assign Parameter". In the parameters dialog box, choose the sys: TargetDir and click OK.

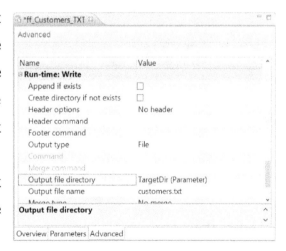

21. Your data object will now look like as shown in the screenshot:

We will now create the mapping:

22. Right click the folder in the object explorer, click New → Mapping.

23. Name the mapping as "m_Lab_11_Flat_Files" and click Finish.

24. From the object explorer, drag the ff_Customers_CSV into the mapping canvas. Choose Read and click OK.

25. From the object explorer, drag the ff_Customers_TXT into the mapping canvas. Choose Write and click OK.

26. Connect all the columns from the source to the target.

27. Save the mapping and run the mapping.

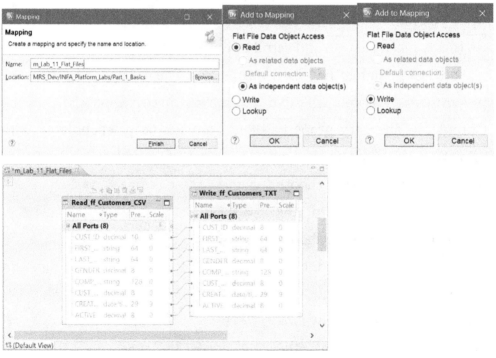

Validate the data:

28. Once the mapping is successfully complete, you can check the OS folder ($INFA_HOME/tomcat/bin/target). You will notice a new file called customers.txt file created. It will have the fixed width format as you specified.

29. Preview the file in a text editor.

In PowerCenter, source and target files/directories are by default present in $INFA_HOME/server/infa_shared. In Informatica Platform, the DIS refers to $INFA_HOME/tomcat/bin/

Chapter 13 – Parameterization

Introduction

Parameters allow you to create a single instance of a mapping and reuse it for multiple purposes by providing the values for several properties at runtime. Parameters allow our mappings and other objects to act like templates and leverage the values that are provided at runtime.

 In PowerCenter, mappings and sessions can be parameterized. In the Informatica Platform, almost every object can be parameterized.

For example, you have "Customers" data object that you want to use in various mappings. However, you may want to use it differently in different mappings. In one mapping you may want to use it to fetch only personal customers. In another mapping you may want to use it to fetch only business customers. In another mapping you may want to fetch all customers. So, instead of maintaining 3 copies of the same table or 3 variations of the same metadata, you will create one data object and parameterize the filter condition. In this chapter, you will learn several ways to parameterize various kinds of objects beginning with relational data objects.

A mapping can receive inputs as well as provide outputs. Inputs can be provided via mapping parameters (simply referred as parameters) and the outputs can be retrieved from mapping outputs (or simply outputs). Mapping can use these inputs at run-time to control various aspects of data reads, processing, and data writes. Mapping can generate outputs that can be leveraged in the workflow and by subsequent tasks in the workflow.

 A mapping / workflow output in Informatica Platform is very similar to Mapping Variable / Workflow Variable in PowerCenter.

You can define parameters in mapping and workflow properties. For example, a mapping has a source filter to fetch only a certain type of customer type and process them. This can be parameterized by creating a parameter pCustType (as shown in the screenshot). The value passed in to this parameter is leveraged in the mapping

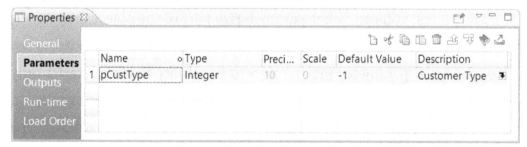

You can parameterize the relational data objects used inside a mapping. You can use parameters – such as the filter condition shown in the screenshot.

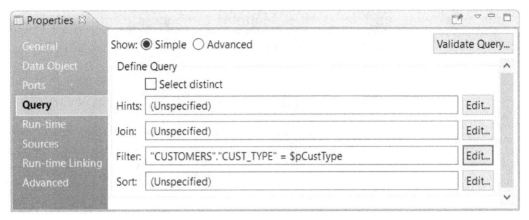

Now when the mapping runs, you can provide the mapping parameter a value that the mapping will pass on to the data object and the data object will use it while applying the filter condition.

Partial and full parameterization

At many places, you can either parameterize part of the object property or the entire object property. At certain places, partial parameterization is not allowed. Partial parameterization refers to the ability to parameterize only a part of the expression. In the screenshot referred here, the expression CUSTOMERS.CUST_TYPE = $pCustType uses the parameter $pCustType as part of the expression. Remainder of the expression is a static constant or expression by itself.

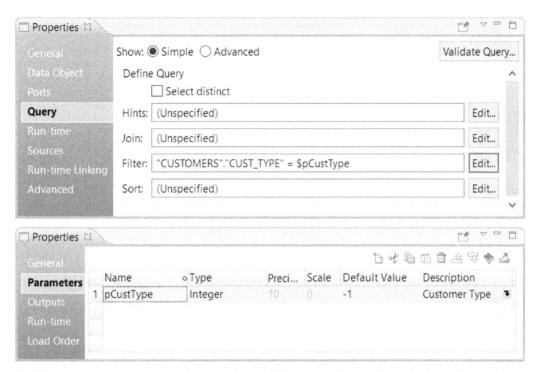

Full parameterization refers to the ability to replace the whole value with a parameter. The example used in the partial parameterization, can also be re-written in full parameterization, by creating a string parameter large enough to hold the expression.

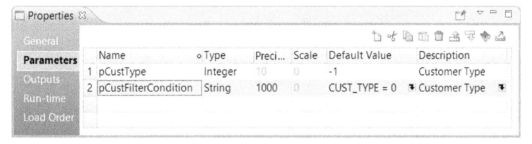

This parameter can then be used in the data object as-is without any expression.

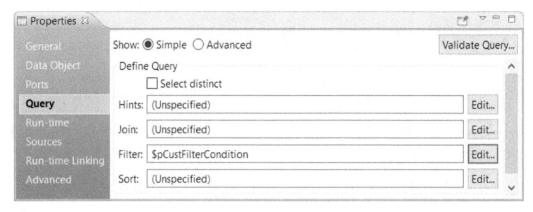

In this earlier example of partial parameterization, the user would have provided only integer value such as zero (0) - that needs to be used in the filter condition. Whereas in the second example of full parameterization, the user would have provided the full condition such as CUST_TYPE = 0. Both types have their own pros and cons. Partial parameterization is less error prone as the DIS is expecting very specific values and as long as the user understands the specific values to be provided, the mappings execute without an error. With full parameterization, the user has greater responsibility of the entire value. In the last example, the user is expected to provide a valid SQL filter clause.

The full parameterization has the advantage of scaling to future needs. In the previous example, user can extend the filter clause from CUST_TYPE = 0 and change it to CUST_TYPE = 0 OR CUST_TYPE =1 and the mapping will honor it. Whereas, with partial parameterization the user would have not been able to provide another value as the expression "CUST_TYPE =" is already present in the data object.

Now, there are some use-cases where partial parameterization does not make a lot of sense and hence it is not allowed. For example, Owner Name (or Schema Name in some databases) is a property where you can either provide a value or parameter (and hence define owner name at run-time), but you cannot partially parameterize it.

Defining parameters

You define parameters in mappings or workflows. You will learn more about workflows in the Workflows chapter, but in this chapter you will look at relevant aspects of the workflows that deal with parameterization.

Parameters can be of the following types:

→ Bigint

→ Connection

→ Date/Time

→ Decimal

→ Double

→ Expression

→ Input Link Set

→ Integer

→ Port

→ Port List

→ Resource

→ Sort List

→ String

→ Time Duration

To create a mapping parameter, go to mapping properties → Parameters tab.

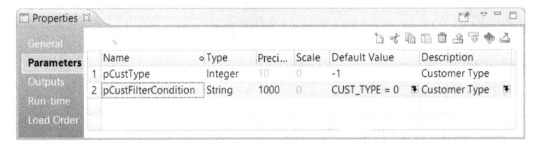

To create a workflow parameter, go to workflow properties → Parameters tab.

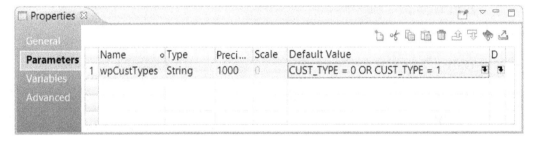

Relational data objects

Informatica Platform is built for reusability – both at the design-time and run-time. When you drag the data object into the mapping, you choose the operation (such as Read / Write / Lookup), and the transformation (operation) is added to the mapping. Once added, you can parameterize the various aspects of the data object's operation such as filter condition and query override.

Defining which data object to choose at run-time

You can parameterize the entire data object. This means that at run-time you can pass the name of the object that should be used as a source. If there is a data object in the MRS that matches the parameter value that you passed, that data object is used in place of the object you used in the mapping.

> The concept of dynamic mapping allows you to parameterize a data object and point the mapping to a data object that is entirely different in structure at run-time. However, dynamic mappings are out-of-scope for this book and hence you will assume that the data object passed at run-time will have to be exactly same structure as the one used in the mapping.

As displayed in the screenshot, you can go to the data object properties → Data Object tab and choose "Parameter" for Specify by property. Then click Browse to browse through existing mapping parameters and assign one. You can also create a new parameter by clicking the New button.

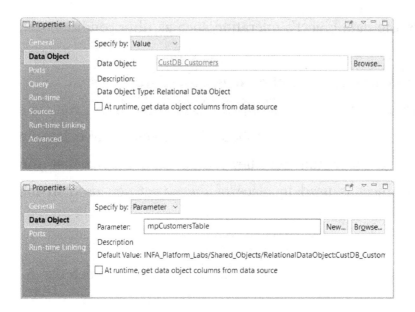

Filter, join conditions, query components

You can also parameterize the query components of a relational data object such as hints, filter condition, join condition, and other source query related components. You can also define an advanced query and parameterize either partially or completely.

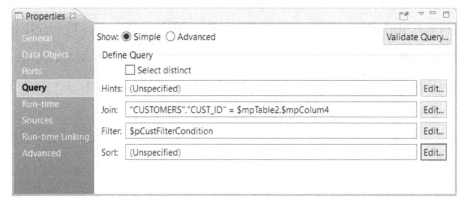

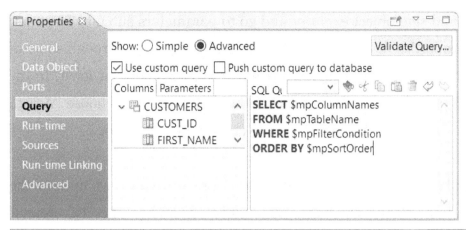

 Though this section focused on the read operation of the relational data objects, similar concepts apply to the write operation as well.

Flat file data objects

Now that you have some understanding of how the parameterization works with the relational data objects, let us take a look at the flat file data objects. Flat file data objects have a very different set of properties as compared to the relational data objects. Parameterization is allowed in the flat file data object itself in addition to what is allowed in the mapping. You can define parameters in the flat file data object itself. To define object level parameters, open the data object form

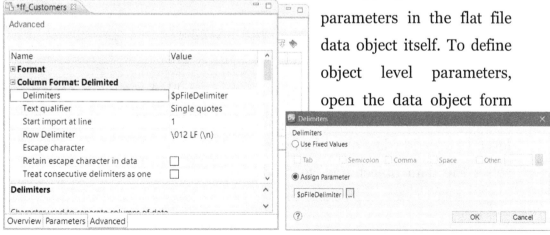

the left hand side object explorer and go to parameters sub tab. There are several properties in the flat file data object. You will go through some of them. For delimiter files, you can parameterize the delimiter itself. In the advanced tab, click the drop down of the delimiters and choose "Assign Parameter" and click the ellipsis icon to choose the parameter.

In the read and write properties, you can parameterize the file name and the file location. Read directory and write directory are by default parameterized and point to SourceDir and TargetDir respectively. You can parameterize the source file name in the "Run-time: Read" properties section and the output file name in the "Run-time: Write" section.

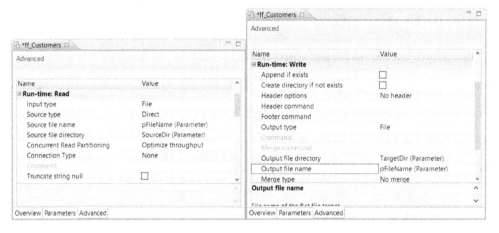

When a data object has parameterization enabled, you can assign the mapping parameters to the data object and override them at the mapping level. To override data object parameters at the mapping, open the mapping select the data object and go to data object properties → data object parameters. Here you will see the parameters used by the object. You will notice that all of them are set to use a default value:

You can change the instance values to Parameter / Use Default / Value. Default means the value for the parameter will be as defined in the data object. When selected as Value, you can provide a static value inside the mapping to override the parameter's default. In the screenshot here, you have overridden the file path from its default value of /data to /output in the mapping.

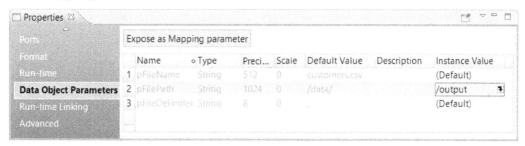

You can also assign a mapping parameter to the data object parameter. When you do so, you can choose the parameter that you want to assign to. For example, you can override the path from /data to SourceDir directory.

You can also choose to expose the data object parameter as Mapping parameter. When you do so, a mapping parameter of same name and type will be created and it will be assigned to the data object parameter as shown in the screenshot here:

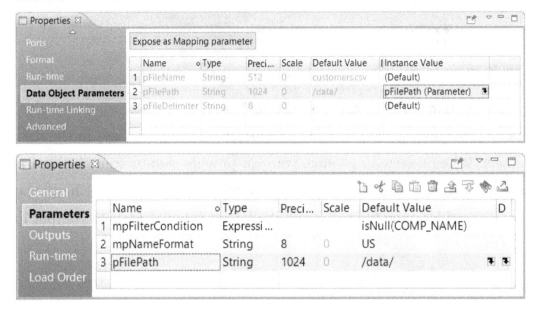

Transformations

This section only covers some transformations to give you a perspective of how powerful parameterization is and how widely you can use it to solve your DI needs. This chapter does not go through every single DI transformation.

Expression

Expressions supports both partial and full parameterization. In variable ports and output ports, you can access the parameters inside an expression

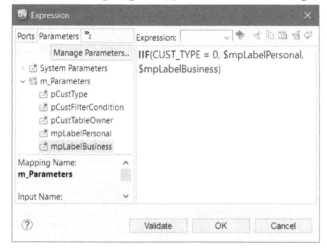

editor. Inside the expression editor, go to the parameter tab on the left and double click any parameter to insert it into the expression. You can also manually type the parameter name in the expression. Validate the expression to ensure there are no typographical errors and the expressions are valid after your changes. If you want to assign a value to a specific port, you can put the parameter name alone (full parameterization).

Expression supports full parameterization for values only. For example, if you set the value of a string port as a parameter, the value of the parameter is assigned to the string. If you use the

> Informatica transformation language inside the parameter value, it will NOT be evaluated and will be treated as string.

Filter

Filter transformation supports both partial and full parameterization. In filter transformation, you can use parameters of type "Expression". These expressions will be evaluated as a filter condition and the result will be applied to the Filter. For such support, the parameters have to be of type "Expression".

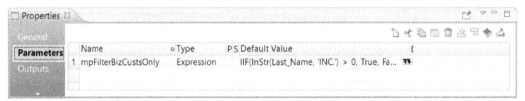

To parameterize the filter condition, go to Filter properties → Filter tab. For partial parameterization, choose the "Specify by" as "Value" and specify the expression (with or without using parameters).

To do full parameterization, set the" specify by" as "Parameter" and choose any parameter that is created of type "Expression".

Aggregator

In an Aggregator transformation, you can parameterize both the group by ports (Port List) and the individual expressions where you use aggregation functions. First, create a mapping parameter of type Port List and define the default ports list that can be used. You can always override them at the runtime.

 While defining the default ports list, you type in the port names manually as the mapping is not aware of the context you want to use these yet. Ensure that these names match to proper port names in the Aggregator or you will have a runtime failure.

By default, you can only specify ports in the Aggregator's group by properties. You can set the "Specify by" property to "Parameter". This will allow you to choose the Port List that you created in the mapping parameters.

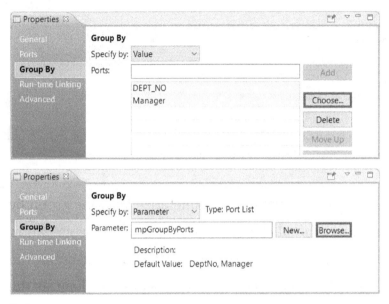

Joiner

Joiner transformation supports full parameterization. You can parameterize the entire join condition and pass in two lists of ports that are used in the join condition. You can define the join condition in three modes: simple, advanced, parameter. In simple mode, you can use the UI to create a grid of which ports in the master table match to which ports in the detail table.

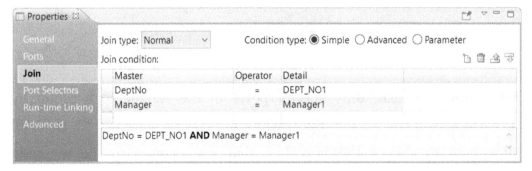

In the advanced mode, you can write an expression to define the join condition. Here you can leverage the full potential of Informatica's transformation language reference as shown in the screenshot. You can also leverage partial parameterization in this mode.

In the parameter mode, you can parameterize the entire join condition by providing a parameter of type expression.

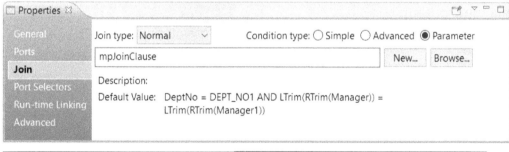

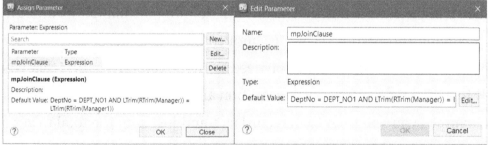

Mapping outputs

Mapping parameters are inputs to the mapping. Parameters are values provided by users to the mapping at run-time. Outputs (or simply outputs) are values that mapping has computed during its execution and are available for the user to consume after the mapping execution is complete. User can pass these values to the subsequent tasks later if they choose to do so.

Let us take a simple use-case of this. Say, you want to the count the number of the rows flowing through the mapping and pass that out as a value to the next mapping / subsequent task in the workflow. You begin by defining the mapping output.

As shown in the screenshot, you begin with defining the mapping output in the mapping properties such as moPersonalCustomerCount.   Since mapping can process in parallel, you need to define the aggregation that you apply to it. There are 3 types of aggregation allowed: Sum, Min and Max. In this example, you will treat each record as 1 and just sum the total to get a count.   you do that inside an expression. Let's go to the expression properties → Mapping Outputs tab. You create a new entry to point to the mapping output you just created (moPersonalCustomerCount). You can write complex expressions here that use the data flowing through the expression.

In this expression editor you can calculate such things as average salary, minimum bonus etc. Any operation that you do on each row here will again get aggregated at the mapping level depending on the aggregation you defined for the mapping output.

Workflows

Workflows support parameterization too. Just like mappings, workflows have the concept of parameters as well as outputs (called as variables). To create workflow variables, open a workflow and go to its properties → Variables tab. Create a new workflow variable – say, called as wvCountOfCustomers and set its initial value as Zero (0).

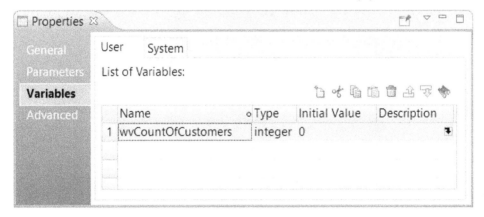

In this example you are associating it with the mapping you just created in the mapping outputs. So, you add that mapping to the workflow and in the mapping task properties → Outputs sub pane. Here in the Mapping Task Outputs → User-defined Mapping Outputs → Current Value → moPersonalCustomerCount – set the workflow variable wvCountOfCustomers. This is where the mapping output is being associated to the workflow variables.

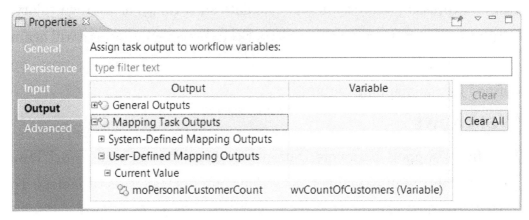

We will now consume this value in a command task subsequent to the mapping task. The command task is configured as shown here in the screenshot. It is printing a static message along with the workflow variable on to a file in the DIS user home directory.

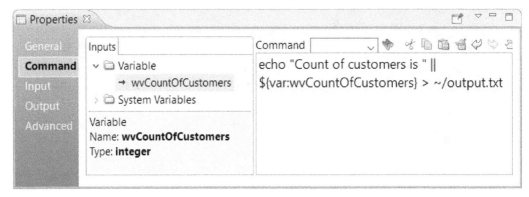

This generates the output:

```
[infa@infa-server~]$ cat output.txt
Count of customers is 5946
```

Parameter files

Parameter files are used to provide values to parameters in a mapping or workflow at runtime. When you execute a deployed mapping or workflow, you can pass a parameter file or parameter set to it. The DIS will read the values from the parameter file and resolve the parameters before executing the mapping or workflow.

Parameter files are of XML format. Let us take a look at a sample parameter file format. The content in the bold is the focus for the current section.

```
<?xml version="1.0" encoding="UTF-8"?><root
xmlns="http://www.informatica.com/Parameterization/1.0"
xmlns:xsi="http://www.w3.org/2001/XMLSchema" version="2.0">
<!--Specify deployed application specific parameters here.-->
<!--
      <application name="app_Params">
            <mapping name="m_Parameters"/>
      </application>
-->
<project name="INFA_Platform_Labs">
<folder name="Part_1_Basics">
<mapping name="m_Parameters">
                  <parameter name="mpFilterCondition">
                        isNull(COMP_NAME)
                  </parameter>
```

```
<parameter name="mpNameFormat">US</parameter>
</mapping>
</folder>
</project>
</root>
```

You can notice that there is an XML tag for project which contains tags for the folders within the project and then the mappings within the project. Each mapping has one or more parameter tags. In the above example there are 2 parameters associated with the mapping. Each parameter has a name attribute and the value is stored in between the open and close tags. For example, for the **mpFilterCondition** parameter the value is **isNull(COMP_NAME)**. Similarly, for the **mpNameFormat** parameter the value is set to **US**.

 You do not have to manually create parameter files for the mappings. You can generate them using Developer tool or using infacmd command line.

Generating a parameter file from mapping

You can generate a parameter file from a mapping. To do so, open the mapping in the Developer tool, go to properties pane → Parameters sub tab. On the properties toolbar, click export Icon (the last one in the toolbar). Choose the file name and click Save. This will create the parameter file. You can open it in any text editor to modify and use it.

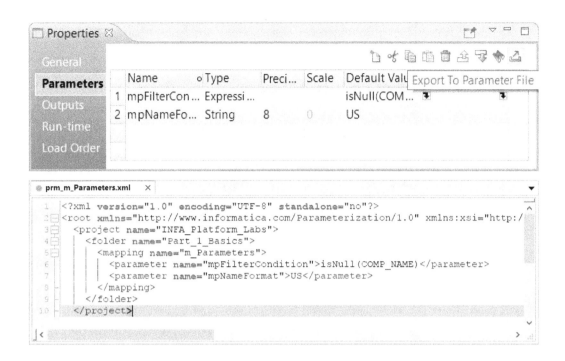

You can also generate a parameter file from mapping. This is discussed in the "Execution, Automation and Monitoring" chapter.

Parameter sets

Parameter sets are objects inside model repository that can be used in place of parameter files. You can associate a parameter set with more than one mapping / workflow. When you deploy your objects to runtime, you can deploy a parameter set as well. Parameter set has various advantages over parameter files.

→ Parameter set is an object inside the MRS, hence the management is very easy.

→ Deployment of a parameter set is easy and streamlined as it is a repository object.

→ Parameter set can be updated using command line interface (CLI) making it easy to automate

Creating a parameter set is easy. Go to file New → Parameter Set or right

click on a project / folder and click New → Parameter Set. Provide a name and description for the parameter set and click Finish. This will create a new parameter set and open it in the workspace. By default, a parameter set is empty. You can add objects (mappings / workflows) to a parameter set and once the object is added, you can add parameters within them. When you add new mapping / workflow, you can choose the parameters from the object that you want to pass a value through parameter set. When you change a mapping / workflow, you can re-add the mapping / workflow to the Parameter set and when prompted, choose to Update. This will refresh the parameters in the parameter set. You can edit a value of the parameter by just double clicking it in the Parameter Set window.

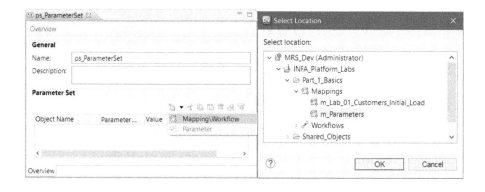

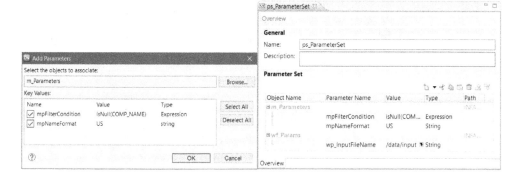

Editing a parameter in parameter set

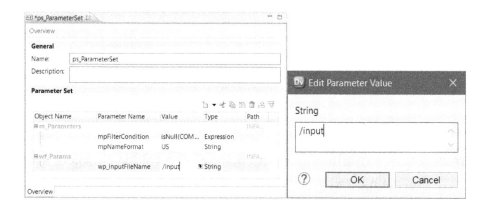

Chapter 14 – Workflows

Introduction

A workflow is an object in the Model Repository that allows you to group mappings and other executable objects to define a business sequence or logical flow of execution. For example, you create a workflow to define Customers load mapping and accounts load mapping can happen in parallel but the transactions mapping can run only after the customers and accounts mapping is finished. This workflow will look like as shown in the screenshot here:

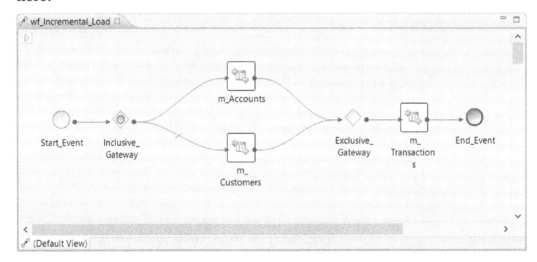

Creating a workflow

You can create a new workflow by right clicking on a folder / project and choosing New → Workflow. You can also create a new workflow by going to the File menu → New → Workflow. When the create workflow dialog box appears, provide a name to the workflow and click Finish. A workflow is by default created with a start event and an end event. All tasks that you want to place inside a workflow must be between the start and end tasks.

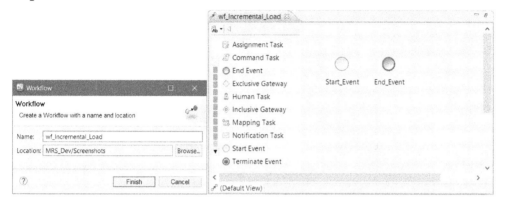

Start and End events

A start event defines the beginning of a workflow. An end event defines the

end of the workflow. All workflow logic must begin with Start Event. Depending on the parallelism that you want to build into the workflow, you can

use gateways to create parallel branches.

 A workflow can have only one start event and only one end event.

For example, see the workflow below. This is an invalid workflow because it has more than one start task. This workflow is trying to execute the P2P payments task in parallel to customers and accounts mapping tasks. The right way of implementing this task is to have the third mapping also as part of the same branch that initiated from the Inclusive Gateway and end into the exclusive gateway. You will learn more about the gateway tasks later.

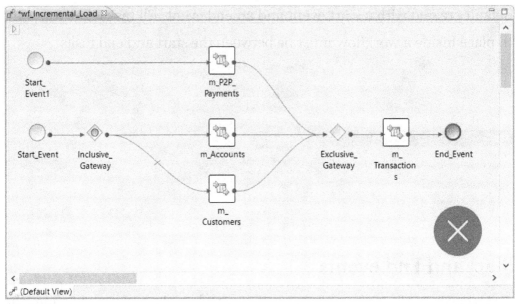

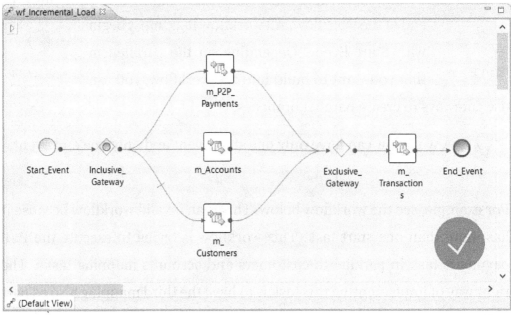

Similarly, a workflow cannot have more than one end event. An end event represents the completion of the workflow. Workflow should be configured

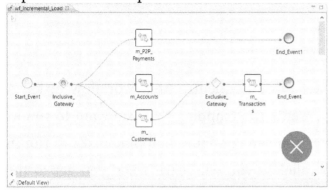

such that the control reaches end event only after tasks are complete. End event represents the completion of the workflow. It represents that all tasks within the

workflow have reached an end state – either successfully completed or completed with a failure. You will learn more about handling failures later. Let's take an example as shown in the screen shot below. The workflow is

attempting to execute the P2P mapping completely independent of the traditional customers,

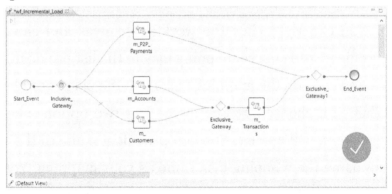

accounts and transactions mapping tasks. This workflow is invalid as it is having more than one end task. The right way of implementing this will be lead the end of the P2P payments also to the same end event as represented in the second screenshot below:

 For a workflow to be valid, there should always be at least one path leading from start event to the end event. At runtime if no

> path leads to the end event, the workflow will remain in a hung
> state.

Mapping tasks

Mapping tasks are one of the most frequently used workflow tasks. A

mapping task represents the mapping that you want to run as part of a workflow. You can configure mapping tasks to run in sequence or in parallel as you will learn when you get to the

Mapping_ Task

gateways section of this chapter. You can add a mapping task to a workflow in couple of different ways:

a. You can drag a mapping from the same or different project / folder into the workflow.

b. You can right click the workflow canvas and choose "Add workflow object" and choose mapping task in the list provided.

c. You can add the mapping task from the palette on the left.

When you choose any one of the last two options above, Mapping Task dialog box will appear. You can provide a name to the mapping task. You can name the mapping task same as your mapping. You can also assign a parameter set in the same dialog box and click Finish.

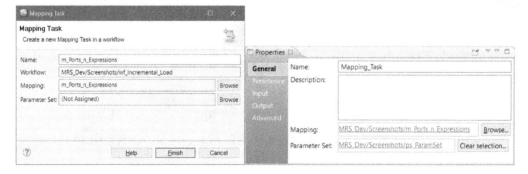

You can go back and change the mapping task name, description, and parameter set in the mapping task properties inside a workflow. To access the mapping task properties, select the mapping task inside the workflow and go to properties pane.

Mapping task properties

Advanced properties

→ Task recovery strategy: You can configure a mapping task for recovery. When you do so, the task recovery strategy defines the recovery of the mapping. It is by default set to restart task. You can change to skip task. Typically, for mappings that process logic and data, restart task is set so that mapping can run again and process the remaining data. For mappings that perform process control and optional clean tasks, skip task is set, where the mapping is expected to not always succeed depending on the task defined inside it.

→ Optimizer level: DIS has various optimizations built into it. This property defines whether or not you want those optimizations to apply to this mapping task. The values can range from 0 – 3. The default value is 2. Value 0 represents no optimization. DIS will run the mapping as-is. Value 1 represents minimal. DIS will apply early projection optimization. Value 2 represents Normal optimization and is the default for all mapping tasks. When set, DIS will apply projection, early selection, pushdown, and predicate optimization methods to the mapping. Value 3 represents full optimization. When selected, DIS will apply all optimization methods available to the mapping.

→ High precision: Enabled by default, mappings will be able to process high precision decimal data that is used for scientific and engineering calculations.

→ Mapping task log directory and file: Mapping task log directory is by default set to the LogDir parameter (in the input tab of the mapping task properties). The log file name is by default same as the mapping name. You can override the directory name in the input tab and the log file name in the advanced properties tab.

→ Java class path: When using Java transformations, you can define the class path for loading any external JAR files.

→ Mapping task log save type: By default, mapping task logs are stored by timestamp. You can also configure to store the mapping task logs by run number. When configured by timestamp, DIS will create the logs with the syntax: <mapping task log file name>_<unique identified>_<timestamp>.log. When configured to save by the run numbers, DIS starts the numbering with 0 and then goes to one less than the number specified (zero index). So, for example, if the numbers of the logs are defined as 10, DIS will create the logs from 0 to 9 and then cycle over to the 0.

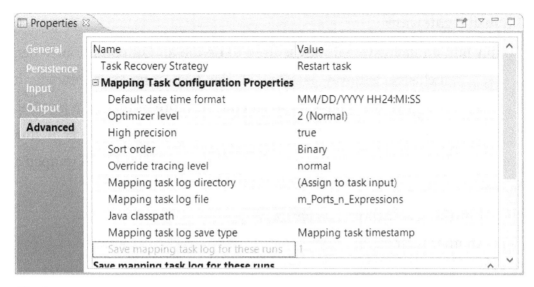

Gateways

Gateways allow you to create and merge branches within a workflow. Branching is used to define which workflow tasks can run in parallel and how. There are two types of gateway tasks available inside a workflow: Inclusive gateway and Exclusive gateway. An inclusive gateway allows you to branch and execute multiple tasks in parallel. Exclusive gateway allows you to branch and execute only among the branches. Similarly, when multiple branches join together, a gateway is used to merge the branches.

 The closing gateway doesn't have to match the corresponding opening gateway. For example, you can use an inclusive gateway to open multiple branches that execute in parallel and then an exclusive gateway to close the branches. In this case, the task after exclusive gateway will execute only when all the branches complete.

Inclusive gateways

Simply put, an inclusive gateway is used to define an OR condition. When

Inclusive_
Gateway

inclusive gateway is used at the beginning of a branch, it indicates that you want to run one or more branches in parallel. You can control the branches that get executed via a link condition. In its simplest form, an inclusive gateway is used both to open a

branch and to close it as shown in the screenshot here. Another screenshot here shows the properties of the inclusive gateway.

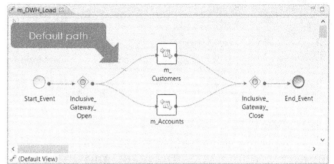

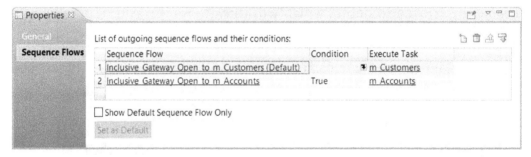

You will notice that one of the links is designated as "Default". Every gateway must have a default path that leads to the closing gateway. This ensures that the control always from the start task to end task. The default link / path always evaluates to true. The default path is represented in the GUI with a slash (/) on the link. If you want to execute all the paths leading from the opening gateway, you can set the condition of all the links to true. If not, you can have user defined conditions. These conditions will be evaluated at runtime to determine whether the tasks following the link should be processed. All links that evaluate to true will be continued. Similarly, when control arrives at the closing gateway, workflow service will wait for all the branches to complete and then move on to the next task.

 The closing gateway can have only one output link.

Exclusive gateways

Exclusive gateways are used when you want to execute only one of the parallel branches that are defined. For example, you have a mapping to load the data to a "Customers" dimension. The mapping is parameterized to determine whether a full reload is required or only incremental load is required. Now, you want to build a workflow such that on the first day of every quarter, you execute the full load / initial load. All other days, you want to execute an incremental load. You can use exclusive gateway in the workflow to determine which path to go to and then you have two mapping tasks to pass different values/parameter sets to the same mapping. Such a workflow will look like the screenshot here. The exclusive gateway acts similar to the inclusive gateway but allows only one path going forward. You can define conditions in the link to determine when that particular link evaluates to true.

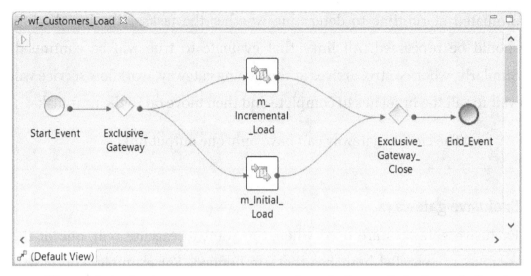

Just like with inclusive gateway, you need to define a default path for the exclusive gateway. The default path (represented by a single / on the link) is chosen when all other link conditions evaluate to false. You cannot define a condition for the default path.

Other workflow tasks

Command task

A command task is used to execute OS commands / scripts. Any command recognized by the OS on which the DIS is running can be executed from the command task. As represented in the screenshot here, a command task can be used anywhere inside a workflow. In the screenshot here, you are using the command task to archive the input files you received into a subfolder, within a predefined archive location.

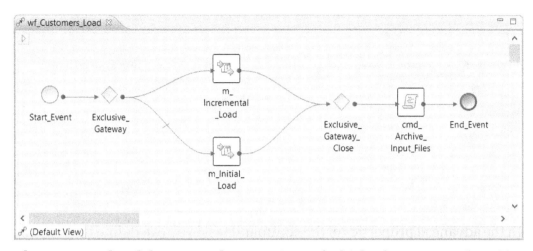

The command task has several properties. Of which, the command itself is of significance. You can set the command in the properties pane → command tab. The screenshot here shows the command task running two Linux commands: mkdir (to create a sub directory within a predefined archive location) and the mv (to move the files into the newly created subdirectory location). The commands are separated by a ";"as the underlying operating system requires multiple commands to be separated by a semi-colon. If you are using windows operating system, you may use different syntax. As shown in the screenshot here, you can use several predefined parameters in the command task.

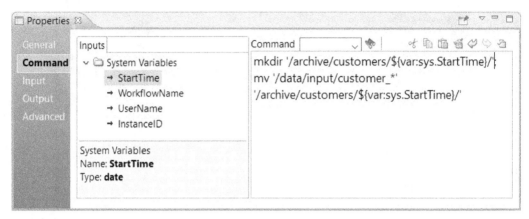

In the advanced properties of the command task, you can define the working directory – the directory where you want these commands to be executed

and whether or not you want to restart this command task in recovery scenarios (Task Recovery Strategy). Standard output and error length is assumed to be 1024 characters, which can also be customized here.

The DIS does not evaluate any commands specified in the Command tasks. It passes the commands as-is after evaluating the parameters inside the task. It is the users' responsibility to ensure that the commands are valid and that they provide the expected result.

Terminate task

A Workflow succeeds as long as it can execute the tasks within – regardless

Terminate_ Event

of the status of the tasks. For example, if a command task is placed inside a workflow, workflow will succeed as long as it can execute that command task. The task itself may have executed successfully or may have failed. But as long as the workflow was able to invoke the commands, workflow will succeed. Similarly, regardless of the mapping task's end state, workflow will succeed. If you want to change this behavior and have the workflow fail when a particular task fails, you can use terminate task for that purpose.

 Terminate task is very similar to "Fail parent if the task fails" functionality in PowerCenter.

Let us take an example of the customers load you discussed earlier in the command task. You will enhance that workflow to showcase the usage of the terminate task. Refer to the screenshot here:

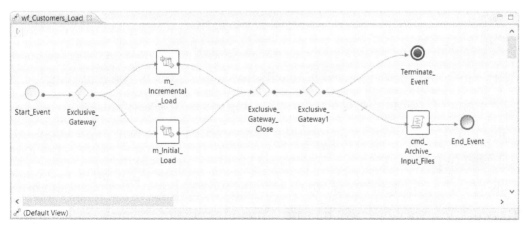

We have an exclusive gateway opening and closing to determine whether you want to execute the initial load mapping or the incremental load mapping. You have defined two workflow outputs (Workflow properties → Variables tab) to hold the status of the customers mapping tasks: custIncrLoadStatus and custInitialLoadStatus. Both of them are of type Boolean and are set to true by default to indicate they are successful.

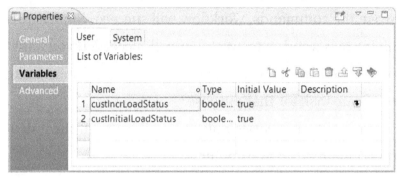

We will then select each of the mapping task and assign their status to the corresponding workflow variable as shown in the screenshots here:

With these changes, the workflow will store the status of the mapping tasks and if one of them fails, the corresponding workflow variable will have the value of FALSE. Now, let us implement an exclusive gateway. This exclusive gateway helps you make a decision on what to do when one of these tasks fails v/s when both of them are successful. You will by default assume both the workflow variables will be true – meaning one of the tasks ran and was successful and the other one never executed. This new exclusive gateway will have two branches – one leading to the command task to execute file archive and the other one leading to a terminate task. The link leading to the terminate task will have the condition to check that one of the workflow variables is FALSE (indicating a session failure). Note that when the expression evaluates to true, the control will flow towards the terminate task which will terminate the workflow. When the expression evaluates to false (when both workflow variables are set to true), you will continue to archive the input files and end the workflow gracefully.

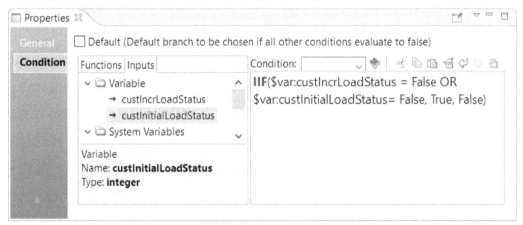

A Terminate terminates the workflow and set its status as "Terminated". A terminate task is an end event – meaning when the control reaches terminate task, it will fail any running mappings in the workflows at that moment. However, unlike End event task, you can have any number of terminate tasks inside a workflow as shown in the screenshot here:

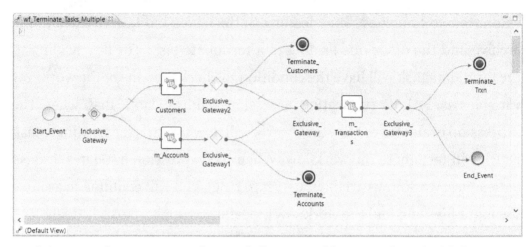

In this example, you created 3 workflow variables – each to hold the status of the one of the mappings. In the non-default links going to each of the terminate tasks, you have the negation of the corresponding mapping status variable. So, if the mapping succeeds the link will evaluate to false. If the mapping fails, the link will evaluate to true. If the terminate tasks evaluate to false, workflow service takes the default paths (the path with the slash - /) and then runs the transactions. At the end of the transactions, you evaluate again to determine the end state of the workflow.

Chapter 15 – Object migration and Deployment

Introduction

So far, you have executed various simple mappings using the "Run Mapping" functionality. You have also seen how you can preview the data mid-stream in a mapping, and how to preview the data of a relational / flat file data object. These features are very handy to quickly test mappings in a non-production scenario. In a production scenario, mappings are often executed hands-free i.e. they are executed in an automated way using Command Line Interface (CLI) or using scheduler service – either using the scheduler service provided by Informatica or external schedulers. In preparation to understand various aspects of executing these mappings / jobs in production scenario, you will look at how to deploy these objects from one environment to another.

 The deployment process in Informatica Platform is quite unique and different than PowerCenter.

Object migration – An overview

Let's look at what happens when multiple Informatica environments are involved. Typically, customers have one Informatica domain to represent one environment. For example, a customer who intends to have 3 unique environments for Development, Quality Assurance (QA) and Production,

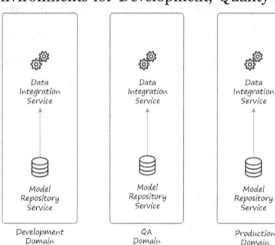

creates 3 Informatica domains – one for each environment. These 3 domains can be on shared hardware (if there are enough resources to hold these domains) or on multiple independent hardware or any combination thereof. Above illustration shows each of those domains having one model repository and one DIS each. Object migration involves copying the objects from one MRS to another MRS. If you want to copy the objects to more than one MRS, you can repeat the same procedure again as shown in the illustration below. At times, you may want to migrate the object to the same repository as well (for example, just to maintain a live backup copy) which is illustrated as a loop-back arrow in the production domain in the below illustration. Note that though the illustration shows this as an example for production domain only, it is applicable for any domain regardless of its usage.

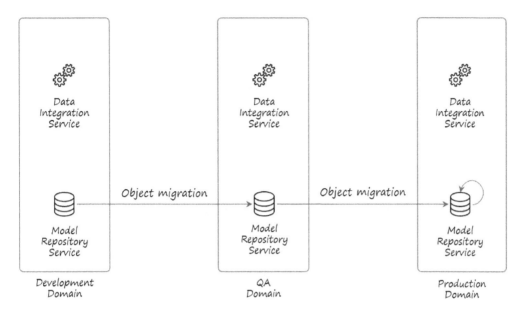

During object migration, the administrator intends to keep the objects as-is. The objects may or may not be available for developers to edit in the target environment, but developers are typically granted read-only access to the objects that are migrated. When objects are migrated from one environment to another, the connections need to be resolved and/or re-assigned.

Steps involved in an object migration

Let's take a quick look at what is involved in migrating objects from one MRS to another. You can export an individual object or a folder or an entire project inside an MRS. When you export the objects, Developer tool creates an XML file. This XML file can be imported in other MRS of the same or compatible version. Let's take a quick look at what's involved in exporting / importing the objects:

You can export only one project at a time. To export more than one project, repeat the steps for each project.

Exporting objects into an XML file:

1. You can export a project by clicking on File menu → Export menu or right click a project and choose Export.

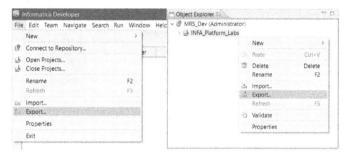

2. Select screen appears. You will be prompted to choose the type of export you want to create. You will choose the "Export Object Metadata File" and click Next.

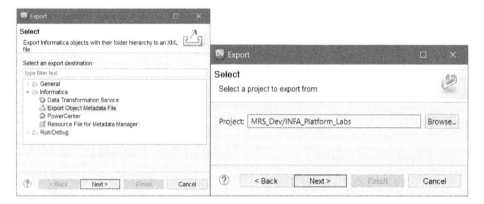

3. In the select project screen, choose a project you want to export. If you already have a project selected in the object explorer or if you initiated this wizard by right clicking an existing project and choosing Export, the project name will appear for you by default.

4. Export to file dialog box appears. Choose all the objects you want to export. Dependencies will be automatically picked up. For example, if you select a mapping, all data objects that are mapping will automatically appear in the next screen. You will also need to specify a export file name. Simply click browse and choose the folder where you want to store this export file and provide a name to the file.

5. Once you click Next, Developer tool will calculate dependencies and show you all the dependencies it will automatically export due to the selection you made in the previous screen. Just click Next.

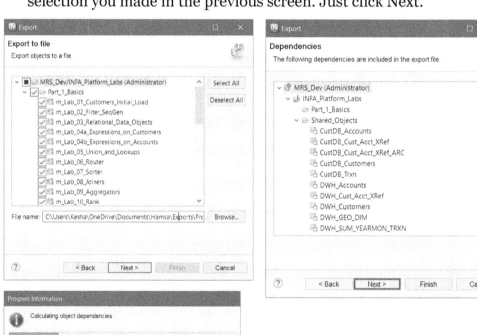

6. If you have any reference tables associated, the developer tool will display those. Otherwise, it shows a message that there are no dependencies with references tables, click Next.

7. Export operation will take several minutes to complete – depending on the number of objects you selected.

8. You will see a success message once the export is complete.

Importing objects from an XML file:

Now, let's take a quick look at how the importing of objects work:

1. Similar to an export process, you can invoke the import process by choosing File menu → Import or by right clicking a project and choosing Import.

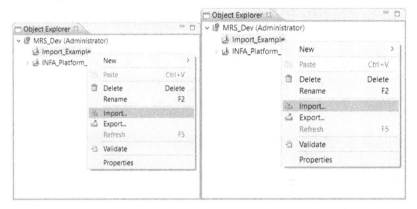

2. In the Import wizard, you can choose Import Object Metadata File (Basic) or Import Object Metadata File (Advanced). Here you will look at the advanced import.

3. Import file screen appears. Click Browse and choose the XML file you want to import and the MRS where you want to import these contents to.

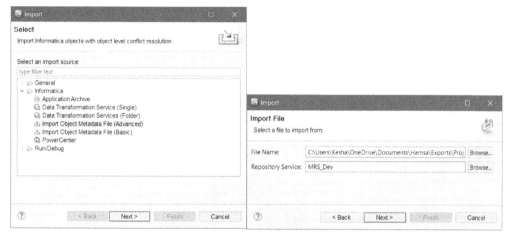

4. Select Objects to Import screen appears.

5. On the left hand side, the contents of the XML file are listed. On the right hand side, projects in the currently connected MRS will appear. Note that this screen only lists the project that you have at least read access to.

6. On the left hand side, choose the entire project or entire folder or choose the individual objects that you want to import. You can choose one or more objects here. To choose a series of continuous objects, use SHIFT key. To choose individual objects that are not continuous, use the CTRL key.

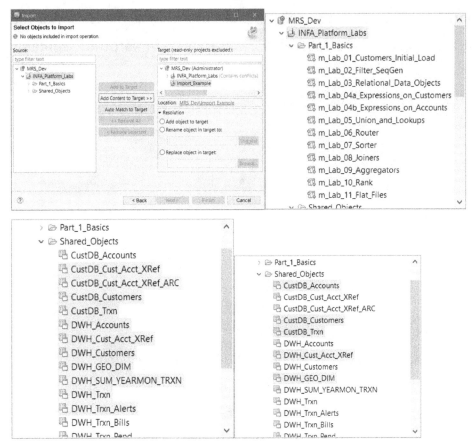

7. Once you have selected the objects to import, on the right hand side, select the target project or folder or MRS you want these objects imported into.

8. In the middle of the screen, you have various actions you can perform for the import. Below is a quick description of those actions:

   1. **Add to Target** → This button will be available if you have selected a parent object on the right hand side. The object on the right hand side should be able to hold the object you selected on the left hand side. For example, it will be enabled when you select

a project on the left and MRS on the right or when you select a folder on the left and project on the right. When this button is clicked, the object on the left and its entire contents are added to the target object. You cannot add a project to a project.

2. **Add content to Target** → This button will be available if you have selected a container object (a project / folder) on the right. Clicking this button will skip the container on the left, but will add all objects inside the left hand side container into the object selected on the right hand side. For example, if you selected a folder on the left and a project on the right, clicking this button will skip the folder but add all folder's objects into the project directly.

3. **Auto Match to Target** → When you click this button, Developer will traverse the target repository (right hand side) and will try to match the objects by name. When it finds the project/folder with the same name as the object you selected on the left, it will try to add the contents of the left hand object into this automatically selected folder / project.

4. **Remove All** → Once you have added objects from the left to the right, if you want to remove them all and start over, click this button.

5. **Remove Selected** → Use this button to remove individual objects from the right (the ones that you have added previously).

 These actions work in conjunction to the resolution you have selected. Read about the resolution before using these.

The primary difference between Add to Target and Add Content to Target is whether or not the selected object (project / folder) will also be added to your target. If you selected a folder on both the sides and choose Add to Target, the folder will be added as a subfolder to the right hand side content and dependencies will be added in the sub folder. If you chose Add Content to Target, the left hand side folder will be NOT added as a subfolder and contents will be directly added to the right hand side folder.

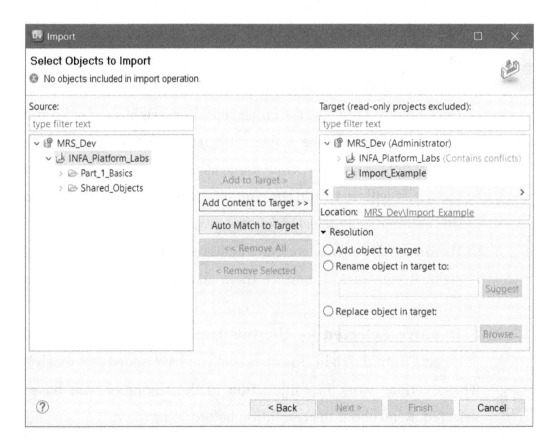

Sample screenshots show the difference between "Add to Target" and "Add content to Target". "Part_1_Basics" is selected on the left and "Import_Example" is selected on the right.

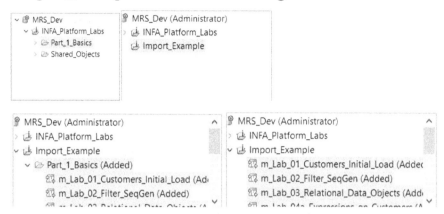

The third screenshot is when "Add to Target" is selected. Notice the folder "Part_1_Basics" is added to the project along with the mappings inside. The fourth screenshot is when "Add content to Target" is selected. Notice that the folder Part_1_Basics is missing. The content inside the folder Part_1_Basics is directly imported into the project selected by skipping the folder itself.

9. Use the Resolution frame to define what actions you want to do when importing objects that already exist in the target. You can choose one of the following:

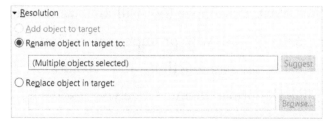

1. **Add object to target** → This is available only when there is no object in the target (right hand side) with the same name(s) as the object(s) selected on the left.

2. **Rename object in target to** → If you select this option, whenever a conflict is found in the object, the object in the target repository will be retained as-is and the new object that is about to be copied will be renamed (by default a suffix of 1 or the first number available is added). Once added, you can select individual objects on the right and change the name to other than what was suggested.

3. **Replace object in target** → If you select this option, whenever a conflict is found, the object on the left will replace the object on the right hand side during deployment.

In the screenshots here, the first one is when the rename option is chosen and the second is when the replace option is chosen.

10. Once you click Next, Developer tool will analyze the dependencies for the selected objects and will prompt you to import the necessary dependences using the same actions and resolutions. This screen will look exactly like the previous one. Once you resolve all the differences, click Next.

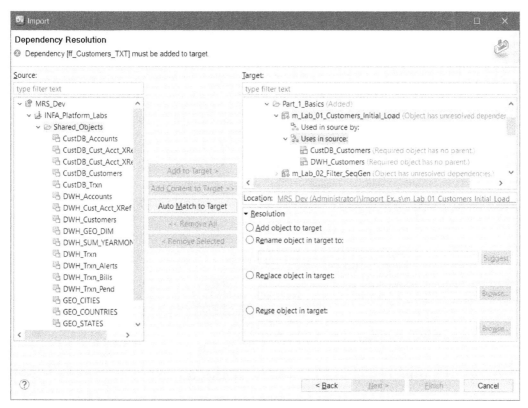

11. The summary screen appears. This screen has 3 main sections: Summary of objects to be imported, parameter set binding, and connection resolution.

1. Summary of objects to be imported → This section displays the summary of all the objects you have selected to import. In this section, you can quickly browse and navigate across various objects. If you check the box that is labeled "Link source and target objects" and the radio button "Source to Target", for any object you select on the left hand side, Developer tool will quickly traverse the right hand tree and select the exact object on the right

hand tree. This gives you a quick way to navigate across and find various objects.

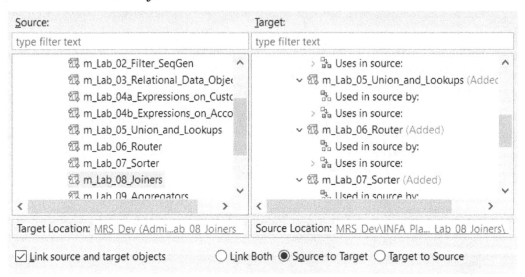

2. Parameter set resolution → If the objects you exported used parameter sets (more on this later), you can map them to the parameter sets you have in target repository.

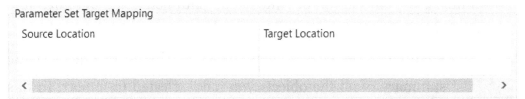

3. Connection resolution → If you have data objects in the import file, you need to assign connections to those objects. In this screen, Developer will show you the name of the source connections, their database type and the third column will be a dropdown for you to choose the database connection to associate to this data object.

Connection Rebinding

The following connections from the source will be mapped to the target domain.

Source Connection	Source Type	Target Connection	Target Type
ora_CustDB	Oracle	ora_CustDB	Oracle
ora_DWH	Oracle	ora_DWH	Oracle

 You must select a connection of the same database type as the object had when it was exported. The name of the connections can be different, but they have to be of same type.

For example, in the screenshot above, both the source connections are of type Oracle. You can assign connections with different names, but they must be of same type as Oracle.

12. Once you click Finish, the objects will be imported. Depending on the number of objects you chose, the import may take longer.

Deployment

In Informatica platform, there is a clear distinction of design time and runtime objects. The objects that the developer designs, build and previews are all design time objects. With proper permissions and privileges, developers can view and modify these objects. When the objects are ready for a hands-free execution such as in production environments, these objects are "deployed" to the DIS. A copy of these design time objects is made (henceforth referred as run time objects) during the deployment process. The runtime objects are managed by the DIS itself and are completely independent of their design time counterparts. Developers can then continue to modify the design time objects in the Developer tool without impacting their runtime copies. In typical design/development environments there will be more design time objects and very few runtime objects. Whereas in production environments such as production, almost all objects will just be runtime objects with minimal or no design time objects. Even if design time objects are maintained in production like environments, their access usually restricted to be read only.

 In the Informatica Platform, there is a clear distinction of the object that is being edited in the Developer tool and the copy or instance that is being executed.

In other words, deployment is a special case of object migration where the intent is to deploy objects from design-time to run-time. Applications are the unit of deployments. Individual objects such as mappings cannot be deployed without an application. Hence deployment can be performed either within the same domain or can be cross-domain. The illustration below shows same-domain deployment and cross-domain deployment:

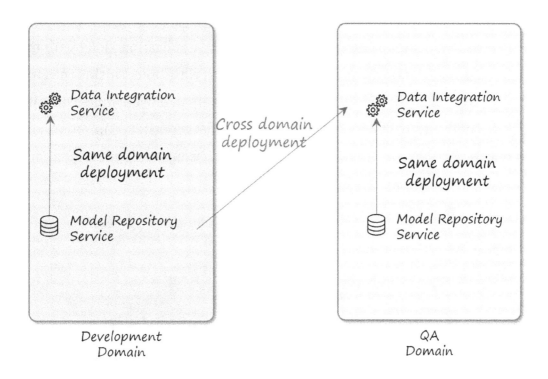

Applications

Applications are an important aspect of the deployment. Application can be defined as a container that holds a group of objects that are intended to be executed together. This doesn't necessarily mean that all the objects inside an application must run at the same time. It just means that all objects inside an application have a purpose to be together.

 To be able to execute objects in the Informatica Platform, they need to be part of an application.

There are two facets to an application: applications in the Developer tool and the applications in the DIS. In Developer tool, applications are containers that contain references to the objects you want to deploy. But when the application is deployed to the DIS, the application along with the mappings and workflows inside it become a first class object inside the DIS. Now, a copy of all the mappings and workflows are deployed in the DIS with no dependencies with or references to the model repository. As soon as an application is deployed to DIS, this application becomes self-contained code along with all the objects that are inside it.

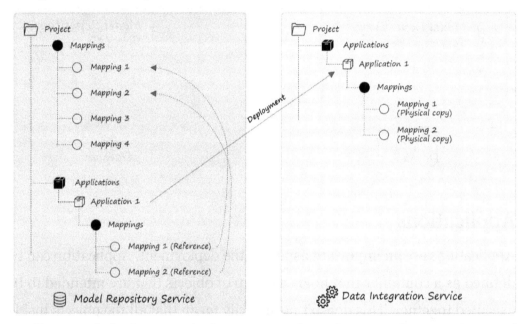

As illustrated, deployment is the process of copying over the mappings and workflows to the DIS. During the deployment, the applications' references are resolved and the corresponding objects are copied on to the DIS. Post deployment, command line, scheduler tools, and all other tools execute the mappings that are deployed on the DIS. A DIS stores all this information internally for persistence. A deployed application has several states as illustrated below:

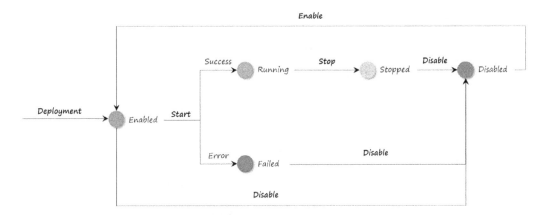

When application is deployed, it goes into ***Enabled*** state. An enabled application is loaded into the DIS memory to serve the mapping execution requests faster. During deployment, you can choose to start the application. If the application is started successfully, it goes in to ***Running*** state. If the application fails to load, it goes to ***Failed*** state. A running application doesn't imply any mapping execution. It just means that the application is ready to take requests to execute mappings and workflows inside it. Once the application is in ***Running*** state, you can stop the application. ***Stopped*** application doesn't take any requests for mapping / workflow execution. As an administrator, you can stop the application to prevent any further execution of the mappings inside it. This will allow you to redeploy the application (with latest / enhanced mappings). You can also disable a stopped application. A ***Disabled*** application is no longer in the DIS memory. When DIS is restarted, it loads all the information related to the applications and their content from an internal persistent store.

 When a developer changes the design-time copy of a mapping or workflow or its dependencies, it needs to be re-deployed to the

> run-time for those changes to take effect. If the changes are not redeployed, developer can continue to make those changes in the MRS without impacting the mapping execution in deployed applications.

Deploying applications

Once the mappings are ready to be deployed to run time, you can create and deploy the applications along with the mappings.

1. To do so, right click one or more mappings and click Deploy.

2. Application screen appears. Provide a name to the application (such as Application_01).

3. In the next screen, choose the deployment method. You can deploy the application to a DIS or to an application archive file. If you choose to deploy to DIS, you will be prompted to select a domain and DIS and click Finish.

4. You will see a confirmation message that the application is deployed.

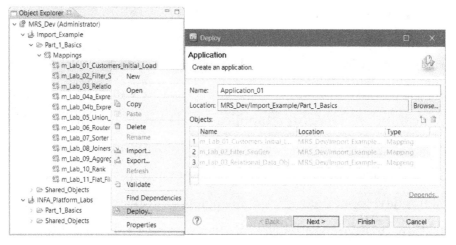

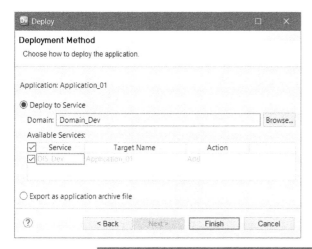

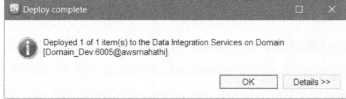

Working with the applications in the DIS

1. You can see the deployed applications in the Informatica Administrator → Manage tab → Services and Nodes sub tab → DIS (Select a DIS on the left hand side). By expanding the application, you can see all the objects deployed inside it.

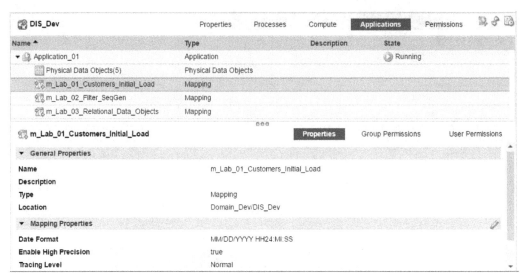

2. To see the application properties, select the application row and click Action menu on the top right corner.

3. You will see the following menu items:

    1. Deploy full application → You can use this menu item to deploy new applications from Informatica Application Archive files (.iar files).

    2. Undeploy application → Use this to undeploy a deployed application. If you do not have a backup of this application, take a backup before undeploying the application. Once undeployed, there is no way to deploy it back unless you have the

         exact same copies of the mappings in the MRS or the Informatica Application Archive file (.iar file).

3. Backup application → Use this to backup application as an XML file.

4. Restore application from file → Allows to restore the application from the XML file that you created by using the "Backup application" menu.

5. Start Application → Use this menu to start an application. Once completed, application will be in Running state.

6. Stop application → Use this menu to stop a running application. You will be prompted to choose whether to wait until any running mappings to complete, or to abort them intermittently.

Application properties

In the DIS properties → application tab, select an application to see its properties. When an application is selected, you will see properties, group permissions, and individual permissions that you can associate for that application. Startup type is a property of significance. Startup type can be set to "Enabled" or "Disabled". Enabled applications are loaded at the DIS startup. "Disabled" applications are not loaded when DIS starts. Such applications need to be explicitly started before mappings inside that applications can be executed.

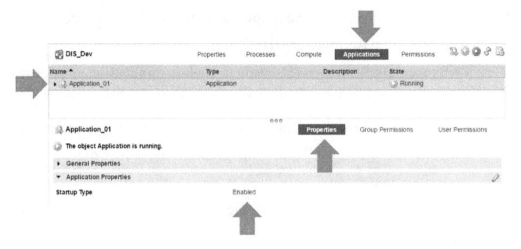

Updating applications

During deployment, the application is copied over to the DIS and hence the copy of the application (deployed application) is independent of the design-time copy of the application in the MRS.

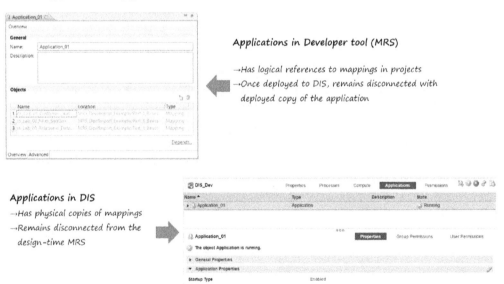

Applications in Developer tool (MRS)

→Has logical references to mappings in projects
→Once deployed to DIS, remains disconnected with
   deployed copy of the application

Applications in DIS

→Has physical copies of mappings
→Remains disconnected from the
   design-time MRS

When mappings in the developer tool (MRS) are updated, the applications in the developer tool no longer refer to older versions of the mappings, they

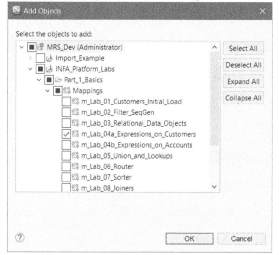

refer to the latest versions of the mappings as they always only store references – not physical objects. Deployed applications (in DIS) however always have a physical copy of the mapping – the copy as of the deployment to the DIS. They are not impacted by any changes in the Developer tool until the application is redeployed. To modify the application, open the application (in Developer). To add additional objects to the application, click the new icon and choose the mappings you want to add to the application and click OK. Again, the changes to the application in developer do not impact the deployed application – hence it remains the same without these additions. For the deployed application to refresh, you will have to redeploy the

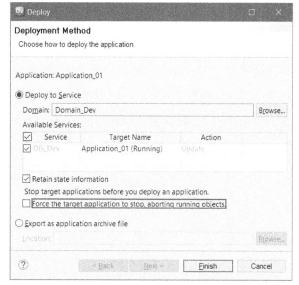

application from the developer tool. To do so, right click the application in the developer tool and click Deploy. Redeployment screen will appear. This screen is very similar to the original deployment screen with two changes. This screen allows you to retain current state information such as Sequence Generator values from the currently deployed application. If the application is running, you can also forcefully stop the application before redeploying. Click finish to deploy the application.

Informatica Application Archive files

You can deploy an application to a DIS or to file system. Customers typically deploy to file system, to version control the applications. When you deploy to file system, Informatica creates an Application Archive file (.iar file). You can then take this iar file and import it into a DIS.

Creating an Informatica Application Archive

In the developer tool, right click an application and choose Deploy. In the deployment method screen that appears, choose "Export as application archive file" and provide a location / folder where this export needs to be created. UNC (network) paths are supported. Once you click finish an application archive file with the same name as the application name with a .iar extension is created and a success message is displayed.

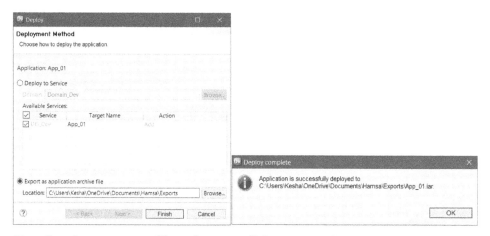

Deploying an application archive to DIS

To deploy an application archive to DIS, go to the Administrator console →
Manage tab → Services and Nodes sub tab. Select a DIS on the left hand
side object explorer. On the right hand side, choose Applications tab.

In the Actions menu, click Deploy Full Application. Deploy Application
dialog box appears. Click Browse to navigate through the file system and
select the application archive file that was created previously. You can add
up to 10 files at the same time. Then click Deploy. Deployment process may
take several minutes, depending on the number of objects to be deployed,

and then summary is displayed. Click Finish to close the dialog box. Application is deployed and started.

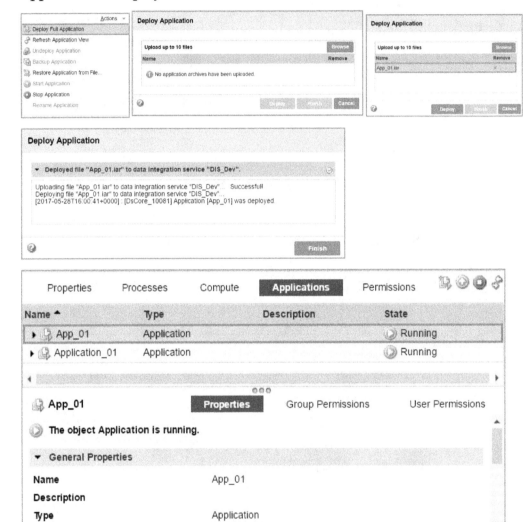

Deploying mappings and workflows

In Informatica Platform, mappings are first class objects and can be

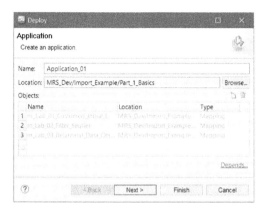

executed by themselves. Hence mappings can be deployed and executed without being part of workflows. There are many such objects that can be deployed without the need of workflows. For example, logical data objects, SQL Data Services, Web Services, etc. In this

book, We will cover only mappings and workflows. You can add mappings and workflows to an application just like any other objects.

Once deployed, you can see these objects in the applications tab in the Administrator console. These deployed mappings can be executed directly and can be monitored by themselves in the monitoring console under the Application → Deployed Mapping Jobs.

Deploying parameter sets

To deploy a parameter set, add it to the application when you deploy an

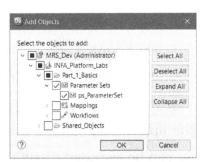

application. Then deploy an application as usual. Since parameter set is not a runnable object by itself. You will not see it in the DIS post deployment. But you can continue to use it in the command line while executing any executable object such as mappings and

workflows – as discussed in the "Execution, Automation and Monitoring" chapter.

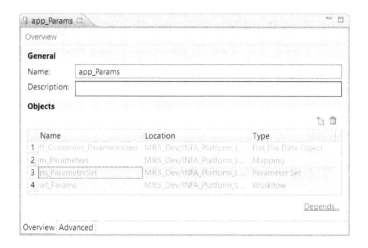

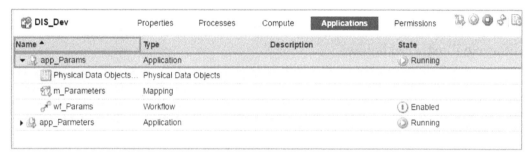

Deployment use-cases

As seen in the above illustrations and sections, Informatica Platform gives you great flexibility in performing both object migration and deployment, and you can use various combinations of these to achieve your organization's needs to manage artifacts in various Informatica environments. In this section, you learn some of the common use-cases around deployment and how they can be achieved.

Since the most common use-case of object migration is to deploy objects to run-time, we will discuss object migration use-case as part of the deployment use-cases itself.

Agile deployment

In agile development, enterprises plan for frequent, smaller releases to production instead of take-longer-and-build-larger approach. In agile methodology it is important to be able to deploy faster and quicker. Maintaining various copies of the same design-objects is also highly discouraged in this approach. Users of such methodology can follow the lifecycle illustrated below:

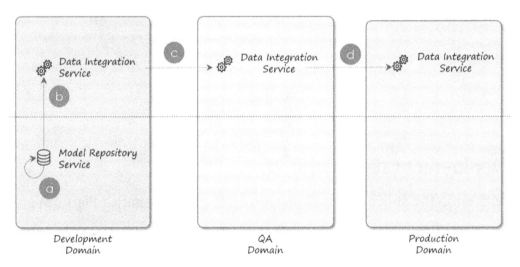

In the agile development use-cases, typically the following steps are performed:

a. When the code is ready to be deployed, it is grouped into containers known as applications. These applications are stored in the MRS. Enterprises that use external, custom version systems, export this application to a file and check-in this file into their versioning system for audit and versioning purposes.

a. The application is then deployed to the DIS, which stores its metadata in a run-time MRS. This application is unit tested and certified to be ready for further deployment.

b. This application is then exported from the DIS and deployed to the DIS in the QA domain. QA team then execute their test cases and certify the code to be ready for production.

c. The application is then exported from the QA domain and deployed to production DIS during the Go-Live window.

 In this use-case, you have taken an example of 3 domains: Dev, QA and Production. In reality an enterprise can have any number of domains/environments and this process can be applied all the same.

Salient features of agile deployment

→ Only one copy of the design-time metadata exists – in the development MRS.

→ Once the application is created and deployed to the DIS in the development, developers can continue to make changes to the mappings and workflows in the MRS, and those changes will not impact the deployed applications.

→ A copy of the application can be exported as Informatica Application Archive (.iar) file and checked in to any version control system of the +administrator's choice.

→ When the application is ready to be deployed from one domain to another, administrator can:

    o Use the export file (.iar) created earlier, or directly export the application from the DIS to create an Informatica application archive file.

    o Deploy directly to the QA DIS and eventually to production DIS.

→ No MRS needed in QA and Production (non-development) environments.

→ QA and Production (non-development) environments remain lean as they don't host any design-time metadata.

→ Though encapsulated into an application, users can still refer and run the mappings and workflows inside an application, directly.

→ End to end process can be automated for hands-free and error-free deployment.

→ Since there is no MRS in the QA and production (non-development) environments, it will not be possible to view the mappings or workflows from Developer tool. To view them, one must import them into a MRS and view them.

Standard deployment

Standard deployment model is often used by customers with PowerCenter background so that they can leverage the automation they already built in PowerCenter, in the Informatica Platform as well. In standard deployment model, a MRS is maintained in every domain as illustrated here:

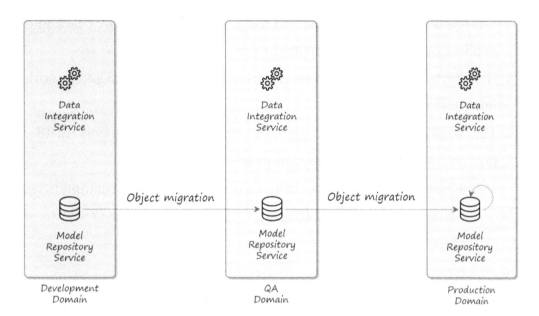

In this deployment model the following steps are performed,

→ When the code is ready to be deployed, a copy of the code is made and – typically in a different project inside the same MRS or in a different MRS exclusively maintained for deployment purposes. This code is then grouped into containers known as applications. These applications are stored in the MRS. Enterprises that use external, custom version systems, export this application to a file and check-in this file into their versioning system for audit and versioning purposes.

→ The application is then deployed to the DIS, which stores its metadata in a run-time MRS. This application is unit tested and certified to be ready for further deployment.

→ This code is then exported (either as an application archive or as object export file) from the MRS in development domain and imported into the MRS of the QA repository.

→ The application is then deployed from the QA MRS to QA DIS and the application is tested and certified there.

→ Once certified, the code is then exported from the QA MRS and imported into production MRS.

→ The application is then deployed from the production MRS to production DIS and the application goes-live.

 While migrating objects from one MRS to another, customers can either use the Informatica application archive file or create an object export file.

Salient features of standard deployment

→ Design-time metadata exists in all domains.

→ If the mappings in the MRS are changed after deploying to development DIS but before deploying to QA MRS, they are no longer the same. Hence the deployment in that scenario must happen from development DIS to QA MRS.

→ A copy of the artifacts to be deployed must be made in the Development MRS first before deploying to any DIS (including development DIS). This prevents from accidentally overwriting any mappings before they are deployed to QA MRS as discussed in the previous point.

→ A copy of the application can be exported as Informatica Application Archive (.iar) file and checked in to any version control system of the administrator's choice.

→ When the application is ready to be deployed from one domain to another, administrator can use the export file (.iar) created earlier or export the application from the DIS directly to create an Informatica application archive file.

→ QA and Production (non-development) environments grow heavily over time as a copy of the previous deployment is also typically maintained for backup / archive purposes.

→ QA and Production (non-development) environments are typically not as lean as in Agile deployment model as you now created a MRS.

→ Though encapsulated into an application, users can still refer and run the mappings and workflows inside an application directly.

→ End to end process can be automated for hands-free and error-free deployment.

→ Since there is MRS in the QA and production (non-development) environments it will be possible to view the mappings or workflows from Developer tool.

→ The number of object migrations, deployments for one end-to-end process, is almost twice as many as compared to the agile deployment process.

Hybrid deployment

The primary difference between an agile deployment and the standard deployment is the maintenance of the MRS in each Informatica domain. There are pros and cons in doing it either way. Hybrid deployment offers the best of both worlds. First, let's take a quick look at some pros and cons between the agile and standard deployments to get a better understanding of the hybrid deployment use-case:

→ MRS

1. Agile deployment model eliminates the need to maintain MRS in non-development environments. This keeps the environments lean.

2. Lack of MRS also means lack of visibility into the mappings / workflow code. Though the mappings and workflows can be executed, they cannot be viewed from the developer tool.

→ Live backups, archive copies

1. Most Informatica Administrators, prefer to maintain a live backup / archive copy inside the Informatica repository itself. For example, some administrators prefer to have last 3 applications deployed still available in non-development environments. This gives them quicker access to code from previous releases in cases of rolling back the deployments or a quick version compare is required.

2. In agile development, lack of MRS makes it very hard to maintain these copies. The copies must now be maintained only at the MRS level.

3. In standard deployment, since a MRS exists, previous applications can be un-deployed from the DIS and maintained just within the MRS.

→ Access controls

1. In agile deployment, access controls are very simple. Since there is no MRS, developers typically have zero access to non-development environments.

2. Even if developers are given access to the runtime monitoring, since the mapping / workflow cannot be viewed from developer tool, developers are limited in their ability to troubleshoot / debug in non-development environments.

3. In standard deployment, developers are often given read-only access to both MRS and run-time monitoring to help with debugging and troubleshooting.

Hybrid deployment mode offers the best of both worlds as illustrated here:

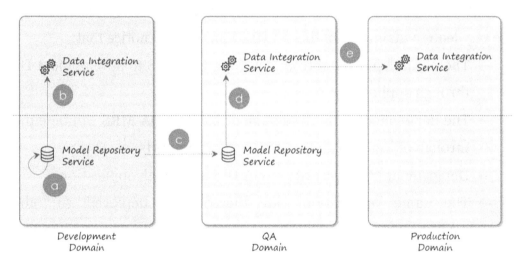

In this deployment model, one non-development environment is chosen to host the golden copy of the code. This environment will have the current code running in production, the new code that has completed development but is not deployed to production yet, and 1 or more previously production deployed applications for quick backup / live archives. Developers will be given read-only access to this environment. This enables them to perform any troubleshooting for any emergency issues found in the production. This gives them a "view" into the mappings and workflows that are running in the production. Though not usually given, even if they are allowed to make any changes here, it will not impact the runtime MRS in the production domain as a re-deployment is required to impact production. Thus hybrid deployment offers lean non-development environments (except for 1 domain) but still retains the capability to "view" or peek into the code that is running in various environments. The illustration here shows a simplified/minified hybrid deployment where more than 3 environments are involved. You will notice that besides one non-development environment, all other environments only need the DIS service and hence are very lean to maintain. In this illustration, you will notice that:

→ There is a deployment from development MRS to development DIS through applications.

→ The deployment from development MRS to QA MRS can be either through object files and/or XML export/imports.

→ Deployment from QA MRS to QA DIS is through application.

→ The same application can thereon be deployed to other environments.

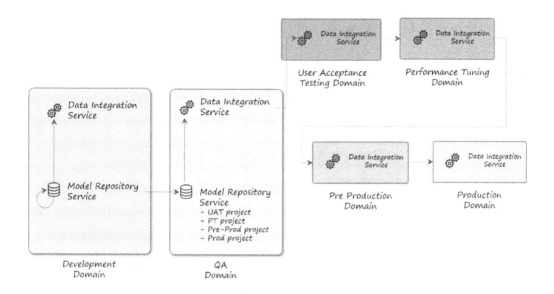

Chapter 16 – Execution, Automation & Monitoring

Introduction

You would have noticed in the chapters related to parameterization, workflows and deployments, you haven't executed any mappings or workflows from the UI. There is a reason for that. Deployed objects can only be executed from Command Line Interface. Once objects are deployed to DIS (run-time), they become a different copy and they may or may not be same as what you see in developer tool (depending on whether those objects changed in the MRS). Hence executing the mapping in the Developer tool may or may not yield the same result as executing a deployed object. In this chapter you look at how to execute the deployed objects. First off, any object can be deployed to DIS only through an application and it remains within the context of the application throughout its lifecycle. To execute jobs you rely on the infacmd command line interface.

infacmd CLI

The infacmd command line interface is a very powerful interface that allows you to interact with several services within the domain. In this chapter you will look at infacmd's capabilities from the execution and monitoring perspective. infacmd CLI resides both on the clients and server. On the client it is available at the **<Default Informatica Path>\clients\DeveloperClient\infacmd** directory as

infacmd.bat. This program is also available on the Informatica Server at

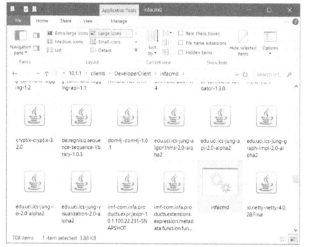

$INFA_HOME/server/bin as **infacmd.sh**. In this book, you are referring to the Informatica Server on Linux; hence all commands use the infcmd.sh. If you are running Informatica on Windows server, adjust the commands accordingly.

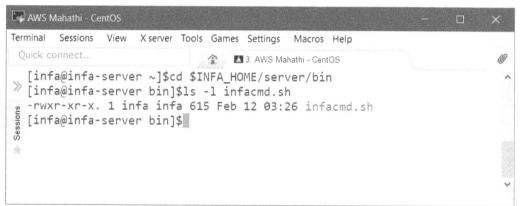

infacmd commands typically have the following components:

→ infacmd – shellor batch invocation

→ pluginName– the plugins that are about to interact with

→ command – the command that you are invoking within the plugin

→ switches – the options that act as input to the command also allow you to control the execution of the command

Parameter sets

Parameter Sets commands are part of the DIS plugin. The commands of this plugin can be invoked in the infacmd using the "**dis**" plugin name.

Getting list of parameter sets

To get a list of all the parameter sets deployed to DIS, use the following command:

```
infacmd.sh dis listParameterSets -dn Domain_Dev  -sn
DIS_Dev  -un userName -pd password -sdn Native -a
app_Params
```

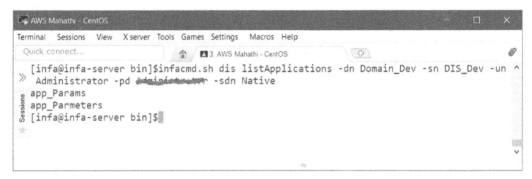

Now, let us try to look at the switches associated with this command:

Switch	Description
-dn	Domain Name
-sn	Service Name – DIS
-un	Username to connect to the repository
-pd	Password for this user
-sdn	Security domain such as Native or LDAP
-a	Application name

Output of this command is:

```
ps_Params
```

Mapping commands

Getting list of deployed mappings

For example, you want to list all the mappings that are deployed as part of a specific application. To do so, you rely on the Mapping Service plugin in the DIS. So, our command invocation will look as shown here:

```
infacmd.sh ms listMappings -dn Domain_Dev -un userName    -
pd password   -sdn Native   -sn DIS_Dev   -a app_Params
```

In this example, you have invoked the command listMappings within the ms plugin (Mapping Service) and have provided the following switches:

→ dn – Domain name

→ un – User name to connect to the domain

→ pd – Password for the user

→ sdn – Security Domain (such as Native or LDAP)

→ sn – Service Name, which in this case is the DIS name (DIS_Dev)

→ a – application name, which in this case is the app_Params

The output of this command is the list of all mappings that are deployed as part of this application in this DIS. There is only one mapping deployed as such and hence only one-line output. You can validate this with the DIS screenshot here:

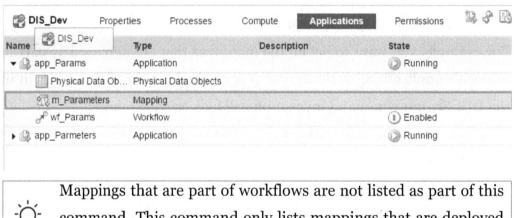

Name	Type	Description	State
▼ 📋 app_Params	Application		⊙ Running
📊 Physical Data Ob...	Physical Data Objects		
🔧 m_Parameters	Mapping		
⚡ wf_Params	Workflow		ⓘ Enabled
▶ 📋 app_Parmeters	Application		⊙ Running

 Mappings that are part of workflows are not listed as part of this command. This command only lists mappings that are deployed by themselves.

Mapping Service module

For many deployed mapping related commands, you rely on the Mapping Service plugin of the DIS. For you to be able to deploy mappings as first class objects into the DIS and to execute them without a workflow, you must have the Mapping Service plugin enabled. You can check this in the DIS properties in the administrator console. Go to Administrator console → Manage tab → Services and Nodes → In the Domain Navigator (on the left), select the DIS → on the right hand side, go to properties pane → Go to the Modules section and check the value next to Mapping Service. True indicates that the plugin is enabled and false indicates that the plugin is disabled.

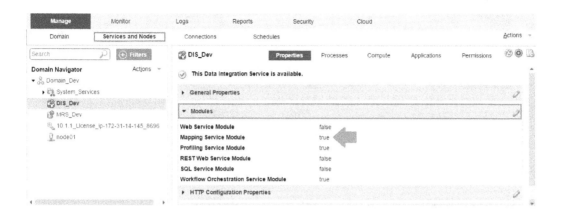

Generating a parameter file for a mapping

When you create a mapping, you may have created several parameters in the mapping. Informatica provides an infacmd command to generate a basic template file with default values as the parameter values. You can take the parameter file and customize it as needed. You use the following command to generate a parameter file for a deployed mapping:

```
infacmd.sh ms listMappingParams -dn Domain_Dev  -sn
DIS_Dev  -un userName  -pd password  -sdn Native -a
app_Params -m m_Parameters
```

```
AWS Mahathi - CentOS                                         —    □    ×
Terminal   Sessions   View   X server   Tools   Games   Settings   Macros   Help
Quick connect...                        ⬆  ▣ 3. AWS Mahathi - CentOS              ⟳             ⫘
[infa@infa-server bin]$infacmd.sh ms listMappingParams -dn Domain_Dev -sn DIS_Dev ^
-un Administrator -pd ~~~~~~~~~~ -sdn Native -a app_Params -m m_Parameters
<?xml version="1.0" encoding="UTF-8"?><root xmlns="http://www.informatica.com/Par
ameterization/1.0" xmlns:xsi="http://www.w3.org/2001/XMLSchema" version="2.0">
    <!--Specify deployed application specific parameters here.-->
    <!--
    <application name="app_Params">
    <mapping name="m_Parameters"/>
</application>
-->
    <project name="INFA_Platform_Labs">
        <folder name="Part_1_Basics">
            <mapping name="m_Parameters">
                <parameter name="mpFilterCondition">isNull(COMP_NAME)</parameter>
                <parameter name="mpNameFormat">US</parameter>
            </mapping>
        </folder>
    </project>
</root>
Command ran successfully.
[infa@infa-server bin]$
```

Let us try to understand the switches associated with this command:

Switch	Description
-dn	Domain Name
-sn	Service Name – DIS
-un	Username to connect to the repository
-pd	Password for this user
-sdn	Security domain such as Native or LDAP
-a	Application name (app_Params)
-m	Mapping name
-o	You can provide an output file for this command to store the mapping parameter XML file

For this command to run successfully, the mapping must have already been deployed to the DIS first.

Let's take a look at the parameter file generated. The mapping section contains the parameters used by the mappings and the values. You can use this XML file:

```
<?xml version="1.0" encoding="UTF-8"?><root
xmlns="http://www.informatica.com/Parameterization/1.0"
xmlns:xsi="http://www.w3.org/2001/XMLSchema" version="2.0">
<!--
    <application name="app_Params">
        <mapping name="m_Parameters"/>
    </application>
    -->
<project name="INFA_Platform_Labs">
<folder name="Part_1_Basics">
<mapping name="m_Parameters">
<parameter name="mpFilterCondition">
                isNull(COMP_NAME)
        </parameter>
        <parameter name="mpNameFormat">
            US
        </parameter>
</mapping>
</folder>
</project>
```

```
</root>
```

Execute a deployed mapping

To execute a deployed mapping, you use the following command:

```
infacmd.sh ms runMapping -dn Domain_Dev  -sn DIS_Dev  -un
userName  -pd password  -sdn Native -a app_Params -m
m_Parameters -wait
```

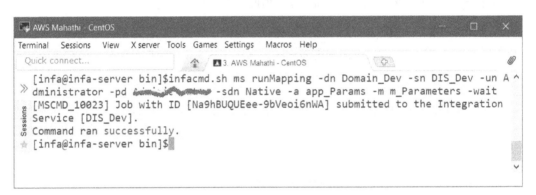

Let us try to understand the switches associated with this command:

Switch	Description
-dn	Domain Name
-sn	Service Name – DIS
-un	Username to connect to the repository
-pd	Password for this user
-sdn	Security domain such as Native or LDAP
-a	Application name (app_Params)
-m	Mapping name

-wait	This switch doesn't have any value associated with it when this switch is added to the CLI, the CLI does not return control to the prompt until the mapping finishes. Otherwise, it returns immediately while the mapping is running in the background.

This is how mapping will look like in the monitoring console. We will cover more on monitoring later in this chapter.

Notice that this mapping has parameters but you did not pass any. You will learn in the subsequent sections on how to do that.

Executing a deployed mapping with parameter file

We can pass a parameter file to a mapping with the -pf switch:

```
infacmd.sh ms runMapping -dn Domain_Dev  -sn DIS_Dev  -un
userName  -pd password  -sdn Native -a app_Params -m
m_Parameters -pf prm_m_Parameters.xml -wait
```

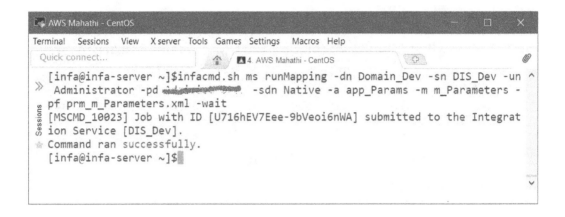

Let us try to understand the switches associated with this command:

Switch	Description
-dn	Domain Name
-sn	Service Name – DIS
-un	Username to connect to the repository
-pd	Password for this user
-sdn	Security domain such as Native or LDAP
-a	Application name (app_Params)
-m	Mapping name
-pf	Parameter file
-wait	Wait until the mapping finishes before passing control back to command line shell

You can verify the parameter file used inside the mapping log. You will see the following message in the logs:

```
2017-05-30 21:02:44.703 <DTFPool-3-thread-1445> INFO:
[MPSVCCMN_10089] The mapping parameters are resolved with
parameter file [/home/infa/prm_m_Parameters.xml] from the
host [infa-server].
```

Executing a deployed mapping with parameter set

We can pass the parameter set to a mapping execution command with the -ps switch:

```
infacmd.sh ms runMapping -dn Domain_Dev  -sn DIS_Dev  -un
userName  -pd password  -sdn Native -a app_Params -m
m_Parameters -ps ps_ParameterSet-wait
```

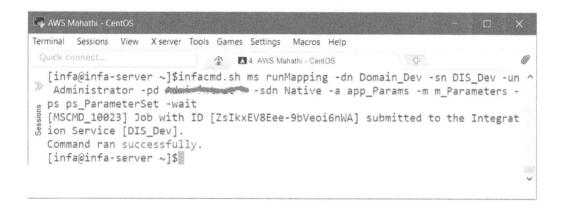

Let us try to understand the switches associated with this command:

Switch	Description
-dn	Domain Name
-sn	Service Name – DIS
-un	Username to connect to the repository

-pd	Password for this user
-sdn	Security domain such as Native or LDAP
-a	Application name (app_Params)
-m	Mapping name
-ps	Parameter set
-wait	Wait until the mapping finishes before passing control back to command line shell

You can verify the parameter file used inside the mapping log. You will see the following message in the logs:

```
2017-05-30 21:10:26.098 <DTFPool-3-thread-1445> INFO:
[MPSVCCMN_10090] The mapping parameters are resolved with
parameter set [ps_ParameterSet].
```

Workflow commands

All the workflow commands are part of the Workflow Service plugin (similar to Mapping Service plugin). The Workflow Service plugin commands can be invoked in the infacmd using the "**wfs**" plugin name.

Getting list of deployed workflows

We can list all of the deployed workflows using the following command:

```
infacmd.sh wfs listWorkflows -dn Domain_Dev -sn DIS_Dev -
un userName -pd password -sdn Native -a app_Params
```

Now, let us try to look at the switches associated with this command:

Switch	Description
-dn	Domain Name
-sn	Service Name – DIS
-un	Username to connect to the repository
-pd	Password for this user
-sdn	Security domain such as Native or LDAP
-a	Application name (app_Params)

Generating a parameter file for a workflow

To generate template parameter file for a given workflow, use the following command:

```
infacmd.sh wfs listWorkflowParams -dn Domain_Dev  -sn
DIS_Dev  -un userName  -pd password  -sdn Native -a
app_Params -wfwf_Params
```

```
AWS Mahathi - CentOS                                              —   □   ✕
Terminal   Sessions   View   X server   Tools   Games   Settings   Macros   Help
Quick connect...                         ⬆    ▲ 3. AWS Mahathi - CentOS           ⊕              🔗
 [infa@infa-server bin]$infacmd.sh wfs listWorkflowParams -dn Domain_Dev -sn DIS_Dev  ^
 -un Administrator -pd ████████████ -sdn Native -a app_Params -wf wf_Params
 <?xml version="1.0" encoding="UTF-8"?><root xmlns="http://www.informatica.com/Parame
 terization/1.0" xmlns:xsi="http://www.w3.org/2001/XMLSchema" version="2.0">
     <!--Specify deployed application specific parameters here.-->
     <!--
     <application name="app_Params">
     <workflow name="wf_Params"/>
 </application>
 -->
 </root>

 Command ran successfully.
 [infa@infa-server bin]$
```

Now, let us try to look at the switches associated with this command:

Switch	Description
-dn	Domain Name
-sn	Service Name – DIS
-un	Username to connect to the repository
-pd	Password for this user
-sdn	Security domain such as Native or LDAP
-a	Application name (app_Params)
-wf	Workflow name (wf_Params)

Execute a deployed workflow

To execute a deployed workflow, you use the following command:

```
infacmd.sh wfs startWorkflow -dn Domain_Dev  -sn DIS_Dev
-un userName  -pd password  -sdn Native -a app_Params -wf
wf_Params -wait
```

```
AWS Mahathi - CentOS                                              —   □   ×
Terminal  Sessions  View  X server  Tools  Games  Settings  Macros  Help
Quick connect...              ⬆   ▲ 3. AWS Mahathi - CentOS            ⬦          📎
  [infa@infa-server bin]$infacmd.sh wfs startWorkflow -dn Domain_Dev -sn DIS_Dev -un ^
  Administrator -pd ~~~~~~~~~~~ -sdn Native -a app_Params -wf wf_Params -wait
  Completed workflow [wf_Params] with instance ID [XcuDOUQgEee-9bVeoi6nWA].
  [infa@infa-server bin]$
```

Now, let us try to look at the switches associated with this command:

Switch	Description
-dn	Domain Name
-sn	Service Name – DIS
-un	Username to connect to the repository
-pd	Password for this user
-sdn	Security domain such as Native or LDAP
-a	Application name (app_Params)
-wf	Workflow name (wf_Params)
-wait	Wait until the workflow execution is complete and do not give the control back to the shell

Execute a deployed workflow with parameter file

To execute a deployed workflow with parameter file, use the -pf switch:

```
infacmd.sh wfs startWorkflow -dn Domain_Dev  -sn DIS_Dev
-un userName  -pd password  -sdn Native -a app_Params -
wfwf_Params -pf prm_wf_Params.xml p-wait
```

Now, let us try to look at the switches associated with this command:

Switch	Description
-dn	Domain Name
-sn	Service Name – DIS
-un	Username to connect to the repository
-pd	Password for this user
-sdn	Security domain such as Native or LDAP
-a	Application name (app_Params)
-wf	Workflow name (wf_Params)
-pf	Parameter file to be used by the workflow
-wait	Wait until the workflow execution is complete and do not give the control back to the shell

Execute a deployed workflow with parameter set

To execute a deployed workflow with parameter set, use the -ps switch:

```
infacmd.sh wfs startWorkflow -dn Domain_Dev   -sn DIS_Dev
-un userName   -pd password   -sdn Native -a app_Params -wf
wf_Params -ps ps_ParameterSet -wait
```

Now, let us try to look at the switches associated with this command:

Switch	Description
-dn	Domain Name
-sn	Service Name – DIS
-un	Username to connect to the repository
-pd	Password for this user
-sdn	Security domain such as Native or LDAP
-a	Application name (app_Params)
-wf	Workflow name (wf_Params)
-ps	Parameter set to be used by the workflow
-wait	Wait until the workflow execution is complete and do not give the control back to the shell

Cancelling a workflow that is executing

To cancel a workflow that is executing you will need the running instance ID. The instance ID (or job ID) is listed when you started the workflow For example, see the two commands below:

```
infacmd.sh wfs startWorkflow -dn Domain_Dev  -sn DIS_Dev
-un Administrator -pd Administrator -sdn Native -a
app_Params -wf wf_Params
```

Output of this command is:

Started workflow [wf_Params] with instance ID [A87w6EQiEee-9bVeoi6nWA].

```
infacmd.sh wfs cancelWorkflow -dn Domain_Dev  -sn DIS_Dev
-un Administrator -pd Administrator -sdn Native -
iidA87w6EQiEee-9bVeoi6nWA
```

Applications

Application commands are part of the DIS plugin. The commands of this plugin can be invoked in the infacmd using the "**dis**" plugin name.

Getting list of applications

To get a list of all the applications deployed to DIS, use the following command:

```
infacmd.sh dis listApplications -dn Domain_Dev  -sn
DIS_Dev  -un userName  -pd password  -sdn Native
```

```
AWS Mahathi - CentOS                                          □  ×
Terminal  Sessions  View  X server  Tools  Games  Settings  Macros  Help
Quick connect...              ⬆  ▲3  AWS Mahathi - CentOS      ⬧           📎
   [infa@infa-server bin]$infacmd.sh dis listApplications -dn Domain_Dev -sn DIS_Dev -un ^
 » Administrator -pd ████████ -sdn Native
   app_Params
   app_Parmeters
   [infa@infa-server bin]$▋
```

Now, let us try to look at the switches associated with this command:

Switch	Description
-dn	Domain Name
-sn	Service Name – DIS
-un	Username to connect to the repository
-pd	Password for this user
-sdn	Security domain such as Native or LDAP

Output of this command is:

```
app_Params
app_Parmeters
```

Start a deployed application

To start an application, use the following command:

```
infacmd.sh dis startApplication -dn Domain_Dev   -sn
DIS_Dev   -un userName   -pd password   -sdn Native -a
app_Params
```

```
AWS Mahathi - CentOS                                        □  ×
Terminal  Sessions  View  X server  Tools  Games  Settings  Macros  Help
Quick connect...            ⬆  ⚠ 3. AWS Mahathi - CentOS              📎
 [infa@infa-server bin]$infacmd.sh dis startApplication -dn Domain_Dev -sn DIS_Dev -un ^
  Administrator -pd ▓▓▓▓▓▓▓▓ -sdn Native -a app_Params
 Command ran successfully.
 [infa@infa-server bin]$
```

Now, let us try to look at the switches associated with this command:

Switch	Description
-dn	Domain Name
-sn	Service Name – DIS
-un	Username to connect to the repository
-pd	Password for this user
-sdn	Security domain such as Native or LDAP
-a	Application name

Output of this command is:

```
Command ran successfully.
```

Stop a running application

To stop a running application, use the following command:

```
infacmd.sh dis stopApplication -dn Domain_Dev  -sn DIS_Dev
-un userName  -pd password  -sdn Native -a app_Params
```

```
AWS Mahathi - CentOS                                           □   X
Terminal   Sessions   View   X server   Tools   Games   Settings   Macros   Help
Quick connect...                    ⤒   ▲ 3. AWS Mahathi - CentOS        ⧉
  [infa@infa-server bin]$infacmd.sh dis stopApplication -dn Domain_Dev -sn DIS_Dev -un ^
  Administrator -pd ▨▨▨▨▨▨▨▨ -sdn Native -a app_Params
  Command ran successfully.
  [infa@infa-server bin]$
```

Now, let us try to look at the switches associated with this command:

Switch	Description
-dn	Domain Name
-sn	Service Name – DIS
-un	Username to connect to the repository
-pd	Password for this user
-sdn	Security domain such as Native or LDAP
-a	Application name

Output of this command is:

```
Command ran successfully.
```

Handling sensitive information

In all the examples so far, you have provided the username and password for the infacmd CLI. This is not a practical solution for enterprises as passwords should never be provided in plain text. In this section, let us take a look at how to address this. infacmd is capable of taking encrypted passwords. You can encrypt a password using pmpasswd utility.

Encrypting passwords with pmpasswd

Executing the pmpasswd utility is plain and simple. Just run the pmpasswd utility by passing the string you want to encrypt as shown in the example here:

```
pmpasswd Administrator
```

The output of this command will be something like this:

```
Copyright (c) Informatica Corporation 1996-2016
All Rights Reserved.
Encrypted string
-->0FDt0tlqNcuXlmS7iwzJAc5zF7ySnY9bJWumuDvMrLM=<--
Will decrypt to -->Administrator<--
```

 pmpasswd generates a different encryption value every time. So, your output may not match what is displayed here.

Environment variables used by infacmd

There are many environment variables that you can set for infacmd to use. Here is a list of few of them. When these environment variables are set, you can skip the corresponding switches when executing the infacmd CLI.

Environment variable	Description	Switch
INFA_DEFAULT_ DOMAIN	Domain name used by infacmd	-dn

INFA_DEFAULT_ DOMAIN_USER	Username passed to infacmd	-un
INFA_DEFAULT_ DOMAIN_PASSWORD	Takes encrypted password.	-pd
INFA_PASSWORD	Same as INFA_DEFAULT_DOMAIN_ PASSWORD	-pd

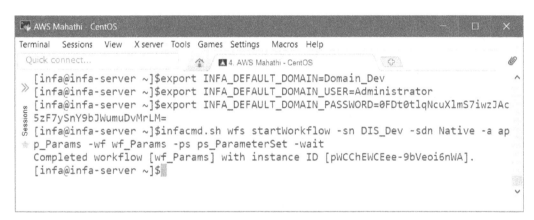

As shown in the screenshot here, when these environment variables are set, you can skip the corresponding switches in infacmd.

Monitoring

Monitoring MRS

Monitoring MRS stores the monitoring statistics of jobs executed on all the Data Integration Services in a domain. Monitoring MRS can be configured in the domain properties. You can configure the number of days the monitoring MRS can preserve the historical statistics and also the purge schedule.

Steps involved in configuring the monitoring MRS

Monitoring MRS is configured at the domain level and is shared by all the Data Integration Services. You can configure this in the domain properties.

1. To configure the monitoring MRS, go to Informatica Administrator console → Manage tab → Services and Nodes → Monitoring configuration.

2. In the Monitoring configuration section, click the pencil icon to edit the monitoring configuration properties.

Monitoring Configuration   ✕

Fields marked with an asterisk (*) are required.

Specify a Model Repository Service to store historical data.

Model Repository Service *	MRS_Dev
User Name *	Administrator
Password *	•••••••••••••
Preserve Summary Historical Data *	180 days
Preserve Detailed Historical Data *	14 days
Purge Statistics Every *	1 days at 1:00 AM
Maximum Number of Sortable Records *	3000
Maximum Delay for Update Notifications *	10 seconds
Date Time Field	☐ Show milliseconds (hr:min:sec:millisec)

                                                          OK   Cancel

3. Here you can select any MRS available in the domain, provide the domain login details to connect to the MRS and the number of the days to preserve both summary and detailed historical data. You can also configure when to purge statistics from the MRS.

4. Once this is configured, the DIS within the domain needs to be restarted for them to start recording the monitoring statistics.

Monitor jobs

To monitor any deployed job (mappings / workflows), go to the monitoring console. Monitoring console runs on the same port as the administrator port. For example, if the Administrator console runs on the port 6008, the Administrator URL is http://infa-server:6008/administrator, then the monitoring console URL is http://infa-server:6008/monitoring.

 Monitoring console offers same content and functionality as the Administrator console's monitor tab and doesn't need elevated privileges to access.

Once logged, into the monitoring console, there are two sub tabs: "Summary Statistics" and "Execution Statistics". Execution statistics tab has the operation details needed to monitor jobs. In the execution statistics tab, on the domain navigator (left hand side tree) expand the domain → DIS. Any execution of the mappings from the developer tool, are listed under Ad Hoc

Jobs. Right below this, all applications are listed. If you expand the applications, you will see the following categories inside them:

→ Deployed Mapping jobs: Mappings that are not part of workflows and will be executed by themselves

→ Logical Data Objects

→ REST Web Services

→ SQL Data Services

→ Web Services

→ Workflows; They may or may not contain mappings inside them. Mappings inside workflows are shown on the right hand side navigator when this option is chosen.

Operations UI

This is where all jobs (per the selection on the left hand side) are displayed. If you selected Deployed Mapping Jobs (inside an application) on the left hand side, the right hand side displays only mappings that are not part of any workflows and are executed by themselves. If you selected workflows (inside an application), this UI shows all workflow executions. On the right hand side, there are two panes - top-pane and bottom-pane. Top pane lists all the mappings' executions. When a row on the top is selected, bottom pane displays the details. On the top row, the following columns are displayed by default:

The top pane

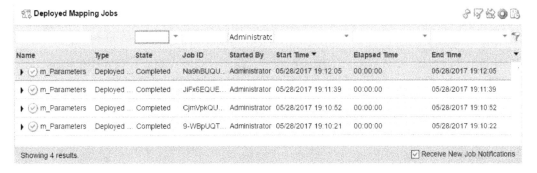

Column name	Description
Name	Deployed mapping name

Column name	Description
Type	Deployed Mapping / Workflow depending on the selection made on the left hand side
State	Can be Running / Completed (Successful) / Failed / Aborted / Canceled / Unknown
Job ID	For every mapping and workflow execution, a unique UUID is generated known as Job ID. It is displayed in this column
Started by	Informatica User that started this job. If executed from CLI -un switch specified the login username
Started time	Time when the job is submitted to the DIS
Elapsed time	Time the job took to complete. If the job is still running, this column will keep changing
End time	Time when the job is finished

You can type or use the drop down in the first row to filter the jobs. For example, by default, the monitoring console only shows the jobs executed by the currently logged in user. You can also use the Job ID and other filters to quickly find a job.

Taking actions on the job

When you select a job in the top pane, you can use the actions menu or the shortcut icons right above the top pane to operate on the job and perform actions such as reissue the job, cancel the running job and so on. You can also use this menu to download the log files for the selected job.

Detailed statistics

When a job is selected on the top, the bottom pane refreshes to show the details of the job. The details pane has 4 tabs:

Properties: Displays the name, start time, end of the job and other general details.

Summary statistics: Displays the source success rows, target success rows, reject rows, throughput, etc. per each source and target in the mapping.

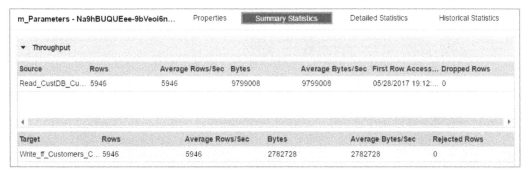

Detailed Statistics show the details of each source and target as timeline for us to understand where most of the time is spent by that data object. This is very useful for long running jobs.

Historical statistics shows the summary of last 500 runs of the mapping in terms of the average elapsed time, CPU and memory usage, average source rows, and target rows. This tab can be very helpful to analyze how the mapping and its objects are performing over a period of time.

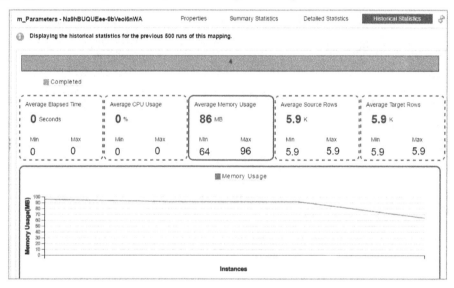

Index

N

O

P

Other books by Keshav Vadrevu

Informatica PowerCenter – The complete reference

Learn about the software that revolutionized the Data Integration industry – Informatica PowerCenter in this easy to learn, self-study guide. With hundreds of screenshots and do-it-yourself labs, learning PowerCenter was never this easy

Applying SOA principles in Informatica®

Learn why architects love Informatica technologies in this book. Sometimes, complex problems are solved by simplest techniques. This book demonstrates how you can use Informatica's simple design patterns to solve complex Service Oriented Architecture principles. By keeping the focus at the concept level, but still staying true to the technology this book is hugely favored by enterprise developers for complex DI use-cases

www.ingramcontent.com/pod-product-compliance
Lightning Source LLC
Chambersburg PA
CBHW060110090326
40690CB00064B/4588